To Larg —

Hope you enjoy the book!

Jo H⸻

Kids' TV Grows Up

*The Path from Howdy Doody
to SpongeBob*

Jo Holz

McFarland & Company, Inc., Publishers
Jefferson, North Carolina

ISBN (print) 978-1-4766-6874-1
ISBN (ebook) 978-1-4766-3060-1

LIBRARY OF CONGRESS CATALOGUING-IN-PUBLICATION DATA

BRITISH LIBRARY CATALOGUING DATA ARE AVAILABLE

Front cover: (on screen) Buffalo Bob Smith and Howdy Doody
(State Library and Archives of Florida); (beside television)
SpongeBob SquarePants (Viacom Media/Photofest)

Printed in the United States of America

McFarland & Company, Inc., Publishers
Box 611, Jefferson, North Carolina 28640
www.mcfarlandpub.com

Acknowledgments

I am deeply grateful to the many people who made this book possible. First and foremost, I owe a great debt to Kathleen Hall Jamieson, Director of the Annenberg Public Policy Center at the University of Pennsylvania, for suggesting I apply for a fellowship as a Professional in Residence at the APPC. This fellowship provided me with the time and resources to research the history of children's television and gave me a home base for my work within a supportive community of colleagues who were always generous with their thoughts and advice. I'm especially grateful to Amy Jordan, now professor and head of undergraduate studies at the Annenberg School for Communication, for her guidance, encouragement, and friendship. Michael X. Delli Carpini, Dean of the Annenberg School, also provided encouragement and made me feel welcome back at my alma mater. Returning to the Annenberg community made it possible for me to reconnect with my mentor and dissertation supervisor, Professor Emeritus Charles R. Wright, to whom I will always be grateful for giving me the intellectual foundation that has shaped all my work.

I was fortunate to have had the privilege of working for Joan Ganz Cooney and Gary Knell at Children's Television Workshop and Geraldine Laybourne at Oxygen Media. Their vision and creativity have been a continued source of inspiration for me.

Linda Simensky, VP of Children's Programming at PBS and an adjunct professor in cinema studies at Penn, generously reached out to me offering wisdom and insights from her experience at PBS, Cartoon Network, and Nickelodeon. Tim Brooks, co-author of *The Complete Directory to Prime Time Network and Cable TV Shows 1946-Present*, whom I met when we were colleagues in the research department at NBC, was perhaps the first person in whom I tentatively confided that I wanted to write about this subject. I am very grateful for Tim's immediate and sustained enthusiasm and his unyielding insistence that I needed to start working on the book. Horst Stipp, also my former colleague at NBC, helped convince me of the value of this work and shared his experiences working on *The Smurfs*. John Carey and Ed Keller, fellow researchers and Annenberg classmates, bolstered my confidence and offered insights from their experiences as book authors. My son, Michael Newman, even as a child provided invaluable insights about the TV shows he watched as he was growing up, and as an adult sharpened my perception of the changing functions children's TV programs now play and the shows that members of his generation still admire.

I would not have been able to complete this book without the help of my husband, Thomas Newman, who threw himself into the role of editor and contributor once the manuscript began to take form. Tom relentlessly challenged me to think more broadly, to interpret more deeply, to connect programs more tightly to their social context, and to articulate my ideas in ways that make this book a richer, more coherent, and more dramatic story than I realized I had it in me to write. The contributions of his eclectic intelligence and his gift for language are manifest throughout the book.

Lastly, I have to thank the many people—friends, colleagues, even unsuspecting casual acquaintances—who shared their memories about the children's shows they watched when they were young. The way that they lit up when they talked about their favorite shows convinced me that I was on the right track in thinking this was a topic that would resonate widely. Thank you all, you know who you are, and I'm grateful to all of you.

Table of Contents

Preface

The idea for this book first came to me when I was head of research for Children's Television Workshop (now Sesame Workshop), the producer of *Sesame Street* and many other wonderful children's shows. Much has been written about the origins of *Sesame Street* and how it was developed to address the concerns and conceptions about children, television, and learning that were prevalent in the late sixties, when the show was created. It occurred to me that all children's shows could be analyzed from that perspective, and that someone should write a sociocultural history of children's television programming, to show how the programs that have been offered to children have changed as the country has changed, as our norms and values have changed, as our culture has changed, and how we think about children has changed.

That was in the 1990s. I didn't think I could undertake such a project at that time, but I did begin writing a blog called *Classic Kids TV* (http://thestarryeye.typepad.com/kidstv/) as a way of starting to describe and analyze some of the earliest children's shows and see how much interest there might be in this topic. The brisk traffic that my blog generated told me that there was an audience for this kind of book and kept me motivated to work on it when the time was right. The impetus to write about this history has only sharpened since then, as the interplay among childhood, social forces, and the media has become even more complex and interesting.

The true origin of this book goes back even further. I came to this country as a refugee from post-war Europe. I was a young child, and television played a large role in my family's socialization, from learning English to learning about American culture and society. The children's shows I watched back then, like *The Howdy Doody Show*, *The Pinky Lee Show*, and *Ding Dong School*, were very important and meaningful to me. The experience of watching TV with my parents, which we did a lot, was full of pleasure and is now a source of fond memories. I think that provided the impetus for my scholarly interest in the mass media, my career in communications, and my decision to write this book.

We don't think about children now the same way that we did in the 1950s, when I was a child. Ideas about what would be entertaining to children, what would be good for them, and what would be harmful to them have changed as our world, our norms, and our culture have changed. This book analyzes the history of children's television as a reflection of those changes.

The book is intended to address what I see as an important gap in our scholarly and popular literature about children's television. While much has been written about the possible effects of television on children, much less attention has been paid to the actual contents of the programs that children watch. Of the few analyses that have looked at the programs produced for children, most have analyzed these shows to support theories about their effects on viewers (usually assumed to be negative). I take a different approach, because I want to understand the other side of the equation—why those kinds of shows were produced in the first place and why they took the form that they did. My analysis is informed by a broad background in media studies and communications research, both theoretical and applied. I have tried to cast an objective eye on these shows, to the extent that this is possible. If anything, this book is probably biased more by my sense of fascination and affection for most of these programs than by negative opinions about their quality or taste level or assumptions about their harmfulness.

In conducting the research for this book, in addition to an extensive literature review, I drew on various directories, guides, and anthologies of television programs, video recordings from DVD collections and YouTube, and my memories of shows I watched as a child and as a mother watching TV with my own child. I focused on shows produced specifically for children, based on the shows' content or the time of day when they aired (in the earliest days of commercial television, all shows initially aired only in the evenings; by the mid–1950s, late weekday afternoons and Saturday mornings became the times when children's shows were usually broadcast). Though children certainly watch other shows intended for general audiences, and such shows can also offer insights into social and cultural trends and conceptions about children that were prevalent at the time, such shows are generally beyond the scope of this analysis, and I have only included a few of them as examples of overall trends in television programming and popular culture, as part of the larger context within which shows for children were created. As for the age range that defines programming aimed at children, in the 1970s the FCC began to identify children's programs as those designed primarily for children aged 2–12, and that is the age range that I have used in this book as a general rule of thumb.

The book begins with an introduction that reviews scholarly thinking about childhood as a socially-constructed concept and briefly outlines the developments in American life that created an environment in which children's TV could take root and quickly flourish. The rest of the book is divided into seven chapters, each covering a specific time period in the history of children's television in the United States. Metaphorically treating the evolution of children's television as similar to a child's "growing up," the chapters have been labeled as if each represents a developmental stage in a child's life (except for the last chapter, whose title refers to a developmental stage in the very conception of childhood). Each chapter presents an overview of key trends in children's programs during that era and attempts to place those trends into the context of historical events, broader television industry trends, government regulation, demographic changes, changes in child-rearing and conceptions of childhood, and other social and cultural milestones of the time. Each chapter also includes detailed descriptions and in-depth analyses of typical, seminal, or iconic TV programs aimed at children during those years.

I have written this book with two different groups of readers in mind. For scholars, I believe this book will provide the first comprehensive sociocultural history of children's television in the United States. I have also tried to make the book approachable and appealing to a wider audience of general interest readers. Watching children's television is something almost all of us have experienced, and the shows we watched as children hold a special place in our hearts. Regardless of which generation of TV viewers you belong to, I hope this book will help you recall and enjoy memories of your favorite shows, see them from a new perspective, and perhaps gain an appreciation for shows that are the touchstones of other generations.

I've tried to capture as many of these shows as possible, but the history of children's television is long and crowded, so this overview is necessarily limited and selective. I know how strongly we all feel about the children's shows we watched growing up. If I have omitted or given short shrift to any of your favorite shows in this book, please accept my sincere apology.

Introduction

"Say kids, what time is it?"

In 1947, when Buffalo Bob first posed this question to America's children on *The Howdy Doody Show*, the answer was twofold. With troops back from the war, the economy booming, and the country firmly established as a world superpower, it was America's time. But for the children to whom the question was explicitly directed, it was *their* time, and they were ready to shout out the answer, the battle cry of the Baby Boom, the first revolution that was, indeed, televised: *"It's Howdy Doody Time!"* It was time to watch TV.

Skip forward seven decades, and *Howdy Doody* has been replaced by a sweet and slightly goofy animated yellow sponge who lives with his pals at the bottom of the sea. In the intervening years, television shows produced for children have taken on many different forms at different times, from fast-paced educational productions like *Sesame Street* to superhero fads like *Mighty Morphin Power Rangers* to surrealist animated parables like *Adventure Time*. Change has been constant and, while the direction may be hard to discern, it has not been random. So what has driven the evolution of children's television? This book suggests that there are patterns of change that mirror, not without distortion but in important ways, how our country, our society, and our culture have changed during that time. Perhaps most importantly, the changing content of these shows reflects fundamental shifts in the ways we think about children and childhood itself.

Purpose of This Book

This book looks at trends in children's television since its inception, both as a product of changing industry practices and government regulations and, more importantly, as a reflection of changes in broader social and cultural norms and changes in what adults have thought about children—their needs, their interests, what is good or bad for them, what might entertain them, and even what it means to be a child. A significant body of scholarship has developed around the idea that childhood is a socially constructed concept. As historian Steven Mintz notes, "Childhood and adolescence as biological phases of human development have always existed. But the ways in which childhood and adolescence are conceptualized and experienced are social and cultural constructions that have changed dramatically over time."[1] Similarly, David Buckingham argues that "childhood is historically, culturally, and socially variable. Children have been regarded—and have regarded themselves—in very different ways in different historical periods, in different cultures and in different social groups."[2]

In early medieval life, children had no special status, rights or privileges and were thoroughly integrated into the larger social milieu.[3] In the 17th century, the Puritans regarded children as potential sinners whose inherent aggressive and willful impulses had to be consistently suppressed. In the early 19th century, this highly religious and moralistic view was replaced by the Romantic concept of children as the embodiment of purity, innocence, and spontaneity. Rather than a condition that should be passed through as quickly as possible, childhood came to be seen as a stage of life to be enjoyed and prolonged, and the role of parents was to see that children's innocence and purity was not prematurely corrupted.[4] In the 20th century, child development experts like Dr. Benjamin Spock refined this approach with the view that children were inherently "good," and that the role of parents and society was to fulfill the child's needs and help children gain independence through self-discovery and self-fulfillment.[5]

This book will explore the changes in our conceptions of childhood since the mid–1940s, together with changes in children's television programs during that time, as dynamic elements that have transformed and reinforced each other. Mintz and other scholars suggest that children's TV shows and the advertising they carry have played a key role in the development of children's mass culture—the shared repository of images, characters, plots, and themes that serve as the basis for children's small talk and play and their sense of identity as distinct from the world of adults. Yet, while there has been a great deal written for both academic and popular audiences about the possible *effects* of television on children, the actual *contents* and the *nature* of the programs that have been produced for children have been given surprisingly short shrift. If one agrees with children's culture historian Stephen Kline that "television has become the undisputed leader in the production of children's culture,"[6] then one must also agree that television shows for children deserve much more careful attention and analysis than they have yet been accorded.

There have been a few excellent analyses of specific children's shows, especially *Sesame Street*, and of TV commercials aimed at children,[7] as well as a history of the children's cable network Nickelodeon,[8] but this book is the first to attempt an analysis of the major trends in children's programs from their earliest beginnings to the present. Given the large scope of this endeavor, this book is necessarily interpretive rather than exhaustive, selective rather than comprehensive. It attempts to identify the major societal events and cultural trends that have occurred during the lifespan of children's television in the U.S., and to draw connections between these events and trends and the kinds of television shows for children that were produced at the time. The goal is to provide a framework for understanding, or at least gaining insight into, the evolution of children's television in its historical, social, and cultural context.

Life in the U.S. at the Dawn of Television

What were some of the key developments and points of inflection that had shaped America in the decades leading up to the birth of the new medium of television? From 1880 until legislation setting quotas aimed at stemming the tide of new immigrants was enacted in 1921 and 1924, the proportion of Americans who were recent immigrants had skyrocketed as more than 22 million people migrated to the United States, filling jobs in mines, mills, and factories, helping to begin the transformation of the U.S. into a leading industrial power. The next few years were ones of tremendous social change. In 1920, for the first time, the majority of the population lived not in the countryside but in cities. Nineteen twenty also saw the passage of the 19th Amendment, which gave women throughout the U.S. the right to vote, prompting politicians to begin emphasizing issues like child health, public schools, and world peace, which were of special interest to women. There was increased support for conservative morality measures that addressed women's concerns, like Prohibition. The prosperity of the Roaring Twenties, when factory output grew by over 50 percent, meant that by 1927, there was electricity in two out of three homes, radios in one out of three, and 25 million new cars on the road. The Great Migration started during this time, when millions of African Americans left the rural South to settle in New York, Detroit, Chicago, Cleveland, Philadelphia, and other cities in the Northeast and Midwest. A global economic collapse, the Great Depression, slowed the growth of the nascent consumer culture to a crawl in the 1930s but only increased the disruption of the social order that had started in the 20s. With more than a quarter of the U.S. population unemployed, people were uprooted, families torn apart, limits of government authority transformed, and the legitimacy of sacred institutions questioned. It would take a cataclysmic event to forge a new national identity from the chaos of so much cultural change.[9]

It was the Second World War and its immediate aftermath that catapulted the country into the modern era and created the conditions that led to the rapid spread of television into the nation's homes. The war intensified the pace of the cultural evolution that the Depression had initiated. When American troops entered combat in 1941, the United States quickly and completely shifted to a war footing, with rationing and large scale militarization of the economy and the society as a whole. Sixteen million men served in uniform, while millions of women filled the labor force slots vacated by men, itself a watershed event with enormous unexpected consequences. The war put a rapid end to the Depression, returning the nation to full employment and locking in the social evolution that had slowly been creating the modern era.[10]

The war also disrupted children's lives. School attendance fell and child labor laws were relaxed during the war, as children were expected to contribute to the war effort and to their families' incomes. With fathers away in the military and many mothers working during the day, there was a relaxation of social restraints on children. Childcare was inadequate and expensive, so children without relatives to care for them were left to fend for themselves during the day.[11] Meanwhile, the civilian population continued to shift from farms and small towns into increasingly crowded urban centers, following work opportunities and the needs of mobilization, so that the generation of children raised during the Depression and war years were increasingly city kids, with an urban outlook very different from their parents' rural or small town upbringing.

These disruptions of normal family life led to growing public concerns about the difficulties of raising well-adjusted children who would become responsible members of society. Childrearing experts blamed the rise of Nazism on Germany's patriarchal and authoritarian family structure and overemphasis on obedience and strict discipline. At the same time, there were concerns about the potential dangers of America's more "democratic" family structure, with its lack of clearly defined roles or lines of authority.[12]

With families under stress during the war, schools took on a heightened role as instruments for building a more democratic society and common American culture. They instituted various rituals for fostering patriotism among their young charges, with a daily salute to the flag and recital of the Pledge of Allegiance chief among these. Sixteen states passed laws making it mandatory for students to participate in this daily morning display of fealty and national solidarity, under threat of expulsion and prosecution of their parents.[13]

The mass media also played a crucial role in teaching children why the country was at war and instilling patriotism and support for sacrifice. Wartime children's media reinforced the dominant message children heard in school, that the war was a struggle of good versus evil, in which everyone, including children, played an important role. Comic books, cartoons, movies, and radio shows aimed at children depicted Japanese and Nazi soldiers and leaders as comical, monstrous, or subhuman, in contrast to the altruism and superior moral mission which guided the Allies in their fight against the Axis.[14]

Wartime conditions also contributed to the growth of a distinctive teen culture. Teenagers and children had already begun to be treated as a distinct market segment during the Great Depression, when comic books, movies, radio shows, and the licensed toys they spawned were targeted to younger consumers, as advertisers searched for potential new areas of growth amidst the stalled economy. The expansion of mandatory high school enrollment during the 1930s also helped to institutionalize the teenage years as a separate stage of life. Conditions during World War II—fragmented families, employment of youth, and rapid urbanization—further enhanced adolescents' development of a distinct social identity, independent of their parents. The jobs that many teenagers took on during the war contributed to family income but also allowed them to pay for their own magazines, go to their own movies, buy their own records, and wear their own, distinctive clothing. Much to their parents' consternation, teens increasingly spent their leisure time outside the home, away from the family, and looked to their peers rather than their parents for guidance on what to think and how to behave.[15]

When the war ended in 1945, demobilized servicemen and women returned to a very different country than that of their Depression-era parents or the one they had known only five years earlier. The resumption of family life after wartime separations, plus the thriving postwar economy, plus perhaps a spirit of optimism following military victory, combined to ignite a population explosion, the demographic surge we know as the Baby Boom, resulting in the largest generation of children the country had ever seen.

Cities, already swollen from more than a generation of immigration from abroad and from within, had absorbed wartime workers to the point of saturation. With housing already in crisis as the war came to an end and soldiers returned home, it was imperative to find a solution. The government responded with postwar low-interest housing loans for returning GI's, and the private sector went into overdrive to build homes to sell to these new families. A new type of housing was developed that had a profound impact on how postwar middle-class families would live their lives—the mass-produced suburban tract house, priced so that even lower-middle-class or blue-collar workers who had never before been able to afford to buy property could purchase their own home.[16]

Waves of middle-class families with young children now eagerly began to migrate to newly-built suburban enclaves with row after row of nearly identical homes. Eleven million of the thirteen million homes constructed in the decade after World War II were in new suburban developments.[17] Here Americans could begin afresh, with a blank slate of limitless possibility before them. Suburban life offered the best of all worlds. It spoke to the normative, idealized, nostalgic, and mythic agrarian and frontier past from which Americans believed they derived their strength and values and from which they could realize their imagined calling to build a better world for their children on the ashes of the old. A new house with a yard, a good job, a big car, and some kids; for postwar families, these became the integral components of the American Dream.[18]

Television was born in this environment, which proved to be the perfect set of conditions for the new medium to thrive. Though initial television broadcasts had occurred in the 1930s, most famously at the 1939 World's Fair in New York, the issuing of television station licenses was suspended during World War II. Once the war was over and the FCC began issuing licenses again, the commercial television industry quickly shifted into high gear. Ownership of TV sets rose from .02 percent of U.S. households in 1946 to 9 percent by 1950, and to 65 percent by 1955.[19] At first, most television shows were produced by local TV stations and only available in their own areas.[20] However, radio network owners NBC, CBS, and ABC (which had been spun off from NBC's radio holdings in 1943 due to new FCC rules), as well as the Dumont Company, which was a manufacturer of TV sets, also owned their own television stations. They soon linked some of their stations together via coaxial cable, so that the same TV shows could be shown at the same time on the interconnected stations. This made it possible for local shows that became especially popular in their own areas to find their way onto the network schedules, where they could reach a larger audience.

Much of the medium's rapid growth was due to the postwar Baby Boom, the strong economy, and the new national preoccupation with domesticity and domestic leisure. In many ways, TV was the perfect medium for the nuclear family in postwar America, where households consisting of a working dad and a stay-at-home mom with young children, living in the suburbs, separated from their extended family, was now the norm. Watching television quickly became the country's favorite leisure activity, providing families with entertainment they could enjoy together in the privacy of their own homes, while at the same time giving them a new simplified surrogate community in the form of the television families who now entered their homes daily.

What they saw in those early TV shows helped viewers make sense of the new world in which they were living. Television taught its viewers the rules and norms of this new world, while presenting them with an idealized version of reality, largely devoid of any unpleasantness. For example, sitcoms like *I Love Lucy*, a huge hit from the day it debuted on CBS in 1951, gave viewers weekly illustrations about how to maneuver the "battle of the sexes," as Lucy and her neighbor Ethel regularly defied their husband's wishes by trying to find jobs or otherwise break out of the limitations of their happy homemaker roles. The women's escapades inevitably resulted in comical catastrophe, and they ended each episode back at home, chastened and promising to abide by the social expectations that their husbands personified. And yet, every following week would find Lucy and Ethel at it all over again. These plotlines let viewers enjoy and identify with Lucy's weekly rebellion, while reinforcing the prevailing social norms about men's and women's proper roles.[21]

The same was true for the role that television played in the lives of children. In TV shows and TV advertising, children saw idealized visions of society and how it expected them to behave. Though the postwar years were considered very family-oriented, other social institutions like schools, churches, and television took on a growing influence in children's socialization. These institutions, together with the commercial marketplace that television fostered, helped to create a separate youth culture in which certain experiences and references were shared by children's peer groups and from which parents were largely excluded.

Stay Tuned...

To understand the birth of children's television, it is vital to know this: television was born into a world of babies, lots and lots of babies, toddlers and youngsters. Families were booming, childhood was booming, and soon children's television would be booming, too.

CHAPTER ONE

The Birth
of Children's Television
(Late 1940s to Mid–1950s)

Life in the U.S.

The Baby Boom and the flight to the suburbs by the middle class at the end of World War II ushered in a new child-centered decade as the country experienced a growing emphasis on the nuclear family and domesticity. The separations and deaths of family members that so many Americans had experienced during the war led to a renewed emphasis on family life once the war ended. Americans with newly-rising incomes were eager to start new lives and enjoy their new-found prosperity, and having children was an important element of that fresh start. Parenthood became a symbol of success and maturity, and childless couples were treated as objects of pity.[1]

Parents sought to put the privations and anxieties they had been through during the Depression and the war behind them and to see that their children would be protected from such hardships and would enjoy the childhood pleasures that they themselves had had to forego. Moving to the suburbs was one way in which parents felt they could give their children a protected and trouble-free childhood. They could make a clean break with the past, with insecurities they associated with either rural or urban lives, with the gloom and difficulties that had filled their own childhoods. But the move to suburbia meant that many parents were now cut off from the extended families and circles of friends they had lived with in the cities and small towns that they left behind. As a result, members of the newly-independent nuclear family had to turn inward for practical and emotional support. At the same time, however, suburban living produced new lifestyle patterns that actually reduced the amount of time families spent with each other. Fathers were now commuting from the suburbs to the city for work, which meant they spent less time at home, while mothers were left to fend for themselves during the day tending to their new children and new homes.[2] Gwendolyn Wright, in her study of American housing, points out, "Now it was expected that the mother be a constant companion and gentle teacher. Since in the early 1950s few young families had a second car for the mother's use, and most new subdivisions had neither parks nor playgrounds, preschool children were home with their attentive mothers all day."[3]

In this environment, public attention to childrearing increased, together with concerns that faulty childrearing, which was conventionally framed as faulty mothering, would lead to serious problems for children and society. With fewer relatives and close friends nearby to turn to for advice about parenting, suburban mothers looked to books and magazine articles from a growing cadre of experts, to make sure they were raising their children properly. The most famous childrearing expert of this era was Dr. Benjamin Spock, whose 25-cent paperback, *The Common Sense Book of Baby and Child Care*, first published in 1946, became an indispensable part of every new mother's household.[4] Spock took Sigmund Freud's ideas about children's psychological development and translated them into terms that any parent could understand. He promoted a newly compassionate and less rigid approach to parenting, one that focused on the essential goodness of children and the importance of showering children with love rather than imposing rigid schedules on them or meting out harsh discipline in order to get children to obey.

Dr. Spock and other childrearing experts of the day also borrowed from Piaget's model of cognitive development, emphasizing the importance of the child's environment and the active achievement of intellectual growth. Experts advised mothers to be sure to provide the right amount of daily stimulation so that their children's minds would develop properly. This model fit the postwar sensibility that virtually unlimited potential was inherent in children and was simply waiting for the right circumstances to reveal it. It also placed the responsibility for creating the proper circumstances for releasing children's unlimited potential squarely on their mothers.[5]

The aim of parenting shifted from the previous generation's goal of raising children who were obedient, submissive, and docile, to raising children who were sociable, outgoing, secure, and adaptable. Being cooperative, congenial, and group-oriented came to be seen as the hallmarks of the well-adjusted child and adult as well as the basis for a successful society.

As for the overall mood and temperament of the country, the end of World War II ushered in what many have described as an age of conformity. The country, if not the world, had a yearning and a need for stability after the enormous disruptions of the war. In a November 5, 1951, cover story, *Time* magazine described the cohort that came of age at the tail end of World War II and were generating the Baby Boom as the "silent generation": "It wants to marry, have children, found homes.... Today's generation, either through fear, passivity, or conviction, is ready to conform." As William Manchester described this group in *The Glory and the Dream*, "They would conform to the dictates of society in their dress, speech, worship, choice of friends, length of hair, and above all, in their thought. In exchange they would receive all the rights and privileges of the good life; viz., economic security."[6]

In their paradigm-shifting 1950 study, *The Lonely Crowd*, sociologists David Reisman, Nathan Glazer and Reuel Denney characterized the predominant personality of postwar mass society as "other-directed," rather than tradition-directed or inner-directed. The authors posited that people who were other-directed tended to seek approval from others, to prefer group over individual action, and to freely subordinate their own needs and desires to the will of the crowd. *The Lonely Crowd* emphasized the growing importance of the "peer group" together with the mass media as primary forces in shaping people's attitudes and behavior.[7]

Life in the new mass-produced suburbs, where residents were under constant pressure to "keep up with the Joneses," further contributed to these conformist tendencies. The prefabricated houses in these suburban developments were often small and built close together, so that the homeowners could easily take the measure of each other's possessions and habits and try to emulate their neighbors' apparent levels of affluence and comfort.[8]

The emphasis on conformity meant that the postwar approach to child-rearing, often labeled as permissive, was quite rigid and restrictive in some ways. For example, gender distinctions were strictly enforced. Though many women had entered the workforce during the war, when the war ended and their husbands returned home, couples tried to reestablish their previous social expectations. Sons were encouraged to be active, tough, messy, and competitive, in order to prepare for their future roles as workers, soldiers, and breadwinners. Daughters were encouraged to be more passive, nurturing, neat, and cooperative, so they would become good wives and mothers. Parents were admonished to strictly reinforce gender norms and to respond negatively to any signs of gender-inappropriate behavior, whether "sissiness" in boys or tomboyish behavior in girls.[9]

Though middle-class life in the suburbs seemed at first idyllic, there were fault lines running below the surface. One of these was the issue of diversity, or lack of it. The GI Bill provided government-backed housing loans to all returning soldiers, but in reality, banks issued few if any mortgages to African American veteran applicants.[10] The Federal Housing Administration "preferred controlled, segregated subdivisions in suburban areas to more complex and diverse urban development," according to Wright, who points out that "until 1968, FHA officials still accepted unwritten agreements and existing 'traditions' of segregation."[11] The new suburban enclaves filled almost uniformly with white families, and suburbanites had minimal exposure to people of diverse ethnicities in their daily lives. Meanwhile, urban cores developed ghettos of concentrated populations of various races and ethnicities, which the dominant culture tried to ignore.[12]

This was not simply an accident. Segregation was the law of the land in the South, as were other forms of racial discrimination throughout the country. Bias against minorities was a deeply held norm in much of the nation. Racism was pervasive and, in most communities, considered socially acceptable as long as people observed various polite customs to simulate tolerance and avoid confronting unpleasant realities. Suburbs simply exacerbated the injustice because they siphoned off resources, including tax money for schools, from areas where minorities lived. It was not until May 1954 that the Supreme Court would hand down its decision that separate but equal schools were inherently unequal and therefore illegal. This was one of the early efforts to reform the culture of racism in the U.S., while decades of social evolution and conflict would pass before most minorities would see much change in their daily interactions with their white fellow citizens. Television would eventually play a role in that social movement, but reluctantly and slowly.

The immediate postwar era also brought new sources of stress and fear for the American public. One of the main sources of anxiety for parents in particular was polio, since children were its most common victims. This highly contagious virus-borne disease, which could cause permanent paralysis and even death, surged in the early 1950s, the ironic result of improved sanitation. Earlier, children had usually contracted the disease as infants, when the likelihood of paralysis was low. As hygiene methods improved, children caught the disease later in life, when the chances of partial or full-body paralysis or death were higher; treatment for severely afflicted children was confinement in an "iron lung," a chamber that facilitated their ability to breathe as their lungs became paralyzed. With no cure for the disease, terror gripped Baby Boomers' parents as polio swept through towns in epidemics during the warm summer months, leaving paralyzed children in its wake. This scourge finally ended when Jonas Salk developed a polio vaccine in 1952 and successfully tested it in a field trial with 1.8 million children nationwide in 1954. It had an immediate impact, and the creation of an oral version of the vaccine in the next decade brought the incidence of polio in the U.S. to virtually zero.[13]

The fear generated by polio was part of a larger atmosphere of anxiety about forces beyond the power of ordinary people to control. The primary source of perceived danger in the world in the 50s and early 60s was war. World War II was still a recent event and people knew what war meant, but at this moment in history, war loomed as a source of terror with a magnitude beyond anything known before. Devastating as the war had been in other countries, the mainland of the U.S. had been relatively untouched, and even the thousands of U.S. military losses paled compared to those experienced elsewhere. A new power had been unleashed, however, that could bring the forces of war to the U.S., and with unimaginably greater destruction.

As Communist forces seized control of governments in Europe and Asia after World War II, a "Cold War" developed between the United States and the Soviet Union. In 1949, the U.S. learned that the Soviet Union had tested an atomic bomb, which altered the military imbalance that had favored the U.S. when the war ended.[14] In China, Communist revolutionaries seized power. These tensions led to actual U.S. military engagement in 1950, when a U.S.-led United Nations force fought to defend a newly-partitioned South Korea against an invasion from North Korea, which was supported by the Soviet Union and China. By the time the Korean War ended, the nuclear powers were starting to produce hydrogen bombs, whose destructive power was a thousand times greater than the atomic weapons that had been used against Japan.[15]

Fear of an apocalyptic nuclear "exchange" and the realization that the nation's defense rested primarily on a policy of assured mutual destruction sent public paranoia into overdrive. Attempts to calm those fears and reassure the nation that such a war was survivable, even winnable, often backfired, spreading greater terror instead of tamping it down. The prevalence and intensity of the public's fear of nuclear war at the time is difficult to convey now, but one example might suggest how almost normal it was in American families to contemplate the imminent possibility of annihilation. A 1958 article in *Good Housekeeping* magazine published for the Thanksgiving issue and presented as a way to encourage rational preparations, vividly described the likely effects of a single atomic blast: "between one breath and the next, a quarter of a million lives are snuffed out. Everybody you know may be dead." It went on in great detail to paint a picture of the expected long-term effects of such a blast on major Midwestern cities and offered practical advice in the form of encouraging readers to prepare a home fallout shelter[16]—just the thing to discuss over the holiday turkey.

Building fallout shelters was well and good, some people thought, but they were angry as well as frightened, and wanted an enemy to blame. Communism was the obvious target for popular anger, and that anger and paranoia grew when government officials began warning the public about possible Soviet infiltrators and spies in their midst. Congressional committees like the House Un-American Activities Committee (HUAC) and private organizations like Counterattack were formed to identify and publicize the names of suspected Communists and Communist sympathizers in American society. One of HUAC's first targets was the Hollywood film industry, which HUAC claimed gave potential subversives a quick way to reach and influence the American public with Communist propaganda. Simply being identified as a possible Communist sympathizer and called in to testify before the Committee was enough to land Hollywood writers, actors, and producers on an unofficial "blacklist," which meant that they could no longer find work in their industry; some were even jailed.[17] The blacklist soon spread to include the television industry as well.[18]

This was the immediate context in which the emerging television industry began to take off. The Baby Boom provided the industry with an enormous new target audience for their programs and ads. TV manufacturers realized that children loved to watch television and that families with children were often the first to buy a TV set, so they advertised the new medium as good for children, something that the entire family could enjoy together in the privacy of their own home, and an "electronic babysitter" that would keep children entertained and out of mom's way as she prepared dinner and performed her housekeeping chores. As *Variety* noted about *Howdy Doody* at the time, "In the middle-class home, there is perhaps nothing as welcome to the mother as something that will keep the small fry intently absorbed and out of possible mischief. This program can almost be guaranteed to pin down the squirmiest of the brood."[19] Television programmers believed that indulgent parents allowed their children to control the TV set until their bedtime, so they placed a priority on offering children's shows in the early evening that would draw the largest audiences, so that the TV set would be tuned to their channel when parents settled down to watch TV later that night.

However, at the same time that the public and critics saw television as a way to engage and entertain children and bring the family together, they also worried about its potential harm to children and to family harmony. Of particular concern was what was seen as TV's encouragement of passive and addictive behavior. With the prewar child-rearing emphasis on submission, obedience, and docility replaced by the postwar focus on children actively achieving developmental milestones, the encouragement of passivity was seen as harmful to children, perhaps even pathological.[20]

These ambivalent attitudes toward television were part of a wider ambivalence about household modernization and all the new domestic technology that transformed the home and housework in the postwar years.[21] Though women's magazines urged their readers to be "up to date" and avail themselves of all the newest labor-saving devices, like vacuum cleaners and clothes driers, they also voiced concerns that these domestic machines could potentially dominate and control their owners. The television set became the focus of much of this concern. For example, *American Mercury* magazine referred to television as the "Giant in the Living Room," who could turn against his human masters at any moment: "He was a mere pip-squeak yesterday, and didn't even exist the day before, but like a genie released from a magic bottle in the *Arabian Nights*, he now looms big as life over our heads."[22] The public was constantly warned, "Don't let the television set dominate you!"[23]

Children were seen as most vulnerable to TV's potential for harm. Experts worried that television would produce passive and addictive behavior in children, who would be "glued to television" or "drugged" by it. Parents were warned to limit their children's television viewing lest it take over too much of their leisure time or cut into time that would be better spent doing homework or engaging in other wholesome or productive activities.

There was another concern about the impact of television viewing on children that added to these worries. Earlier mass media like comic books, dime novels, movies, and radio had all been criticized for their ability to expose children to types of knowledge that adults considered inappropriate or corrupting. Television now became the primary focus of these concerns, and it was often cited as a key factor in the perceived rise of juvenile delinquency in the early 1950s. Whether crimes by teenagers were actually increasing or had just become more likely to lead to arrests, there was a social panic over juvenile delinquency that may have been based in growing fears about changes in how young people behaved and the rapid changes in broader postwar society. The popular wisdom at the time was that juvenile delinquency was the result of two interrelated forces—a dysfunctional postwar family life and the corrupting influence of the mass media, primarily television. Anxiety about psychologically unbalanced families with weak, hen-pecked fathers and smothering, overindulgent mothers permeated popular culture. Experts argued that this left children vulnerable to the influence of unsavory outside forces like television, resulting in immoral and criminal behavior.[24]

The producers of the first television shows for children lived in this environment and were inevitably influenced by it. Together with market forces and government regulations, the prevailing values, norms, and preoccupations of the country, as well as ideas about children and what would be appropriate entertainment for them, all contributed to the types of children's shows that were first produced and broadcast into the country's homes.

The First TV Shows for Children

If there is a single birthday for children's television, it would have to be March 11, 1947, the day that *Movies for Small Fry* debuted on the Dumont television network. As described by TV historians Tim Brooks and Earle Marsh,[25] the show initially consisted of just theatrical cartoons and other movies for children, with an off-screen voiceover by "Big Brother" Bob Emery. Emery had previously had a successful career in radio, entertaining children with wholesome shows that included lessons in good behavior along with the fun and games.

Movies for Small Fry soon evolved into the *Small Fry Club*, adding a studio setting with a live audience of children and incorporating most of the elements that would become typical of many other early children's shows—a variety format with cartoons and silent films, puppets, songs, demonstrations, and sketches by a studio cast of actors representing different animals, like Honey the Bunny, Mr. Mischief the Panda, Peggy the Penguin, and Trina the Kitten. As with Emery's prior radio show, the *Small Fry Club* was both entertaining and educational, including segments about current events, literature, travel, and music, as well as lessons about health and nutrition, good manners, self-discipline, and respect for others.

Emery referred to himself as "Big Brother," but from the perspective of his young viewers, he seemed more like a kindly uncle. He always appeared in a business suit, wore dark-rimmed glasses, and comported himself in a gentle, respectful manner. He sang and played the banjo, beginning each show with a rendition of "The Grass Is Always Greener in the Other Fellow's Yard," a song from the 1920s about being satisfied with what you have and not being envious of others.

True to the show's "club" title and Emery's interest in encouraging active viewer participation, the *Small Fry Club* offered membership cards to its viewers so that they could officially join the "club," and thousands of children wrote in for them. They also sent in letters, pictures and drawings, and joined in contests that the show held. By 1950, the "club" could claim 150,000 "active" members.

The *Small Fry Club*, which had aired weekly at first, soon expanded to five days a week at 7–7:30 p.m., beginning the television day for those families who were lucky enough to have a TV set at home. It became one of the most successful series on the Dumont network and aired there for more than four seasons before it was cancelled in 1951. After the show's network cancellation, host Bob Emery went on to do a popular local version of the show in Boston, until he finally retired in 1968.

The *Small Fry Club* became a common template for early children's shows that followed it onto the air in the late 1940s and early 1950s. The fact that it had originated as a radio show was also typical of many of the first shows on television for both children and adults, since television was structured, managed and controlled by the same people and companies responsible for commercial radio. Many successful radio shows were repurposed for television, but in this exploratory stage in the evolution of children's television, program creators also freely borrowed from earlier forms of live entertainment as well as other media and genres for both adults and children, including those drawn from movies, comics, and literature. With no track record of what types of shows would be most successful, program creators tried every kind of show and format that they thought might possibly appeal to children and families. There were storytelling shows, puppet shows, circus shows, variety shows, talent shows, animal shows, quiz and game shows, Westerns, science fiction shows, educational shows, news shows, cartoons, and more, some hard to pigeonhole.

Most of the earliest children's shows were produced in studios and broadcast live, as was all local programming and most network shows, since relatively inexpensive recording technology like videotape had yet to be invented. Budgets for these early shows were minimal, and audiences, thrilled by the idea that there were moving pictures in their living rooms, had low expectations for production quality.

While shows for children were primarily designed to entertain their

young audiences, these shows also incorporated moral lessons and guidance on good behavior. Children's shows avoided content that included
violence, sex, or anything considered excessively scary, suspenseful, or
otherwise too intense for children's delicate sensibilities, though the latter
was subject to broad interpretation. Scripted stories or plots were usually
morality tales in which heroes always vanquished villains and good always
prevailed over evil. The National Association of Broadcasters, the main
trade organization for the radio and TV industry, formally incorporated
these restrictions in its first television code, adopted in 1951. The code
also specified that on shows for children, criminals should always be pun-
ished and social institutions like marriage should always be depicted
respectfully.[26]

As was the case with the *Small Fry Club*, program creators often tried
to address concerns about television being a passive experience that did
not contribute to children's cognitive development by including forms of
audience participation, like contests that required viewers to write or
phone in, or by encouraging viewers to play along at home with activities
on the show. A live studio audience of children was an on-screen element
of many of these shows, and they often referred to the studio audience or
the viewers at home as a "club," further promoting the group-oriented
values and focus on peer orientation that were so prevalent then. In line
with racial and ethnic prejudices at the time, the makeup of these on-
screen viewer "clubs" was almost exclusively white, with few if any children
of color in the studio audience or among the characters or performers on
the shows.

Gender role expectations at that time were also reflected on the air.
Though there were a few notable exceptions, the hosts or stars of the earliest children's shows, whether humans, puppets, or cartoon figures, were
invariably male, while girls and women played supportive secondary roles.

As Lynn Spigel, a scholar of early children's television, notes, many
of these early children's shows presented a fantasy world where there were
few if any differences between children and adults and the social con-
straints and harsh realities of adult life did not exist.[27] Though the popular
press and advice literature of the day emphasized the need to maintain
age-based hierarchies and adult authority over children, "the actual children's television programs that emerged in this period played with the
culturally prescribed distinctions between adults and children. Drawing
upon the fantasy figures of children's literature, puppet shows, the circus,
movies, and radio programs, these television shows engaged the hearts of
children (and often adults as well) by presenting a topsy-turvy world

where the lines between young and old were blurred and literally represented by clowns, fairies, and cowboys who functioned as modern-day Peter Pans."[28]

Children's Show Genres

"Reality" Shows

Many of the earliest children's shows took activities or forms of live entertainment that had long been popular with children and families—story-telling, drawing and sketching, games, puppets, circuses, vaudeville shows, and talent contests—and staged them for broadcast, often including a studio audience of children and sometimes also parents who were shown on the air. Today, we would probably refer to this television category as "reality" shows. Programs sometimes blended together two or three of these types of entertainment, so there were shows that combined story-telling with drawing and sketching, vaudeville or variety shows that included puppets or circus acts, and so on.

Story-Telling and Drawing/Sketching Shows

Some of the earliest shows for children featured a host or hostess telling stories, sometimes accompanied by music, puppets, or child actors illustrating the stories. The first TV series of this type was *The Singing Lady*, which debuted on ABC in 1948. Based on a highly successful earlier radio show, each episode featured the Singing Lady, Ireene Wicker, singing songs and reciting stories drawn from Native American legends, fairy tales, or childhood events in the lives of world and national leaders, composers, artists, and writers, often acted out by marionettes. The stories emphasized the importance of courtesy, compassion, and the avoidance of cruelty or violence. In an unfortunate turn of events that was all too common at the time, the show was abruptly cancelled in 1950, when *Red Channels* magazine accused Wicker of being a Communist sympathizer. Though her accusers later admitted that they might have been mistaken, Wicker's TV career never recovered.[29]

Along with simple storytelling, some of these shows also took advantage of TV's visual dimension by adding drawing and sketching to their storytelling. These shows sometimes included an element of audience participation by providing instructions for how to draw or by encouraging viewers to sketch along with the program. By adding these participatory features, these shows tried to counter the public concern that watching TV was a passive experience which would have negative effects on child viewers. And in fact, shows like these were recommended for children by such trusted sources as *Parents Magazine*: "The idea of the drawing program ... promises to become very popular on television. WJZ-TV and its affiliates show *Cartoon Teletales*, with one artist drawing illustrations for stories told by his companion. On WABD New York's *Small Fry Club*, and WTMJ Milwaukee's *Children's Corner*, drawings sent in by children are shown on the screen. And on WCBS-TV there is a program which shows real television originality and inspires creative activity by the young audience: *Scrapbook, Jr. Edition*; among its features is a cartoon strip beginning a new adventure story, and the children are asked to write in their ideas for an ending; then the winning conclusion is drawn by the artist in another cartoon strip shown the following week."[30]

Winky Dink and You, which debuted on CBS in 1953, was one of the most interesting and unusual shows of this type. It starred host Jack Barry, who showed clips of the animated adventures of a crudely-drawn star-headed, big-eyed little boy named Winky Dink and his dog Woofer. What made the show unique was the use of a "magic drawing screen" and set of special crayons that came in a kit that children could send away for in order to interact with the show. The magic screen was actually a large TV-shaped piece of see-through plastic that could be made to stick to the television screen by static electricity. At several points throughout the show, young

Winky Dink and You, which debuted on CBS in 1953, starred host Jack Barry, who showed clips of the animated adventures of a crudely-drawn star-headed, big-eyed little boy named Winky Dink. Children were urged to order a kit that included a "magic drawing screen" (a sheet of clear plastic) and set of special crayons so they could draw on the TV screen during the show.

viewers were instructed to use their crayons to draw on the plastic sheets attached to their TV screens in order to complete various scenes that were shown with key visual elements missing.

For example, Winky Dink would sometimes encounter some obstacle or danger, along with a connect-the-dots picture included in the scene. Winky would then ask the children at home to help him out by connecting the dots on the screen with their crayons, and the resulting drawing would turn out to be a rope, ladder, bridge, or whatever Winky needed to get out of his predicament.

The interactive screen was also used to send secret messages to the audience. A message would appear on the screen, but only the vertical lines of the letters in the message were visible. Viewers at home would quickly trace these lines onto their magic screen. Then a second television image would appear showing only the horizontal lines of the message, and when viewers also traced these onto their magic screens, the full message would appear.

Winky Dink and You took advantage of the public's concerns about television viewing leading to passivity in children by touting the use of its magic screen as a form of active engagement. In one of his frequent on-air sales pitches urging children to get their parents to buy them the magic screen kit, host Jack Barry put it this way: "Now, I know you're just used to watching television shows and you just sit back and watch all the other shows, but not this show. This show, you really get a chance to be a part of 'cause it's different. You get a chance at home to play right along with us, and what you at home draw actually becomes part of the program."[31]

Because of the ingenious magic screen, *Winky Dink and You* became a big hit in the early 1950s. And the producers profited handsomely from sales of the screen and crayon kits, which every child had to have. In fact, by 1955, over 2 million kits had been sold. If parents wouldn't buy the kits, some children resorted to getting out their own crayons and drawing directly on their TV screens. Understandably, this caused some parental backlash. There was also concern that children were harming their eyesight by sitting so close to the TV when they were drawing on the screen, or that they were being exposed to "radiation" emanating from TV sets. Radiation was a grave concern that was poorly understood in these times, when tests of atomic bombs were known to be producing actual radioactive fallout. These concerns led to the show's cancellation in 1957, despite its popularity.

Variety Shows

Variety is a genre dating back to the days of vaudeville, a type of popular live entertainment which had thrived at the turn of the century in special theaters called vaudeville houses, like New York City's famed Palace Theater. The vaudeville format consisted of a series of different acts of various kinds—musical performances, dance routines, magic acts, comedy skits, etc.—introduced by a master of ceremonies who provided continuity and managed the flow of the performances. Variety shows on radio had proven popular, and live TV variety shows like *Texaco Star Theater* with Milton Berle on NBC and *The Toast of the Town* with host Ed Sullivan on CBS, which both debuted in 1948, quickly became big hits. As TV historian Gary Edgerton aptly notes, even in their day, shows like these were forms of "throwback entertainment from an earlier America, providing viewers with the kind of comforting escape and amusement that they temporarily craved in the immediate wake of World War II."[32]

The variety format also lent itself well to early TV shows for children, like *The Small Fry Club*. Beginning in the late 1940s, ventriloquist Paul Winchell and his dummy Jerry Mahoney starred in several popular variety and puppet shows that remained on the air in one form or another through 1965. Their best-known show, initially called the *Speidel Show*, after the show's sponsor, the Speidel watch company, and later called the *Paul Winchell Show* and then the *Paul Winchell and Jerry Mahoney* show, presented a mix of puppetry, comedy, music, quizzes, guest star appearances, and even drama segments, all performed in front of a live studio audience. The show would open with a comedy routine by Winchell and Mahoney. Jerry's personality was that of a sassy wise-cracking child or adolescent. Winchell, acting the role of a rational adult, would try to have a conversation with Jerry, but as Jerry responded with provocative smart-aleck comments, Winchell would become increasingly exasperated with his dummy's antics and insolence. After this opening comedy routine, the two would then act as emcees for a quiz segment called "What's My Name?" in which contestants drawn from the studio audience and viewers called at home would try to guess the identity of a famous personality as guest stars acted out or sang the clues. For a while, the show also included a brief dramatic vignette starring a well-known actor or actress in a serious short story, but that odd segment was soon dropped. The Winchell-Mahoney variety show aired in the evenings, where it would reach a family audience. In 1954, Winchell and Mahoney moved to a weekend daytime show called *Jerry Mahoney's Club House*, aimed specifically at child viewers.[33]

The children's show that probably captured the essence of the variety genre best was the *Pinky Lee Show*. The show premiered on NBC in 1950 as a live half-hour variety show for adults starring vaudevillian entertainer Pinky Lee but transitioned to a children's show in 1954. The star was a multi-talented child-like performer in baggy pants, a loud checkered jacket, a bow-tie, and a little Porkpie hat, who could sing, dance, and perform slapstick comedy routines. Pinky's persona was an example of what Lynn Spigel refers to as "liminal characters" typical of many children's shows, "characters that existed somewhere in between child and adult," who often acted out playful forms of rebellion against social norms about proper behavior.[34] Such characters would have been especially appealing as escapist fantasies for audiences in the 1950s. Whenever conformity is highly valued, people seek relief in sanctioned forms of symbolic deviancy. That was Pinky's appeal in a nutshell.

Pinky was in constant motion, dancing and running around the stage and jumping into the studio audience to interact with the children and mothers there. In the sketches on his show, Pinky played a mischievous character who was always doing what he was told not to do, and he often teased and played jokes on the mothers and children in his studio audience, evoking constant gales of laughter. The frenetic pace of the show and Pinky's naughty behavior drew criticism from TV critics and commentators like *New York Times* television reviewer Jack Gould, reflecting the views of some child-rearing experts that this kind of overstimulation was not healthy for children: "The screen lights up and there is hysterical bedlam—screaming and wild jumping up and down by Mr. Lee. He induces little children to do the same, and even worse, their mothers. The whole operation is a sort of organized frenzy designed to whip children into a high emotional pitch."[35] In fact, Lee collapsed on the air during a live telecast of his show in 1955, apparently from exhaustion. He recovered and later returned to the air, but his show was cancelled soon after.

PUPPET SHOWS

Puppets have been entertaining children and adults for centuries, and they were a central element in many of the earliest television shows for children. With their diminutive size and often unruly behavior, puppets encourage children to identify with them, and they can act out behavior and adventures that children (and adults) wish they could engage in.

One of the most famous puppet shows of this era was *Kukla, Fran, and Ollie.* Created by puppeteer Burr Tillstrom, who handled all the puppets on the program, the show made its debut in 1947 as *Junior Jamboree* on the NBC station in Chicago, the source of many children's programs in the early days of television. From 1949 to 1954, NBC put the show on their national network schedule. After that it moved to ABC, where it ran until 1957.

The show's format consisted simply of female host Fran Allison standing in front of a puppet stage and interacting with Kukla and Ollie, the two hand puppet stars of the show, and a rich array of other puppet characters who were called the Kuklapolitans. Kukla was a sweet and gentle red-nosed clown who served as the sensible though somewhat over-earnest leader of the group. Ollie was a mischievous snaggle-toothed dragon who often instigated the funnier interchanges on the show. The other puppet characters included Fletcher Rabbit, the town mailman and fussbudget; Madame Ophelia Oglepuss, a former opera diva; Beulah Witch, a hideous but lovable witch who rode a jet-propelled broomstick; stage manager Cecil Bill, who spoke a language that only the other puppets understood; Colonel R.H. Crackie, a courtly Southern gentleman; Ollie's mother Olivia Dragon; and Ollie's cousin, Dolores Dragon, who started out as a toddler and grew into a teenager during the years that the show ran. Host Fran Allison, who was the only human who appeared on air, served as straight man to the puppets.

Kukla, Fran, and Ollie combined a simple format and gentle, sweet atmosphere with adult-level wit and sly satire, and it quickly became a hit among both children and adults. Producer and head puppeteer Burr Tillstrom insisted that his show was not intended just for children, and he sometimes dealt with topics that would have been difficult for children to understand. For example, one episode focused on the concept of "taste cultures," the idea that artistic or cultural creations and interests could be categorized as lowbrow, middlebrow, or highbrow, which had been the controversial focus of an issue of *Life* magazine at the time. Though each episode had a pre-established theme and general storyline, the dialogue between Fran Allison and the puppets, all played by Tillstrom, was largely improvised, giving the show a large dose of spontaneity.

Unlike *Kukla, Fran, and Ollie*, most of the other early puppet shows that debuted in the late 1940s and early 1950s were simpler and aimed at a level that young children could easily understand. These shows, like the *Adventures of Oky Doky, Lucky Pup, Uncle Mistletoe and His Adventures, Judy Splinters, Alkali Ike, Paddy the Pelican, Life with Snarky Parker*, and many others were fun for children to watch but also often conveyed lessons about proper behavior, good manners, self-discipline, or health and nutrition. For example, *The Whistling Wizard*, which aired on CBS from 1951 to 1952, featured Bil and Cora Baird's marionettes in a show set in the magical "Land of Beyond," where young hero J.P., his horse Heathcliffe, and their protector, Dooley, a leprechaun with a magic flute, who was known as the Whistling Wizard, battled villains like Kohlrabi and his mistress, the Spider Lady. The show tried to convey lessons about the ups and downs of life and the need for perseverance.

Kukla, Fran, and Ollie was a sophisticated puppet show aimed at both adults and children. The show's puppet stars were little clown Kukla (left) and snaggle-toothed dragon Ollie, seen here bundled up for winter weather.

Early puppet shows reached their quintessential form with *Howdy Doody*. Undoubtedly the most famous and successful show of this type, the *Howdy Doody* show had its roots in a prior radio program called *Triple B Ranch*. The television version debuted in December 1947 as a weekly program on NBC called *Puppet Playhouse*, where it quickly became a hit. By August 1948, NBC was airing the *Howdy Doody* show five days a week. Set in the fictional Western circus town of Doodyville, the show starred Howdy Doody, an ever-smiling, red-headed, freckle-faced, all-American boy marionette in a Western outfit that included a plaid shirt, blue jeans, cowboy boots, and a red bandanna around his neck. Buffalo Bob was the show's human buckskin-clad host (he also provided the voices for Howdy as well as several other marionettes on the show). The show also featured a live studio audience of young children, referred to as the Peanut Gallery. Each show began with Buffalo Bob asking, "Say kids, what time is it?" and the Peanut Gallery yelling in unison, "It's Howdy Doody time!" A typical episode of the show consisted of a film short, a musical number or two, and a skit involving Doodyville residents. There were also games and contests with children from the Peanut Gallery.

Besides host Buffalo Bob, there were a number of other human characters on the show, who all came from the circus or Wild West shows. Buffalo Bob's assistant was Clarabell, a voiceless clown who communicated via body language and by honking a horn attached to his/her belt (Clara-

bell's gender was indetermi-
nate, though the character was
played by a male performer). In
true circus and vaudeville tradition, Clarabell always carried
a seltzer bottle and sometimes
squirted people with it. Other
human characters on the show
included Chief Thunderthud, a
Native American tribal leader
who originated the exclama-
tion "Kowabunga!"; Princess
Summer-Fall-Winter-Spring, a
Native American princess of
the fictional Tinka Tonka tribe;
Bison Bill, who filled in as host
when Buffalo Bob was absent;
and Ugly Sam, a wrestler.

There was also a colorful
assortment of distinctive marionette characters, including
Phineas T. Bluster, the mayor
of Doodyville and Howdy and
Buffalo Bill's cranky nemesis;

NBC's *Howdy Doody* show was the quintessential TV puppet show. Seen here are
buckskin-clad host Buffalo Bob and Howdy
Doody.

Dilly Dally, a dim-witted carpenter who was usually tricked by Bluster into doing his dirty work for him; Flub-a-dub, a creature composed of parts of several different animals; Captain Scuttlebutt, a sea captain who piloted an old scow; John J. Fadoozle, a detective; Don Jose Bluster and Hector Hamhock Bluster, Phineas' triplet brothers; Double Doody, Howdy's twin brother; Heidi Doody, Howdy's sister; and Sandra, a witch. In 1956, the filmed adventures of Gumby, a Claymation figure, were added to the show and became so popular that Gumby later was given his own series.

Lynn Spigel points out that host Buffalo Bob, like many other hosts of children's shows, was both a grown-up and a cowboy, an adult who had not abandoned the land of make-believe.[36] Though Howdy Doody was apparently a child, Buffalo Bob's interactions with him did not take the form of adult-to-child behavior but rather seemed like the interactions of two peers. In fact, all the characters on the show, whether representing adults or children, treated each other as peers.

The *Howdy Doody* show integrated moral lessons and instruction in good behavior throughout the show. Every episode would feature skits in which scheming amoral characters like Phineas T. Bluster would try to get the better of good characters like Howdy but would be thwarted by Howdy and his friends' superior intelligence and higher morality.

The *Howdy Doody* show combined two popular themes and settings in American culture—the Western and the circus—and many children's shows that followed used these settings. Other puppet shows placed their characters in fantasy settings where they had adventures and sometimes confronted evil villains. For example, *Time for Beany* starred a little boy hand puppet named Beany who sailed the seas with his sea captain uncle, together with Cecil, a sea serpent who was Beany's friend. The hand puppet star of the *Rootie Kazootie Show* was a kazoo-playing baseball cap-wearing Little Leaguer, accompanied by his pet dog Gala Poochie and his girlfriend Polka Dottie, and they regularly tangled with evil villain Poison Zoomack.

Smilin' Ed's Gang/Andy's Gang is noteworthy in that it was one of the few early children's variety/puppet shows that was not broadcast live but rather shot on film. The show was originally hosted by "Smilin' Ed" McConnell and was based on his popular radio show. When McConnell died of a heart attack in 1954, he was replaced as host by the folksy character actor Andy Devine, and the show was renamed *Andy's Gang*.

True to the variety show format, *Smilin' Ed's Gang/Andy's Gang* was a mixture of stories, film clips, and onstage skits involving the host and several puppets. The show would begin with Smilin' Ed or Andy sitting in a big easy chair, reading from a book of stories, which were illustrated by film clips. The setting was a vaudeville theater, with the action taking place on a stage and an audience of children sitting in the theater seats. However, the numerous reaction shots of the audience that were interspersed throughout the show were always the same, having been filmed separately and simply edited into each episode of the show.

The main character on the show was Froggy the Gremlin, a rubbery frog hand puppet who lived inside a grandfather clock on the stage and, through the magic of film, would suddenly appear when the host said the words, "Plunk your magic twanger, Froggy!" Froggy was a rascal who usually misbehaved while the host wasn't looking. He had some kind of magical power over people, since he could get the host to smash cream pies into his own face or do other silly or bizarre things. Froggy would engage in increasingly wilder pranks behind the host's back, which were intercut with canned scenes of a theater full of children laughing and shrieking, louder and louder, until finally Froggy would begin to vibrate and then suddenly disappeared in a puff of smoke.

Unlike most other children's shows at the time, in which good behavior was encouraged and bad behavior usually led to negative consequences, Froggy's shenanigans went unpunished and ended up making the adult host of the show look foolish or embarrass himself by losing his temper. Froggy was a character very much in the tradition of the "trickster" from folklore and mythology, who would appeal to a child's natural desire to subvert authority and celebrate naughtiness. Like other tricksters, by giving children a "safe" outlet for their fantasies of breaking social rules and getting the better of their parents and other adult authority figures, Froggy ultimately served the purpose of maintaining and reinforcing the established rules and norms.

Puppet show *Johnny Jupiter* was an unusually sophisticated show that took a satirical look at the foibles of our civilization through the eyes of inhabitants from another planet. The premise was that a teenage techno-nerd named Ernest P. Duckweather had invented a magic TV set through which he made contact with beings on the planet Jupiter—Johnny Jupiter, B-12, and B-12's robot, Major Domo—and they became long-distance friends. The Jupiter inhabitants could observe Earth through the interplanetary TV connection and were bewildered by what they saw of human behavior, since social norms on Jupiter were often the opposite of those on Earth. For example, on Jupiter, being forced to watch TV was used as a form of punishment for children who spent too much time reading books. The show skewered many aspects of American culture, from the political system to taxation to the new American space program. By satirizing American norms and behavior that children were taught to follow, *Johnny Jupiter* was a transgressive show that would have appealed to children's sense of absurdity about the social rules they had learned and their secret desire to flout those rules.

CIRCUS SHOWS

Like puppets, a classic form of entertainment for children and families, the visual spectacle of the circus made it another natural genre for early television shows. Two live shows with circus elements, *The Magic Clown* on NBC and *Super Circus* on ABC, debuted in 1949 and were successful enough to remain on the air through the mid–1950s. Both shows featured classic circus acts like cyclists, trampoline artists, clowns, and magicians, as well as audience participation games, humorous skits, singing acts, and so on. One of the stars of *Super Circus*, blonde baton twirler/band leader Mary Hartline, became one of TV's first popular heartthrobs and fan idols.

Talent Shows

Having demonstrated their popularity on the radio, talent shows aimed at general audiences, like *Arthur Godfrey's Talent Scouts* and *Ted Mack's Original Amateur Hour*, were among the first shows on television when they debuted in 1948 and became instant hits. They quickly spawned other shows with similar formats, including several featuring or aimed at children. These talent contests were broadcast live and usually included live studio audiences. Two early versions which went on the air in 1951 were *Grand Chance Roundup*, in which young contestants performed in a Western setting (actually an outdoor set in Philadelphia), and *The Talent Shop*, which was set in a New York City drugstore. Other entries in this genre included *M & M Candy Carnival*, which debuted in 1952, and *Contest Carnival* in 1954.

Game/Contest Shows

Game shows had been popular on the radio and were easily transferred to TV, where they were among the first shows on the air. Some were aimed specifically at children and families.

One of the earliest entries was *Juvenile Jury*, which debuted on NBC in 1947. Based on a successful radio show, *Juvenile Jury* was a live show that featured a panel of children who gave spontaneous advice in response to questions about social problems that viewers had mailed in. The advice that the young panelists provided to questions about proper etiquette, how to discipline children, and how to handle awkward social situations was often very funny. For example, one mother wrote in about her daughter's habit of waking up so early for school each day that she would arrive at school before the doors opened and have to wait outside, after having woken the rest of the family unnecessarily. A six-year-old boy panelist offered this response to the situation: "Maybe she gets ready fast and early now, but wait till she gets older. Wait till she starts putting lipstick on and wearing a girdle."[37]

Scrapbook, Jr. Edition aired on CBS beginning in 1948. Viewers mailed in information or examples of their hobbies, so that others could learn from them. Each telecast also featured a contest in which a child viewing at home would be called on the phone and asked to identify what was wrong with a picture that represented a nursery rhyme. If they answered correctly, they won a prize, which could be anything from a bicycle to a pet dog.

Like *Juvenile Jury*, *The Quiz Kids*, which premiered on NBC in 1949, had also begun as a radio show. It featured a panel of five child prodigies ages six to sixteen answering difficult questions on a range of topics. Viewers could send in questions for the panelists and received cash prizes if their questions stumped the panel. Child panelists remained on the show as long as they continued to answer the questions correctly, and some stayed on for weeks or months.

Hail the Champ was a game show in which teams of children competed in various athletic stunts in front of a studio audience. Each episode featured three qualifying rounds in which boys competed against girls. The three finalists then competed against each other in a timed set of activities, and the champ received a prize, like a bicycle.

Another early ABC show, *Your Pet Parade*, featured a different type of contest. Each week, three or four children would put their trained pets through their paces, while a professional trainer of movie animals would judge their performance. The winner would get prizes, including a year's supply of the sponsor Ralston-Purina's dog or cat food.

Educational Shows

While many early TV shows for children had an indirect educational element in the sense that they tried to inculcate morals, values, and good behavior as a secondary goal to providing entertainment, other shows had a more explicit educational objective. One of the earliest educational shows was *Mr. I. Magination*, which debuted on CBS in 1948. As its name suggests, this live show was aimed at stimulating children's creativity and encouraging them to use their imagination. The host of the show was Paul Tripp, author of the successful children's book *Tubby the Tuba*, who had once worked at a settlement house on New York's Lower East Side. Tripp played the role of a magical train engineer dressed in overalls and cap. Each week he took young "passengers" on a musical journey to places like Imagination Town, Ambition Town, and I-Wish-I-Were Land, where any child's wish could come true. Viewers wrote in about dreams and fantasies they wanted to see, which were often acted out on the show.

Several early educational shows pioneered ways to present science on television, which would become a recurring subject in children's programming, often recycling similar formats over the years. *Science Circus* on ABC starred an absent-minded professor host who performed scientific experiments in front of a live studio audience. *Adventure* on CBS was produced in partnership with the American Museum of Natural History in New York. *Exploring God's World* on CBS also focused on natural history by showing documentary films about nature topics.

Other natural history shows were broadcast live from local zoos, where a host would take viewers on a tour of select exhibits each week while discussing animal behavior and answering children's questions. There was *Sunday at the Bronx Zoo* on ABC, *Zoo Parade* from Chicago's Lincoln Park Zoo on NBC, and *Meet Me at the Zoo* on CBS, telecast from the Philadelphia Zoo.

The most successful and long-lived of the early science education shows was NBC's *Watch Mr. Wizard*, which debuted in 1951 and aired continuously until 1965, with a brief revival in 1971–1972 and a later incarnation on Nickelodeon from 1983 to 2000. Host Don Herbert played the role of Mr. Wizard, a friendly scientist whom the neighborhood kids loved to visit at his home. On each episode, a visiting child would ring Mr. Wizard's doorbell, and Mr. Wizard would let them in and have them assist him in carrying out simple scientific experiments with everyday objects. Mr. Wizard's child assistants were an equal mix of girls and boys, an approach to gender parity that was highly unusual at the time.

Watch Mr. Wizard was a TV sensation and reportedly generated an interest in science for many children. By 1953, there were 4,400 Mr. Wizard science clubs all across the country, and 200 schools had made the program required homework.[38]

Two other early educational shows, *Ding Dong School* and *Romper Room*, were aimed at preschoolers. Both shows simulated a preschool or kindergarten setting, and unlike most other children's shows at the time, both shows starred female hosts, who were apparently considered more appropriate than male hosts in playing the role of kindergarten teacher.

Airing nationally from 1952 to 1956 and in syndication until 1965, *Ding Dong School* set the standard for preschool shows to come and was a clear influence on series that followed in its footsteps. By watching *Ding Dong School*, children could get a preview of what preschool or kindergarten would be like, without leaving the comfort of their home and mom's reassuring presence.

The show was simplicity itself. Unlike other children's shows with in-studio audiences or with large casts of characters, its only host/character/performer was Dr. Frances Rappaport Horwich ("Miss Frances"), a former classroom teacher and head of the education department at Chicago's Roosevelt College. Miss Frances engaged her young viewers by talking directly to the camera, addressing the home audience as if they were there in the room with her, slowly and carefully explaining things, asking questions and even pausing for the response. For the young child viewing at home, this would have felt as if they were having their own one-on-one conversation with the motherly Miss Francis, who gave them her undivided attention.

Like a typical kindergarten, the show presented a mix of education and play. Miss Frances would discuss some of the new experiences and challenges that preschoolers would be facing, like going to the dentist, and tell them what to expect. She showed them how to play games or do various simple arts and crafts activities, like making a bunny doll from one of their father's handkerchiefs. Her manner was quiet, gentle, and low-key, and the pacing of the show was slow and deliberate. For example, one episode featured a segment with Miss Frances quietly blowing a bubble pipe for over a minute. That may not sound like a long time, but on television, it is.

Ding Dong School was designed as an educational show for parents as well as children. At the end of each episode, Miss Frances would ask her young viewers to go get whichever adult was at home with them and bring them to the TV. Since most mothers did not work outside the home in those days, this adult would usually be the child's mother. Miss Frances would tell her child viewers to go and play, so that she could talk to mom privately. Miss Frances would then tell mom about what she had talked about and done during that day's show, so that mom would be prepared for any follow-up questions her child might have or requests to play the games or do the activities that were covered during that episode. She would also talk more broadly about preschoolers' educational, social, and developmental needs and interests, and give parents suggestions and pointers about how to address these needs.

For NBC, *Ding Dong School* was a way to counter the growing public criticism of television as a source of crime, violence, and deterioration in children's reading and language skills. The network even appointed Dr. Horwich to be head of their new Children's Program Review Committee.

Another educational show for preschoolers, *Romper Room*, debuted a year after *Ding Dong School* and remained on the air for the next five decades, giving millions of young children their first exposure to a pre-

NURSERY CENTER has the newest TV star..

Tiny Tears

See her with
Miss Frances
on famous
Ding Dong School
T.V. show on
N.B.C.

AN AMERICAN
CHARACTER DOLL

THE DOLL THAT CRIES TEARS

LIKE A REAL BABY • BLOWS BUBBLES

BATHES • FEEDS • WETS • SLEEPS

TINY TEARS IS UNBELIEVABLY HUMAN

YOU'LL LOVE HER . . .

$5.95 up

Countless hours of joyous play value. Teaches your child to be self reliant and self sufficient. Approved by teachers and educators everywhere.

USE OUR CONVENIENT LAYAWAY PLAN

Nursery Center

johnsonia bldg. 524 main st. fitchburg

Ding Dong School on NBC was the first educational show for preschoolers. Its host, Miss Francis, is seen here as a product endorser in a newspaper ad for a doll. In the early days of children's TV, hosts often pitched sponsors' products during the program.

school/kindergarten environment. The show featured a female teacher/host who would lead a group of about eight young children in various educational and play activities. Rather than being broadcast by a particular network, *Romper Room* was franchised to local stations, which means that stations could produce their own versions of the show instead of airing a national telecast. As a result, viewers in different parts of the country would see a different host and different children on the set, though the format of the show remained the same.

Many of the *Romper Room* hosts were former kindergarten teachers who knew how to deal with young children. They were always women, and they were always addressed as "Miss" plus their first name. When *Romper Room* debuted in Baltimore, its first host was Nancy Claster ("Miss Nancy"), who helped produce the original series together with her husband.

As in real schoolrooms in those days, each episode of *Romper Room* would begin with the host leading the children in reciting the Pledge of Allegiance to the flag. Then the host would read books to the children, teach them the alphabet, and direct them in playing games, doing exercises, singing songs, and learning moral lessons and polite behavior, all accompanied by lively background music. Unlike *Ding Dong School*, *Romper Room* featured a group of children participating in the activities led by the host/teacher, so that viewers at home could identify with these on-air "schoolmates" and get a vicarious sense of what it would be like to attend such a school.

The show also featured helpers Mr. Do-Bee and Mr. Don't-Bee, recurring characters in bumblebee costumes, whose roles were to teach good manners and proper behavior. Mr. Doo-Bee would always start his sentences with "Do Bee..." and then add a statement about how children should behave (e.g., "Do Bee polite to your parents!"). Mr. Don't-Bee would tell young viewers what not to do, like "Don't Bee a nasty tongue!"[39]

The show had an "interactive" feature at the end of each telecast, when the host would hold a "magic mirror" in front of her face (actually just a hand mirror frame, without the mirror) and look through it to see all the viewers out in "television land." She would then recite this rhyme: "Romper, bomper, stomper, boo! Tell me, tell me, tell me do. Magic Mirror, tell me today, have all my friends had fun at play?" Then she would start naming some of the children that she could "see" watching at home: "I can see Scotty and Kimberly and Julie and Jimmy and Kelly and all of you boys and girls out there!" Parents would mail in their children's names, hoping that they would be read out loud on the show. Of course, if a child viewer had a relatively common first name, chances were good that they would eventually hear their own name called out, making it seem as if the host could really "see" them.

News and Public Affairs Shows

Among the different genres of shows for children that the TV networks experimented with early on were several shows that dealt with news and public affairs. These shows were modeled after *Meet the Press*, which debuted on NBC in 1947, where a well-known guest, usually a political figure, would be interviewed by a panel of journalists each week. *Junior Press Conference* on ABC, *The New York Times Youth Forum* on the Dumont network, *Youth Wants to Know* on NBC, and *Youth Takes a Stand* on CBS all featured panels of children interviewing newsmakers of the day. Like *Meet the Press*, these shows all aired on Sunday.

SCRIPTED DRAMAS

Live dramas for adult audiences were a popular radio genre and made a natural transition to primetime television, reliably attracting viewers from the first days of regular broadcasting. *NBC Television Theater* debuted in 1945 with a three-part adaptation of Robert Sherwood's *Abe Lincoln in Illinois*. Later renamed *Kraft Television Theater*, this critically acclaimed drama anthology series won top ratings and inspired a host of other distinguished live drama series like the *Hallmark Hall of Fame* that characterized what we now think of as the "golden age of television."

Crime dramas were another program type that had been popular with adults in the movies and on radio. Television versions like *The Plainclothesman*, *Rocky King*, and the iconic *Dragnet* debuted in the late 1940s and early 1950s.

For drama series aimed at children, serious theater or crime shows were apparently considered inappropriate. But several other drama genres were produced primarily for children and families, and some met with considerable success.

OUTER SPACE/SCIENCE FICTION ADVENTURE SHOWS

Space adventures like those featuring Flash Gordon and Buck Rogers had proved popular with children in comic books, movies, and radio programs, and soon proliferated on TV as well. The postwar television versions of this genre reflected the country's fascination with science and new technology, including television itself. It was a time when these magical new inventions and the growing possibility of space exploration made it seem as if nothing was impossible, and that technology would lead to a future in which evil would be vanquished and the planets of the universe would live together in peace. As the Cold War and accompanying "space race" between the U.S. and the Soviet Union heated up, these shows added elements of patriotism, anti–Communism and counter-espionage to their plots.

The earliest show in this category was *Captain Video and His Video Rangers*, which ran five or sometimes six days a week on the Dumont Network from 1949 to 1955 and was so popular that it soon spawned numerous copycat programs. Set in the distant future, the series followed the adventures of Captain Video, leader of the Video Rangers, an elite group of fighters for truth and justice, and his assistant Video Ranger, a teenage boy, as they battled evil scientists and other nefarious villains throughout the solar system. The use of the word "video" in the captain's and show's title seemed to reflect the idea that television itself had recently been considered a futuristic technology that existed only in the realm of science fiction.

Each episode of *Captain Video* began with this voice-over announcement: "Captain Video! Electronic wizard! Master of time and space! Guardian of the safety of the world! Fighting for law and order, Captain Video operates from a mountain retreat with secret agents at all points of the globe. Possessing scientific secrets and scientific weapons, Captain Video asks no quarter and gives none to the forces of evil. Stand by for Captain Video and his Video Rangers!"

Reflecting the country's fascination with new technology, the show's hero was depicted as a technological genius who had invented a variety of communication devices, like the Opticon Scillometer, a long-range X-ray machine used to see through walls; the Discatron, a portable television screen which served as an intercom; and the Radio Scillograph, a palm-sized two-way radio. Captain Video's weapons were also futuristic inventions, designed not to kill but to capture his opponents, like the Cosmic Ray Vibrator, a static beam of electricity that temporarily paralyzed its target, and the Electronic Strait Jacket, which placed captives in invisible restraints. Captain Video's uses of science and technology for good contrasted with the evil pur-

"Captain Video! Electronic wizard! Master of time and space! Guardian of the safety of the world! Fighting for law and order, Captain Video operates from a mountain retreat with secret agents at all points of the globe. Possessing scientific secrets and scientific weapons, Captain Video asks no quarter and gives none to the forces of evil." Al Hodge starred as Captain Video (left) and Don Hastings was his assistant Video Ranger.

poses to which science was put by such villains as Dr. Pauli, a genius inventor who dressed in gangster-like pinstripe suits and spoke with a foreign-accented snarl.

The show was performed, shot and broadcast live, which posed great technical challenges. Without the luxury of editing, or even pausing, *Captain Video* employed the new real-time electronic capabilities of television to accomplish dissolves, superimpositions, and other crude special effects, to place Captain Video in fantasy surroundings and show his travel through space and time. To pick up the pace and allow time for the crew to frantically change sets and prepare special effects, at some point in each episode Captain Video or his young assistant Video Ranger would stop to show short action-filled clips from cowboy movies, described as the adventures of Captain Video's undercover agents on earth. Other breaks between scenes were filled with commercials for Post Cereal, the series' sponsor; Ranger Messages, which dealt with moral issues like freedom, the Golden Rule, and nondiscrimination; or ads for Video Ranger merchandise, like space helmets, secret code guns, flying saucer rings, decoder badges, and toy Viking rockets complete with launchers.

Another popular early space adventure was *Tom Corbett Space Cadet*, which debuted on CBS in 1950. The setting was the world of 2350, a utopian future in which the formerly feuding countries of the world had formed the peaceful Commonwealth of Earth, where there was no war and where deadly weapons had been outlawed. Tom Corbett was a teenage cadet in the Space Academy, who joined the other cadets in battling dangerous natural phenomena like asteroid storms. Unlike *Captain Video*, which it was clearly designed to imitate, the teenage character on this show was the star rather than a sidekick, enhancing his appeal as someone with whom young viewers could identify. Employing a consulting science advisor who was an expert on rockets, the show was notable for its scientific authenticity. With a larger budget than *Captain Video*, *Tom Corbett* was also able to incorporate more realistic and sophisticated special effects.

Commando Cody—Sky Marshall of the Universe starred masked super-scientist Commando Cody and his assistants Joan and Ted as they battled against space-alien villains and Earth-born criminals led by a mysterious "Ruler" of unknown planetary origin. Like Captain Video, Commando Cody had various high-tech gadgets and inventions at his disposal, including a sonic-powered flying suit with rocket back-pack and an innovative rocket ship he had designed and built.

As the Cold War intensified through the early 1950s, more explicit patriotic and anti–Communist elements appeared in these types of shows.

The premise for *Atom Squad*, which debuted in 1953, was that there was a secret Manhattan-based organization that battled villains while protecting U.S. atomic secrets. On *Rod Brown of the Rocket Rangers*, which also premiered in 1953, young viewers were asked to take an oath of loyalty to the U.S. constitution and to promise to obey their parents and teachers. The star of *Captain Midnight*, which debuted on CBS in 1954, combed the globe on his "Silver Dart" aircraft, flushing out spies, rescuing captured nuclear scientists, and vanquishing secret enemy agents.

A key attribute of these space adventure series was the fact that they depicted an overwhelmingly masculine world. Though women did sometimes appear as members of the various patrols and space academies and occasionally as villains, the shows' heroes were always male.

WESTERNS

The Wild West and the cowboys and other frontiersmen who inhabited it had been longtime staples of American literature, movies, and radio, so it was to be expected that Westerns would be among the first TV shows aimed at children and families. Though the genre had wide appeal, the depiction of a still-young country being tamed and taught to follow the law seemed likely to resonate strongly with children, who were just learning to follow rules and social norms. These stories could show children what happens when rules are broken and teach them to respect and admire the authorities, in the form of frontier law enforcers, who were the stars of these shows and were invariably polite, kind, and morally upright.

Unlike many other early children's TV genres, Westerns were usually filmed rather than broadcast live, since they were largely shot outdoors. In fact, one of the first of these series, *Hopalong Cassidy*, which went on the air in 1949, initially consisted of old theatrical features that were simply repurposed for television, though new episodes were later filmed for broadcast. Each episode ended with Hopalong delivering a personal message directly to young viewers, about safety awareness, personal responsibility, or other moral lessons.

The ABC TV network found its first big hit with *The Lone Ranger*, which debuted in 1949 and would become one of the most distinctive programs of early television. Each episode dramatically opened with the Lone Ranger galloping across the screen to the show's signature theme music, the finale of Rossini's William Tell Overture, and the announcer intoning, "A fiery horse with the speed of light, a cloud of dust, and a hearty 'Hiyo, Silver!'"

Based on an earlier radio series, the show's premise was that our hero, left for dead by outlaws, was rescued and nursed back to health by Tonto, a Native American. Since the hero was the sole survivor from a posse of Texas Rangers, he was dubbed the Lone Ranger. Tonto and the Lone Ranger roamed the frontier, bringing evildoers to justice on their own, following a strict formula: The Lone Ranger wore a mask and never

"Who was that masked man?" Actor Clayton Moore starred in *The Lone Ranger*, an early "kiddie Western" on ABC. The Lone Ranger and his partner Tonto vanquished the bad guys through the strength of their moral code and with very little violence.

revealed his identity; he never killed, and he used minimal violence (his excellent marksmanship allowed him to disarm adversaries by shooting their guns from their hands, and he was very skilled with a lariat); he used bullets made of silver; and his horse was named Silver.

Similar to superhero stories like *Superman* and *Batman*, the appeal of *The Lone Ranger* revolved around the main character's hidden identity, providing a powerful lesson in humility and altruism. At the end of each episode, the Lone Ranger would rear up on Silver, and he and Tonto would gallop away as someone would ask, "Who was that masked man?" to which the response was always "Why, he's the Lone Ranger!"

Native Americans were the stereotypical enemy in many other Westerns, but the Lone Ranger's close partnership with Tonto showed that respecting the rights and beliefs of others was an important part of his moral code and one of the lessons that the show tried to convey. The role of Tonto was played by a Native American actor, Jay Silverheels, and unlike traditional sidekicks who were usually comic foils, Tonto was portrayed as a courageous hero who was just as skilled, morally upright, and worthy of respect as the Lone Ranger.

The *Adventures of Kit Carson* was another popular early Western. The series was based on the life of the famous Kentucky-born trapper, guide, and scout. It depicted Carson as a frontier hero with a simple code of honesty, upholding justice with the help of El Toro, his Mexican sidekick.

Among the many other "kiddie Westerns" that were broadcast in the early 1950s, several deserve mention for their special characteristics. *The Cisco Kid*, based on earlier movies and a radio show, featured a Hispanic hero and was the first TV western to be filmed in color. *The Gene Autry Show* and the *Roy Rogers Show*, both based on successful theatrical film series, starred "singing cowboys" who would assist a rancher menaced by robbers, expose a corrupt sheriff, or otherwise right some wrongs, and then perform a musical number. *Sky King*, based on an earlier radio series, was a Western set in contemporary times and starred a rancher who piloted his own small plane, The Songbird, which he often used to pursue and catch criminals. King was assisted by his teenage niece Penny and young nephew Clipper, who lived with him on his ranch.

Cowboy G-Men applied the anti–Communist paranoia of the 1950s to the classic Western. Set in the West of the 19th century, it featured a pair of undercover government agents whose job was to discover and thwart revolutionaries and spies who were plotting to take control of the country.

Unlike adult-oriented Westerns like *Gunsmoke* and *Rawhide* that began to air later in the decade, these early Westerns were child and family-oriented series that sought to teach lessons about morals and values to their viewers. *The Lone Ranger*'s creator, a prosperous Detroit businessman, said that the show should "teach patriotism, tolerance, fairness, and a sympathetic understanding of fellow men and their rights and privileges … without arousing unwholesome desires and instincts."[40] It was the star characters' strict moral code that enabled them to prevail over the bad guys who preyed upon the good people of the Old West.

Like the space adventure series with which they shared the airwaves, the world of the "kiddie Westerns" was largely ruled by men and gave the boys in the audience masculine role models to emulate. The exception was the *Annie Oakley Show*, the first TV show of any genre to depict a woman as an action hero. Annie lived with her kid brother in the little frontier town of Diablo and helped her friend the sheriff keep the town free of desperadoes. She was played by actress Gail Davis, a skilled horseback rider and sharpshooter who performed many of her own stunts on the show.

ANIMAL ADVENTURE DRAMAS

Two filmed shows featuring the adventures of heroic animals debuted on television in 1954—*Lassie* and *Rin Tin Tin*. Both series starred pet dogs and their boy owners. As in other dramas aimed at children and families, the plotlines on both *Lassie* and *Rin Tin Tin* were morality plays in which the innocent and good, in the form of children and their brave, loyal pets, prevailed over danger and evil.

Lassie was based on a best-selling 1940 novel, *Lassie Come Home*, which was made into a series of successful movies and a radio show before migrating to television. It starred a daring and resourceful collie that lived on a modern-day farm with a young boy, his widowed mother, and his grandfather. In each episode, Lassie would use her amazing intelligence, resourcefulness, and tenacity to rescue her masters or other local good people from accidents, natural disasters, criminals, and other forms of danger. During the many years that the series remained on the air, it went on to feature different families and different situations, but the central plotline always focused on Lassie's heroic adventures.

The other show featuring a heroic dog, *The Adventures of Rin Tin Tin*, started life as a series of silent films in the 1920s and a radio show in the 1930s. *Rin Tin Tin* was set in the Old West of the 1880s and starred a German shepherd and his young master, Rusty, who were the only survivors of an Indian raid in which Rusty's parents had been killed. Rusty

Lassie was the first of several TV dramas that featured brave, loyal animals and the boys who owned them. The show went through several cast and setting changes, but the plots always revolved around Lassie rescuing people from danger. The original cast included (clockwise from bottom left) Tommy Rettig as young Jeff Miller, Jan Clayton as widowed mom Ellen Miller, George Cleveland as Gramps (George Miller), and intrepid collie Lassie.

and his dog were adopted by members of the 101st Cavalry and commissioned as honorary troopers. Similar to the plotlines in *Lassie*, Rusty and Rin Tin Tin's adventures involved helping the cavalry and the local townspeople establish and maintain law and order on the frontier.

SUPERHERO SHOWS

There was only one drama in the early days of television that starred a hero with superhuman powers, but it became such a success that it spawned an entire genre of children's shows that would become prolific in later decades. *The Adventures of Superman* debuted in 1952 as a syndicated show sold directly to local TV stations. The star character had first appeared in the June 1938 issue of *Action Comics* and was later featured in a radio series, movie serials, and a feature-length film. The TV show became extremely popular and, though production of new episodes ended in 1957, it remained on the air in syndication for several decades, long enough for its introductory sequence to become iconic: *"Faster than a speeding bullet! More powerful than a locomotive! Able to leap tall buildings in a single bound! Look! Up in the sky! It's a bird! It's a plane! It's Superman!"*

The television series, which was produced on film, was based on the same premise as the comic book, movies, and radio show. Superman, an infant from another planet, was sent to Earth by his parents as their planet was about to be destroyed, and raised as Clark Kent. As an alien on Earth, he discovered that he had unusual powers and abilities, like superhuman strength, extraordinarily acute hearing and sight, the ability to fly, and imperviousness to bullets, which just bounced off his manly chest. Superman decided to use his powers to secretly fight evildoers in "a never-ending battle for truth, justice, and the American way." When he was in his Superman persona, he wore a mask to hide his identity and a special form-fitting costume with a cape, which, thanks to the writers, was also impervious to damage. To further hide his real identity, when he was in his human persona as Clark Kent, he took on a "mild-mannered" and meek demeanor. *Superman's* appeal to children undoubtedly rested in part on the premise that he possessed great powers that were not apparent from his unremarkable exterior appearance. Children could have easily identified with that concept.

CARTOON SHOWS

Animated shorts produced by movie studios like Warner Brothers, MGM, and Disney had been popular since the 1920s as accompaniments to longer features in movie theaters. These vintage theatrical cartoons, like *Krazy Kat*, *Bugs Bunny*, and *Farmer Alfalfa*, were shown on some of the earliest local and network television shows for children. They were rarely programmed on their own since they were only six to seven minutes long but were usually presented by the host as one of several elements in an otherwise live variety show. Originally intended for a general audience, some were edited for television to change or remove overtly erotic, racist or excessively violent content or other images considered unfit for viewing by children, like scenes of smoking, drinking, or gambling.

Cartoons made specifically for the small screen did not begin to proliferate until the later 1950s, but there were a couple of early entries in this genre that debuted in 1949—*Telecomics* and *Crusader Rabbit*. *Telecomics* began as a syndicated show sold directly to local stations, though it was later picked up by NBC and retitled *NBC Comics*. Like the old theatrical cartoon shorts, *Telecomics* featured a variety of short animated segments starring different characters, including Danny March, a tough self-reliant orphan crime-fighter who became the Mayor's personal detective; Johnny and Mr. Do-Right, about the adventures of a young boy and his dog; and Kid Champion, about a boy who dreamed of becoming a musician but became a prize fighter in accordance with his father's wishes.

Crusader Rabbit was produced for syndication by Jay Ward, who later went on to create *Rocky and His Friends*, and by Alexander Anderson, nephew of famous film animator Paul Terry (creator of Terrytoons). *Crusader Rabbit* was designed as a series of five-minute cliffhangers with five installments making up a complete story. Each of the five installments could be shown separately on weekdays as part of a larger show or shown together as a weekly program.

The series featured Crusader Rabbit and his partner Ragland T. Tiger as mock-Arthurian characters who fought dragons, evil villains, and other bad characters while they pursued their quest. Foreshadowing the later style of *Rocky and His Friends*, the humor on *Crusader Rabbit* did not rely on slapstick violence, as in most of the early theatrical cartoons, but on situation comedy, satire, comical antagonists, clever puns, contemporary dialogue, and insider references to television and popular culture that were probably over the heads of most of its child viewers. Episodes bore titles like "West We Forget" and "Gullible's Travels," and characters included the Brimstone Brothers, Bigot and Blackheart, Archilles the Heel, Babyface Barracuda, Belfry Q. Bat, Whetstone Whiplash, and Dudley Nightshade. In one episode, a two-headed fire-breathing dragon justified its bad behavior by explaining, "A job's a job, and think of the residuals we'll get!"[41]

ANTHOLOGY SHOWS

There was only one early show for children that could be categorized as an anthology, but that show—*Disneyland*—was in a league of its own in many ways. It was a seminal series that had some of the characteristics of a variety show but was produced on film. From its debut on ABC in October 1954, through its final telecast on Christmas Eve 2008, *Disneyland* appeared on all three broadcast TV channels at various times under a variety of names, becoming one of the longest-running primetime programs on American television.

Walt Disney, founder and head of Disney Studios, and by any measure a marketing genius, initially approached both NBC and CBS with his plans for producing a family-oriented TV series, but he ultimately chose third-place network ABC for the debut of *Disneyland*, because ABC was willing to give him what he wanted in exchange—a $500,000 investment in the amusement park he dreamed of opening in Anaheim, California. ABC executives were desperate to obtain programming that would give them an edge against their two more established rivals, NBC and CBS, and they were also very interested in attracting the growing family market. ABC's investment paid off quickly, as *Disneyland* became the network's first series to hit the top ten in ratings.

Disneyland's format was a mixture of filmed segments—cartoons, live-action adventures, documentaries, and nature stories—all initially hosted by the affable Walt Disney himself. Much of the material came from the Disney studio library, including one-hour edits or multi-part miniseries of recent Disney films. Unlike the heads of the other major Hollywood movie studios at the time, Walt Disney didn't worry that the new television medium would destroy his movie business. On the contrary, he understood that he could use his TV show to promote and extend the life of his theatrical releases, and vice versa. The TV series, the Disney studio's theatrical films, and the new Disneyland theme park were all designed to cross-promote and market each other and strengthen the overall Disney brand.

A good example of this marketing synergy was the phenomenal cross-market success of the three-part miniseries about the historical American frontiersman Davy Crockett that aired on *Disneyland* in 1955. It ignited a nationwide Davy Crockett craze. The show's theme song, "The Ballad of Davy Crockett," became a huge hit record, and Disney sold millions of dollars of Davy Crockett merchandise. It seemed as if every child in America had a Davy Crockett lunch box, coonskin hat, fringed jacket or pants, or similar paraphernalia. Disney subsequently edited the TV episodes into two theatrical films that were quickly released to benefit from and build upon the TV show's popularity.

When the Disneyland theme park opened in July of 1955, ABC aired a live television special honoring the new tourist mecca and its founder. Within a year, millions of *Disneyland* viewers who saw the park constantly promoted on the TV show poured into Disneyland. In its first year, the theme park grossed $10 million. Walt Disney and his company had shaped two new cultural forms, both based on providing wholesome, high-quality entertainment to families, and interlinked them in a strategy that continued to generate millions of dollars in profits over the ensuing decades.

Television Advertising and Marketing to Children

Television was born as a commercial enterprise following the profitable radio model, in which entertainment programs cultivated audiences who were valuable to businesses with something to sell. Defining and monetizing markets, which is the function of marketing, was an integral part of TV programming from its earliest days, and children's TV had to build a market.

It was unclear at first how best to use TV to sell into markets in general, much less the children's market. The first shows were often sponsored by single advertisers, referred to as sponsors. In fact, some of the earliest shows were actually produced by ad agencies as advertising vehicles for their clients. Within a few years, however, single sponsorship became so expensive that most shows carried commercials from multiple advertisers, who paid only for the airtime in which their ads ran.

Though TV shows for children were designed to be wholesome and moralistic, when it came to advertising practices, shows for children were treated no differently than shows for adults. Advertising was thoroughly integrated into the programming on these shows, with sponsor names often included in the shows' titles, children in studio audiences singing the sponsor's jingles, and trusted hosts and beloved characters on live broadcasts pausing mid-show to pitch their sponsor's products.

Before commercial television first began to enter the homes of American families, print or radio advertising for products consumed by children, like toys, candy, breakfast cereal, or clothing, was mostly aimed at parents, since children controlled little or no money and were not seen as a potential market segment. Television advertising for children's products initially followed the same pattern, with program hosts directing their pitches to the parents watching TV with their children. For example, Miss Frances, the host of *Ding Dong School*, spent several minutes at the end of each broadcast telling mothers how important a breakfast of sugary

Kix Cereal would be for their children's health and well-being. Kix was her show's sponsor.

But advertisers began to realize that children were often watching television on their own, without their parents in the room, and that they could aim their ads directly at child viewers. Since parents still held the purse strings, hosts would often try to take advantage of what was called the "nag factor," urging children to ask their parents to buy them the advertised product. A typical example was Buffalo Bob on the *Howdy Doody Show* telling children to "make sure to tell your mom to put a package of Hostess Cupcakes in your lunch box when you go to school, or ask her to buy some as a special reward sometime during the week."[42]

Some advertisers got viewers to use more of their products by creating marketing campaigns in which young viewers could send in a specified number of cereal box tops, candy bar wrappers, or other evidence of using their product, together with ten cents or so to cover the costs of postage, in exchange for inexpensive program-related merchandise that would be mailed back to them. For example, Ovaltine, the sponsor of *Captain Midnight*, gave viewers the opportunity to send in Ovaltine box tops in order to receive a "secret" decoder ring.

Besides extolling their sponsor's products, advertising on children's shows would often play upon children's desires to own the same popular products that their friends had, to not feel different or left out. For example, on *Winky Dink and You*, host Jack Barry urged children to send in for the *Winky Dink* kit in these terms: "I tell you what, if you had your Winky Dink kits and played along with us, well, there's no reason for any of us to miss all the fun…. You can't really be a part of the program without 'em, and you can't have the fun that the other boys and girls who have their Winky Dink kits do have…. Now boys and girls, you <u>must</u> have this kit! … Now, I do hope you'll all get your Winky Dink kit right away because you really can't have as much fun as if you have a kit."[43]

In addition to sponsorship and advertising, children's television programs and networks profited through the sale of licensed products which were heavily promoted during the show, like the *Winky Dink* magic screen kit. One of the first highly successful pioneers of this strategy for children's shows was *Hopalong Cassidy*. The *Hopalong Cassidy* show sold some $70 million worth of cowboy gear, pajamas, wallpaper, bicycles, candy bars, toothpaste, and myriad other program-related products annually.[44] That translates into nearly three-quarters of a billion in current dollars. According to television historian Gary Grossman, the *Lone Ranger*, following in the hoofprints of *Hopalong*, generated so much income from licensed products like records, toy guns, hobby horses, and cereal, that contemporary accounts described the show as a "corporation on horseback."[45]

The *Howdy Doody* show quickly became a licensing juggernaut, after a toy buyer for Macy's department store contacted the producers in 1948 to tell them that customers were asking for Howdy Doody dolls to buy for their children. The dolls were manufactured, sales took off, and the show's producers were soon inundated with other product licensing requests. Buffalo Bob Smith and other actors and puppets from the show helped to market their licensed products by making personal appearances at Macy's and other stores carrying their products, which generated huge crowds and increased sales. By the end of 1957, total gross sales of *Howdy Doody* merchandise were estimated at $25 million.[46]

Stay Tuned...

As the country entered the latter half of the 1950s, television had already become a pervasive force in children's lives, exerting a nationwide pull on millions of children simultaneously, often without parental mediation. Advertising and marketing industries were finding ways to harness this force for profit by stoking the consumer-based kids' culture that had its beginnings earlier in the century. By watching the same shows and owning the same products advertised on those shows, children around the country began to share the same fashions, vocabulary, interests, and reference points, and to feel more strongly than ever before that they belonged to the same peer group. These trends would only intensify as children's television continued to grow and develop over the next few years, until childhood itself became defined by them. As childhood was altered by these forces, children were no longer the same. This was a true point of inflection. The first generation of children raised by television would be unlike any that had come before.

CHAPTER TWO

The Infancy
of Children's Television
(Mid to Late 1950s)

Life in the U.S.

In the latter half of the 1950s, as many middle-class families enjoyed the fruits of postwar peace and prosperity, what seemed like an idyllic life in the suburbs belied growing undercurrents of anxiety. Events were taking place in the country and elsewhere in the world that many perceived as potential threats to their way of life.

The Cold War, sustaining the public's fear of Communism abroad, with its nightmarish potential for nuclear annihilation, and at home, as subversion from within, created a constant background of barely suppressed terror among Americans, both old and young. On October 4, 1957, the Soviet Union stunned the U.S. by successfully launching Sputnik I, the first satellite to orbit the Earth. Sputnik's launch caused a profound crisis of confidence across the country. Not only did Russia suddenly seem to displace the U.S. as the world leader in technology, math and science; worse still, the idea of a Soviet spacecraft passing over the U.S. homeland was widely considered a violation of American territorial integrity. It seemed only a small step to imagine Sputniks capable of raining down hydrogen bombs on U.S. cities, against which the nation's vaunted military had no defense.[1]

In fact, the same rocket that could launch a satellite could lob a hydrogen bomb anywhere in the world, with best-case warning of maybe half an hour. Evacuation, previously considered a viable form of civil defense, wasn't going to work.[2] The fear of nuclear war, already intense, continued to build, but in hawkish government circles it was considered vital to project a confident image of a nation prepared to return fire if attacked; the same image served to bolster domestic political support. There was a concerted effort to get out that message in the mass media. A government-produced animated film, "Duck and Cover," was the cornerstone of a campaign to teach children that they could easily protect themselves against a nuclear blast; schools held regular drills across the country to reinforce its message.[3] *Life* magazine, in September of 1961, wrote that only 3 percent of the population would die in a nuclear attack if there were fallout shelters available, a figure that one could arrive at only through the most torturously optimistic assumptions, such as imagining that cities would not be targeted.[4]

Given the tepid sales of bomb shelters, it seems Americans did not find this rosy (if it can be called that) scenario convincing. Newsreel footage and TV and movie dramatizations, of which there were many, even some that were officially sanctioned, reflected a far less favorable outcome and had greater emotional resonance. The message of safety was further eroded by press coverage like this headline in the *New York Times*: "H-BOMB CAN WIPE OUT ANY CITY," quoting no less an authority than the head of the Atomic Energy Commission at a Presidential press conference.[5] It appears that, in spite of efforts to bolster morale, people sensibly concluded that their lives after a thermonuclear war would be, to borrow the words of Thomas Hobbes, nasty, brutish and short.[6]

While the U.S. may not have been able to win an old-school propaganda war in the face of overwhelming evidence, a different, more modern strategy was far more successful. Instead of the "stick" of the fear of obliteration, the country responded readily to the "carrot" of regaining lost prestige. When the issue of the Soviet threat was framed not as a confrontation but instead as a competition, the country threw its support into the "space race," in which it was our status as leader of the free world that was at stake. Congress allocated huge resources in an attempt to surpass Russia's new dominance in space exploration, with better missile technology as an ancillary benefit. A key part of this undertaking was a major initiative to improve the U.S. educational system. The federal government quickly approved a billion dollars in direct aid to public schools, aimed at raising educational standards in math, science, and foreign language study.[7]

Anxieties darkening the American psyche were not only about foreign threats. Domestic life was unsettled by growing public concerns about juvenile delinquency.[8] Teenage gangs were a particular source of worry. Street gang membership had been a normal part of life for many working-class boys in America's urban centers before World War II, providing their members with a protective and supportive peer group, a sense of identity, and a feeling of manliness and power. After the war, the number of gangs in big cities mushroomed, as did violent turf battles among them. Movies called "teenpics," which focused on gangs and troubled adolescents, flourished in the mid–1950s, perhaps best exemplified by the 1955 *Rebel without a Cause*. This film, starring James Dean, gave full-throated representation to the belief that American teenagers were "out of control" as a result of growing up in dysfunctional families where bad parenting was widely prevalent, specifically pinning blame on the collapse of paternal authority.[9] Dean's death in a car accident just before the release of the film helped infuse the story, which includes a character dying in a drag-racing incident, with an element of realism for audiences of the time. *Rebel without a Cause* followed only two years after Marlon Brando's star-making role in *The Wild Ones*, in which a nomadic motorcycle gang of anomic youth run roughshod over a weak sheriff and terrorize a town. Together, these movies and other teenpics created a foundation myth for postwar adolescent rebellion, basing its origins on the breakdown of authority and disrespect for tradition. The lesson American audiences were given by movies like these was that teenagers were members of a dangerous alien culture, the bad seeds of inadequately strict schooling, permissiveness of failed authority at the family and civic levels, the decline of religion, and the negative influence of the media, including comic books and television.[10] The concept of the generation gap had begun to emerge.

Against this background of threats to traditional ways American society had defined itself, the emerging Civil Rights movement in the 1950s forced the country to confront the disgraceful legacy of slavery and the continued racist attitudes toward black citizens. Though there had been previous acts of protest and resistance to public policies which treated minorities as second-class citizens, a series of events in the mid–1950s catalyzed a more organized social movement that gained strength and numbers in subsequent years. Together with newspapers and radio, television played an important role in publicizing these events, bringing disturbing images of brutality and protest into white middle-class homes.

On May 17, 1954, in the case of *Brown v. Board of Education*, the U.S. Supreme Court struck down the legal framework that supported racial segregation in public schools. The Court further ordered that segregated public schools begin an active process of desegregation, which led to numerous local conflicts in which black school children were often caught in the middle. The next year would see growing racial unrest and strife as those with conflicting stakes in the pivotal battle for equal rights fought to enforce their incompatible visions of what America stood for.

In August 1955, Emmett Till, a 14-year-old African American boy visiting Mississippi from his hometown of Chicago, was lynched after a white female store clerk accused him of flirting with her. When Till's mutilated body was sent back to Chicago for burial, his mother insisted on having an open-casket funeral so that the public could see the brutality he had suffered. Thousands attended the funeral, and the public agonized over the image of Till's body that was published in newspapers. The woman's husband and brother-in-law were tried for the murder, and after deliberating for little over one hour, the all-male all-white jury (people of color were legally barred from jury service in Mississippi then) declared them not guilty. Protests ignited around the country. The national press, historian David Halberstam writes, made the Till murder and the trial the "first great media event of the civil rights movement."[11] Protected from prosecution by laws against double indemnity, the killers confessed four months later for an article in *Look* magazine but expressed no remorse.[12]

In December 1955, the Montgomery bus boycott began when Rosa Parks was arrested for refusing to give up her bus seat to a white man, as required by Montgomery Alabama's bus segregation law. She reportedly told civil rights leader Jesse Jackson that at the moment she was ordered to move, she thought of Till's murder and hardened her resolve to disobey.[13] African American residents of Montgomery, organized by Ralph Abernathy and Martin Luther King, Jr., protested Parks' arrest by refusing to ride the city buses, which caused serious economic repercussions in Montgomery. King was arrested for his role in the boycott, and when he refused to pay a fine, he was thrown in jail. In contrast to the reticence of local newspapers, a new local NBC TV station, WSFA-TV, reported the news about King's arrest aggressively. NBC picked up their coverage and fed it to the national network. A deluge of national and international media coverage followed, which focused public attention on the young, charismatic Reverend King and his framing of the story as a nonviolent struggle of ordinary citizens for their basic rights. It placed the recent Till story in a larger context and amplified it into an example of institutionalized injustice, assigned to King a central role in the Civil Rights movement, and illustrated the decisive influence that television could wield. The boycott and protests lasted for a year and resulted in the peaceful desegregation of Montgomery's public transit system. The historical significance of this victory would gradually become evident, as years of continued struggle unfolded.[14]

Concerns about the Cold War, juvenile delinquency, and the emerging Civil Rights movement were harbingers of even greater social change and turmoil that would characterize the 1960s, all of which would play out in various ways in the mass media. But it was not only news coverage that reflected and reinforced the emerging transformation of American society. Another American cultural form seems in retrospect to have best embodied the vital spirit of the change that was occurring. Initially ignored by world leaders, trivialized by reporters and scholars, and decried by parents, its impact would blaze a trail for youth culture in the U.S. and around the world for years to come. It was called rock 'n' roll.

Rock 'n' roll emerged out of the blending of rhythm and blues and other forms of African American music with country and western music, precipitated by the Great Migration of southerners to urban centers where whites and blacks lived in proximity and could hear and be influenced by each other's music. The new genre gained its name and national traction in the mid–1950s, with the release of Bill Haley and the Comets' recording of "Rock Around the Clock" in 1954, the same year that Elvis Presley recorded "That's All Right." These white performers brought rock 'n' roll to the attention of a white audience, compounding the artistic momentum being generated by African American artists like Chuck Berry, Little Richard, and Bo Diddley. The wildfire resulting from the commercial success of music springing from these roots spread rapidly, and with it came a whole new way of thinking. Rock 'n' roll was not just a musical innovation and some catchy lyrics. It contained a package of ideas about relationships, about authority, about emotions, and about the self. The music cut across racial lines and supported a new vocabulary for tolerance. In time it provided a medium for poetry that articulated new attitudes toward war, poverty, injustice and alienation. It drew its energy from sex even as it reinforced romance. It set to music the turmoil and conflicts of a generation, rendering them both more powerful and more comprehensible.

Rock 'n' roll soon became integral to teenagers' rebellion against the emotional repression that many of them felt in the conformist atmosphere of the 1950s. Its lyrics celebrated the teen years and legitimized interests that many teenagers could relate to, like school (bad), dating (challenging), cars (thrilling), clothes (important), and even sex (not just imaginary). "Rock and roll provided a vehicle through which urban, rural, and suburban youths declared their independence from parental standards and expressed their desire for pleasure.… It offered an expressive outlet for all the pent-up energy, sexuality, and individualism that teens experienced.... The new music exuded sexuality; indeed, *rock and roll* was a slang term in certain black communities referring to sexual intercourse."[15]

It also generated a backlash from parents and government authorities, who viewed the new music as a threat to America's traditions. Their criticism tended to emphasize the dangers that rock 'n' roll posed for the country's youth, although in hindsight it is obvious that it was adult authority that was at risk. Many adults thought rock 'n' roll contributed to juvenile delinquency and social rebellion, not just because of its sexuality but also because the music and its culture were shared by different racial and social groups. FBI Director J. Edgar Hoover called it "a corrupting impulse," and there were numerous crusades to ban rock 'n' roll from the airwaves. The major record companies responded by producing more socially-acceptable sanitized versions of sexually explicit songs, sung by white performers.[16]

Rock 'n' roll precipitated a dramatic shift in the radio and music industries. Radio stations with traditional radio dramas and comedy programs were already losing market share to television. Their survival now hinged on how quickly they could pivot to popular music as their core programming and how accurately they could gauge the rapidly shifting desires of these large new audiences of young consumers. New technologies took the music out of the home and into the streets. The invention of portable transistor radios and inexpensive 45-rpm records made it possible for teens to share their music and take it with them wherever they went.[17] Car radios provided an unprecedented level of mobility for the teen music audience, becoming a public expression, at high volume, of musical taste-making and youthful rebellion.

The rapid growth in the popularity of rock 'n' roll among a young audience created enormous new market opportunities. Adults, previously the only game in town for advertisers, were becoming just one demographic, and not necessarily the primary one, for marketers of consumer goods.[18] The resulting resentment of ascendant Baby Boomers by the shrinking older generation would become a central focus for attention in the coming decade and would feature often in popular media. The necessary conditions and the mechanisms required to foster a sustainable distinct youth audience with its own media, its own norms, and its own economy were now starting to work in synergy. The only weak link was a more efficient visual component, and that is what television would bring to the party.

Television

The music industry's success in creating and catering to a youth market blazed a trail for television to follow. An early trendsetter was *American Bandstand*, a local Philadelphia TV show that was picked up by the ABC network and debuted nationally in 1957. *Bandstand*, which aired daily in the late afternoon or early evening, had a simple format. It featured a young disc jockey named Dick Clark, who played the latest hit records as local teenagers in the studio danced to the music. There were occasional guest performances by rock 'n' roll performers, who usually lip-synched the vocals to their own records. With his neat, clean-cut looks and polite demeanor, Dick Clark made rock 'n' roll "safe" for national consumption, even as his show featured a racially integrated group of teenagers dancing and guest performances by African American performers. *American Bandstand* became a huge hit, bringing rock 'n' roll and the latest dances and fashion styles into millions of American homes.[19] Though the show was aimed at teens, it was viewed by children as well, helping to make rock 'n' roll the theme music for an entire generation of Baby Boomers.

Bandstand's rise from a local to a national phenomenon typified the arc of successful television programs in the 1950s. The late 1940s and early 1950s had been a time of innovation and experimentation in television programming, as writers, producers, and networks tried to develop shows that worked best in the new medium and would appeal to the most viewers. There was minimal risk involved in trying out various types of programs at that time, since few families owned TV sets and those who did were happy to watch whatever was on the air. Most programs originated locally or were seen first on regional networks. But television ownership quickly spread. By 1955, when a majority of households in all parts of the country owned TV sets,[20] television had become a true mass medium, a household fixture in most homes and able to influence American culture in broad and profound ways.

Unlike some of the "teenpic" movies discussed earlier, television shows designed for national audiences sought to avoid content that was remotely problematic. The world of entertainment television in the 1950s generally insulated itself from external social and political influences, and programming aimed at children was particularly scrubbed clean. The values of patriotism, religiosity, and good manners were directly or indirectly promoted. Ethnic, gender, racial and other stereotypes that would be unacceptable a generation or two later were routinely depicted in ways that reflected commonly accepted standards and were rarely an explicit matter of concern.

Though the movie industry had initially looked at television as the enemy, the success of filmed shows like *Disneyland* and *The Lone Ranger* earlier in the decade inspired key Hollywood studios to put aside their hostility to the new medium and begin producing shows for television. Throughout the late 1950s, TV production gravitated to Hollywood, with its deep bench of talented writers, producers and film studio infrastructure for cinema-style storytelling, and away from New York City, where most of the earlier live TV shows had been produced in relatively cramped theater-style studios. Filmed sitcoms, action adventure shows, and westerns began to fill the airwaves. Unlike earlier wholesome cowboy shows aimed at children, the newer westerns aired in the late evening and were intended for viewing by adults. Shows like *Gunsmoke, Wagon Train, Maverick,* and *Have Gun Will Travel,* featuring grittier characters and plotlines and more violence, proliferated in prime time, rising from sixteen in 1957–58 to a peak of twenty-eight in 1960–61.[21]

One type of live TV—quiz shows— remained popular and continued to air through the late 1950s, until the entire genre came crashing down in 1959. After the Supreme Court ruled that give-away quiz shows were not lotteries and were therefore legal, CBS debuted *The $64,000 Question* in 1955, exponentially raising the stakes from the popular radio show on which it was based, *The $64 Question. The $64,000 Question* quickly became the most popular show on television, and other quiz shows like *The Big Game, Dotto,* and *Twenty-One* soon followed, offering ever-higher prizes. But several former contestants charged that they had secretly been given the answers to their questions ahead of time, and the New York District Attorney began to subpoena witnesses as he looked into the allegations. When Charles Van Doren, a respected Columbia University college professor and popular winner on *Twenty-One,* admitted that, in his case, the allegations were true, the networks cancelled all their quiz shows, ending the genre's run for decades to come.[22]

Among the many sitcoms that aired in this era, family sitcom *Leave It to Beaver,* which debuted in 1957, was groundbreaking in its comparatively realistic depiction of middle-class children's everyday lives at the time. Unlike the children on *Father Knows Best,* another popular family sitcom which had premiered in 1954, Beaver and his pre-teen brother Wally were not portrayed as adults' idealized visions of perfect children. As TV historians Castleman and Podrazik describe it, "The children in *Leave it to Beaver* were just like real kids: flawed and confused, usually good, but not above some exciting petty larceny. As a result, *Leave it to Beaver* emerged as a warm family show that offered real-life kids the opportunity to actually identify with children portrayed in a television series. More than any other sitcom at the time, it captured the essence of a child's everyday life in the late 1950s..."[23]

Children's Television

If you were a child growing up in the latter half of the 1950s, you would rush home from school every day to watch *The Mickey Mouse Club*, another iconic hit show from Walt Disney Productions, which had launched the popular *Disneyland* series a year earlier. With its debut in 1955, *The Mickey Mouse Club*, named for the Disney studio's best-known cartoon character, quickly became the defining children's TV show of its day. Every child in America could sing the lyrics to the show's theme song (if you are of a certain age, you are probably hearing the refrain in your mind now).

Airing weekdays in the late afternoon, *The Mickey Mouse Club* had a variety show format that featured singing, dancing, guest stars, classic Disney cartoons, a newsreel, and continuing serials like *The Hardy Boys* and *Spin and Marty*, in which teens usually faced and overcame difficult situations in their everyday lives. Mickey Mouse was prominently featured throughout the show, in its opening and closing segments, in old Mickey Mouse cartoons originally made for showing in movie theaters, and in interstitial segments between other show elements.

The show's most distinctive feature was its cast—a group of wholesome, talented teenagers called the Mouseketeers, who wore mouse-ear hats and sang and danced their way into the hearts of the viewing public. There were also two adult regulars, "head Mouseketeer" Jimmie Dodd, who served as the host and also provided short segments giving viewers moral advice and guidance, and "Big Mooseketeer" Roy Williams, a rotund performer who had previously worked as a staff artist at Disney.

Every episode of the show would start with the Mouseketeer Roll Call, a musical number in which each of the Mouseketeers would announce themselves by name. Though many of the Mouseketeers gained name recognition and loyal fans, the most popular Mouseketeer was Annette Funicello, a talented teen who was given her own serial on the show and later went on to a successful movie career. Annette was TV's first real child star. Her dark Italian features gave her an "ethnic" look that was unusual for TV in those days, which largely favored blond, blue-eyed actors. In fact, all the Mouseketeers on the original series were white.[24]

While Disney's earlier hit show, *Disneyland*, was intended for viewing by the entire family, *The Mickey Mouse Club* was designed to appeal specifically and exclusively to children. The large cast of Mouseketeers gave young viewers teenage role models they could idolize and emulate if they wanted to feel like part of the "club." Children could also get themselves their own mouse-ear hats and other licensed products to proclaim their club membership, and millions did, providing a supplementary source of profits for the burgeoning Disney empire and its astute business partners.

On the same day in 1955 that the *Mickey Mouse Club* premiered on ABC, CBS introduced a new daily morning show for children, *Captain Kangaroo*, that went on to become one of the longest-running series on television. CBS advertised the show in these terms: "Good news for parents! (and for children). Starting tomorrow morning at 8, CBS Television presents the gentlest children's show on the air as the kindly Captain Kangaroo re-creates [sic] the private wonderland of childhood in his Treasure House. It is a 'live' and enthralling hour-long program."[25] The show starred Bob Keeshan, who had played the original Clarabell on the *Howdy Doody Show*, as Captain Kangaroo, named for the large pockets on his jacket. True to CBS's advertising, the Captain did seem gentle and kind, and the show exuded a calm and peaceful atmosphere. *Newsweek* magazine published a positive review of the new show that praised it for offering a counterpoint to some of the other more frenetic children's programs of the day, like the *Pinky Lee Show*: "There is, mercifully, no studio audience of hyper-stimulated youngsters."[26] Keeshan himself noted, "Any abundance of excitement is not good. Children can't be at a high pitch all the time; it's just not healthy. There must be balance, just as there is in life itself."[27]

The *Captain Kangaroo* show had a loosely-structured variety format, with puppets, sketches, games, cartoons, and occasional guest stars. It emphasized social learning and good behavior as it taught young children about the world around them. The show was built around life in the "Treasure House," where the Captain would tell stories, introduce guests, and engage in skits and silly stunts. Another important human character on the show was Mr. Green Jeans, a farmer and amateur inventor, who would introduce viewers to different animals and demonstrate his various inventions. Puppet characters included the mischievous Mr. Moose, the thoughtful Bunny Rabbit, the curious Miss Frog, the quiet Mr. Whispers, and the scholarly Word Bird. Regular features included "The Magic Drawing Board" and "Reading Stories," which introduced viewers to children's literature classics like *Curious George* and *Make Way for Ducklings*. Like Miss Francis before him on *Ding Dong School*, the Captain would end each episode of his show by encouraging parents to spend quality time with their children every day and showing them various creative activities they could do together.

Another educational show for children, *Children's Corner*, debuted on NBC in 1955. Created, produced, and hosted by Fred Rogers and Josie Carey, it was similar to a show the two had created for community-supported local television station WQED in Pittsburgh a year earlier. It featured puppet animals and live performers in a cozy and reassuring environment, with stories that emphasized morality and decency and introduced children to foreign

CBS described *Captain Kangaroo* as "the gentlest children's show on the air." The show starred Bob Keeshan as Captain Kangaroo, named for the large pockets on his jacket.

languages and other cultures. Though it lasted only one season on NBC, *Children's Corner* was a significant show because it became the blueprint for *Mr. Rogers' Neighborhood*, which would debut in the next decade and last much, much longer.

The circus show tradition from the early 1950s was carried on later in the decade, largely in the form of *Bozo the Clown*. The character of Bozo originally appeared in a series of children's story-telling record albums and accompanying books and comic books produced by Capitol Records in the 1940s. In the comic books and on the TV show, Bozo was depicted in typical white-faced clown makeup, but it was his bright-orange hair that stuck out in a wing-tipped halo around his otherwise bald head that made him distinctive and became his defining physical feature.

Bozo was a franchised show, which means that the Bozo character and format were licensed to individual TV stations around the country, which produced their own versions of the show with local performers. Generally airing live, the shows had a variety format, and most featured comedy sketches, circus acts, cartoons, games, and a studio audience. Ver-

Bozo the Clown **was a circus variety show that was franchised to local stations, which each produced their own version of the show, with different performers starring as Bozo. Larry Harmon, seen here as Bozo, was the show's originator.**

sions of the show were produced around the world, and it remained on the air through the 1990s.

There was another live show that debuted in the mid–1950s which provided a counterpoint to shows like *Bozo the Clown*, one with a style and sensibility that seemed more in tune with the following decade than the conformist 1950s. *The Soupy Sales Show*, which made its network debut on ABC in 1955, was one of several local and national children's shows created and hosted by comic Soupy Sales. Soupy was a multi-talented performer who hosted a number of local, national, and syndicated children's shows from the 1950s through the 1970s, with broadcasts originating from Detroit, Los Angeles, and New York. He reached the height of his popularity with a syndicated show produced in New York City beginning in 1964, but his earlier network show already embodied his hip, ironic approach to children's entertainment.

Soupy's shows had a variety format which included vaudeville antics, puppets, jokes and puns, fast-paced comedy sketches, musical numbers, and guest appearances by major stars of the day. Though the format was familiar, the show's elements were all a little "off," and Soupy presented them in a self-amused and knowing manner that made them seem like an ironic twist on the standard conventions of children's TV shows. For example, the puppets on the show were rather strange. White Fang, billed as "the biggest and meanest dog in the USA," appeared only as a giant shaggy white paw at the edge of the TV screen. Fang spoke only in grunts and growls, which Soupy hilariously translated for the viewers. When Soupy told bad jokes, Fang would throw cream pies at Soupy's face. There was also Black Tooth, "the biggest and sweetest dog in the USA,"

who appeared as a giant furry black paw extending from the edge of the TV screen and spoke with equally unintelligible but somewhat more feminine-sounding doggy noises, and who would pull Soupy off-screen to give him what sounded like loud, wet kisses. Pookie the Lion was a little hand-puppet who appeared on a puppet stage behind Soupy. Despite his cuddly appearance, Pookie was a beatnik type who engaged in rapid-fire repartee with Soupy. He usually

Comedian Soupy Sales starred in a series of hip children's variety shows in the 1950s and 60s. He is seen here on his *Lunch with Soupy Sales* program in 1960.

greeted Soupy with "Hey, bubby, want a kiss?" Pookie would mouth the words to jazz, soul, or pop recordings from Soupy's extensive record collection while he and Soupy bopped around to the music.

The show also featured a number of live characters, including Peaches, Soupy's girlfriend, played by Soupy in drag; Philo Kvetch, a private detective played by Soupy; The Mask, Philo's evil nemesis, also played by Soupy (and later revealed to be deposed USSR leader Nikita Khrushchev); and Onions Oregano, The Mask's henchman, played by actor Frank Nastasi, who was always eating onions. Every time he breathed in Philo's direction, Philo would choke and make faces, spray air freshener around, and exclaim, "Get those onions out of here!" There were also frequent guest appearances by major stars of the day, like Frank Sinatra, Sammy Davis, Jr., and singing groups the Shangri-Las and the Supremes.

Much of the live show was ad-libbed, which gave it a loose, edgy, and slightly dangerous feeling. Viewers knew that Soupy was unpredictable and that anything could happen on the show, and it often did. In one of several notorious incidents that occurred on the show, Soupy was apparently annoyed at having to do his show on New Year's Day, when he would rather have had the day off. So, at the end of the broadcast, he urged his young viewers to tiptoe into their still-sleeping parents' bedrooms, remove the "little green pieces of paper" from their parents' wallets and mail them to him, which many children did. Though Soupy later insisted that he had only been joking, he was suspended from the show for a week.[28]

Though new live shows like *Captain Kangaroo*, *Bozo*, and *Soupy Sales* were still being produced, many children's shows, like *The Mickey Mouse Club*, were now being shot on film. One children's TV genre that became typical of this era was the filmed action-adventure series, like *Sergeant Preston of the Yukon*, *Brave Eagle*, *The Adventures of Robin Hood*, and *Tales of the Texas Rangers*. Following the model set by *Lassie* and *Rin Tin Tin*, several of these series, like *Fury* and *My Friend Flicka*, featured heroic animals, in this case horses, and the boys who owned them, and continued the practice of providing moral lessons about responsibility, good sportsmanship, and the triumph of good over evil.

In a significant development that presaged the direction that commercial children's television would take over the next few decades, the first program-length made-for-TV cartoons appeared in the mid-1950s. *Mighty Mouse Playhouse*, which aired Saturday mornings on CBS, debuted in 1955. It starred a caped flying rodent crime-fighter who blended Mickey Mouse with Superman. The show's operatic theme song gave it a distinct and memorable quality. In 1957, *Mighty Mouse* was joined on Saturday mornings by cartoon series *Ruff and Reddy*, the first network television show from Hanna-Barbera Productions. The show featured the adventures of Ruff, a quick-thinking cat, and Reddy, his lovable but dim-witted canine friend. The following year, Hanna-Barbera followed up with the *Huckleberry Hound Show*, featuring another lovable animated mutt. Hanna-Barbera went on to produce dozens of successful TV cartoons, including *The Flintstones*, *The Jetsons*, *The Yogi Bear Show*, *Jonny Quest*, and *Quick Draw McGraw*.

Other cartoon series that debuted at this time included *The Woody Woodpecker Show* and the *Gerald McBoing-Boing Show*, both based on animated shorts that had been shown in movie theaters. Gerald McBoing-Boing was a little boy who had first appeared as a Dr. Seuss book character. He didn't talk but communicated in the form of sound effects that sounded like "boing-boing." The show also included educational segments "Meet the Artist," "Meet the Inventor," and "Legends of Americans in the World." Original music written for the show was a key element throughout.

Another kind of animated show that made its first appearance at this time was the *Gumby Show*. Created by animator Art Clokey, *Gumby* first appeared in 1956 as a regular short segment on the *Howdy Doody Show* and was so popular that it became a full-length series on NBC the following year. The show used a unique style of stop-motion clay animation developed by Clokey when he was a film student at the University of Southern California. *The Gumby Show* went into syndication after it ended its run on NBC, and there were 233 episodes of the show produced over the course of its 40-year history, all featuring a green clay robot-like little boy with a slanted head and big feet, and his sidekick Pokey, a talking

The *Huckleberry Hound Show* was one of the earliest program-length cartoons from Hanna-Barbera Productions. It starred a lovable but dim-witted mutt.

pony. Other regular characters on the series were the Blockheads, a duo of red humanoid figures who created mischief and mayhem; Gumby's parents Gumba and Gumbo, and his sister, Minga; Goo, a flying blue mermaid; Tilly, a chicken; and Denali, a mastodon. Each episode hinged on the fact that the characters and settings were made out of clay and could melt into various shapes and then reconfigure to their original forms. Many episodes included a sequence in which Gumby and Pokey would physically slip into a book and then have an adventure in the world of the book's story.

The claymation style of the show had a primitive look that didn't try to make the characters or settings look realistic. Gumby and the other characters seemed like clay figures made by a child and brought to life to play out a child's imaginary stories. Gumby's personality was like that of a real child, but he existed in a magical, surreal world where anything could happen.

Debuting on ABC in November 1959, *Rocky and His Friends* (often referred to as the *Rocky and Bullwinkle Show*) was a cartoon series from

Rocky and His Friends (often referred to as *Rocky and Bullwinkle*) was a transitional program that poked fun at the conventions of the 1950s, including the Cold War with Russia. It starred Rocky, a flying squirrel, and his dim-witted sidekick Bullwinkle, a moose. Rocky and Bullwinkle were constantly battling Soviet spies Boris Badenov and Natasha Fatale.

animator Jay Ward, the co-creator of *Crusader Rabbit*. Like *The Soupy Sales Show*, *Rocky and His Friends* was a transitional program that poked fun at the conventions of the 1950s, including the Cold War with Russia. It starred Rocky, a flying squirrel wearing an aviator's hat, and his dim-witted sidekick Bullwinkle, a moose. Rocky and Bullwinkle were constantly battling and outwitting Russian espionage mastermind Mr. Big and the two Soviet spies who worked for him, Boris Badenov and Natasha Fatale. There were also other tongue-in-cheek segments on the show, including "Fractured Fairytales," which added modern twists to classic children's stories; "Bullwinkle's Corner," where Bullwinkle tried to introduce some culture into the show by reciting and acting out classic poems, which he only succeeded in butchering; "Dudley Do-Right of the Mounties," a parody of damsel-in-distress movie melodramas; and "Peabody's Improbable History," about the adventures of Peabody, a pedantic genius dog, and his pet boy Sherman, who traveled through time via the Wayback Machine, one of Peabody's inventions. With its satirical format and timely cultural references, *Rocky and His Friends* attracted a cult following of both children and adults, as *The Soupy Sales Show* and *Crusader Rabbit* had also done.

Television Advertising and Marketing to Children

Television advertising to children in the latter half of the 1950s continued the practice from the earlier part of the decade in which children's show hosts and characters often directly promoted their sponsors' products during the show. Even the gentle, high-minded Captain Kangaroo took part in this practice, pitching Schwinn bicycles on his program.[29]

On the *Mickey Mouse Club*, however, a new age of TV advertising to children began when the Mattel toy company made the audacious decision to invest a half-million dollars to air three commercials for Mattel on each episode of the show for a year. As advertising executive Cy Schneider recounts in his book about the children's television business,[30] Mattel created the first filmed TV commercials for toys to advertise two of their musical products, a Jack-in-the-Box and a "Getar," and their Burp Gun, an automatic cap-firing machine gun modeled after the machine guns used in World War II jungle combat. For the Burp Gun commercial, instead of just showing the toy or showing a child demonstrating how to play with it, Mattel's advertising agency filmed a young boy pretending to stalk a herd of elephants in his living room, while rear-screen projectors showed the elephants advancing and then retreating whenever the boy fired his Burp Gun. The commercial was intended to show how the toy gun would help a child play out the fantasies that the toy gun would engender. At the time, no one really questioned the appropriateness of selling or advertising toy guns to children, or the fact that the toy and its advertising were aimed only at boys.

The Burp Gun commercial began airing on the *Mickey Mouse Club* in November 1955. By Christmas of that year, Mattel had shipped over a million Burp Guns to toy stores and distributors, more than doubling their prior sales volume. Still, many stores ran out of the gun, and even President Eisenhower wrote to Mattel to try to find a Burp Gun to give his grandson for Christmas. The success of Mattel's TV ads shifted the toy industry's thinking about how to evaluate the sales potential of toys, from a focus on the appeal of the toy's own features to a focus on how successfully the toy could be shown in TV commercials. As Schneider describes this paradigm shift in marketing to children, "Presenting the product on television became part of the product. We realized early on that, for children, the product as seen in a television commercial *was* the product."[31]

Their commercials on the *Mickey Mouse Club* quickly established Mattel as the toy industry leader in musical toys and toy guns. It also laid the groundwork for Mattel's launch in 1958 of what would become arguably the most popular branded toy product in history, the Barbie doll. Barbie's success was inextricably tied to television advertising. The doll itself embodied a significant break from the kinds of dolls that most girls played with at that time. Rather than a baby doll with which girls could imagine and practice their future roles as mothers, Barbie allowed girls to fantasize about their future lives as fashionable teenagers and young women. The television commercials for the doll were designed to facilitate these fantasies by not depicting Barbie as a doll but rather as a real-life teenage fashion model. Each commercial told a story in Barbie's life, with the doll filmed in various fashion poses against a realistic background, so that children would think of Barbie as a real person. In essence, each commercial was like a short episode in a TV show starring Barbie as a beautiful teenage fashion model. As a result of this advertising campaign, the Barbie doll was an immediate success, and Mattel initially struggled to keep up with demand for the doll. Mattel went on to build on Barbie's success by creating a boyfriend doll for Barbie named Ken, producing an endless supply of different clothes, accessories, and environments for the doll, and creating different models of Barbie to reflect changing tastes and interests.[32]

The success of Mattel's Burp Gun and Barbie doll illustrated the power of television advertising aimed at children and, in the case of the Barbie doll, the role that TV advertising could play in creating a cultural touchstone that became an icon in children's lives. It also offers insight into how gender roles were depicted and reinforced through children's television in the 1950s. While boys were encouraged to imagine themselves as soldiers and wild game hunters killing elephants in the jungle, girls were encouraged to fantasize about themselves as sexy and fashionable young women leading lives filled with glamour, wealth, and stardom. On the other hand, Barbie commercials featured a female as its star rather than as a supporting player, something that girls would rarely have seen in most TV shows for children at that time.

As for depicting people of color, TV commercials aimed at children reflected the same racial prejudices seen in TV shows in the 1950s. Even as news coverage of continued discrimination and violence against African Americans and the emerging Civil Rights Movement intruded into the lives of middle-class white Americans, the world depicted on television shows remained oblivious to the shifting social and cultural tides. Nonwhite characters were rarely if ever shown in TV ads, and it would be years before Mattel began producing Barbie dolls of different races and ethnicities.

Stay Tuned...

Though the moods, trends, and attitudes of the 1950s remained prevalent through the early years of the following decade, American society and culture were changing, and both adults' and children's television would soon begin to reflect those changes. As TV historians Castleman and Podrazik note, there were three events that occurred during the 1959–60 television season that seemed to mark the passing of an era in television culture. In 1959, George Reeve, the star of *The Adventures of Superman* since its debut six years earlier, committed suicide, and millions of children learned that television was not reality and that Superman was in fact only human. In March 1960, Lucille Ball filed for divorce from Desi Arnaz, officially ending a marriage whose fictionalized portrayal on television had been a cultural touchstone of the 1950s. Then, on September 24, 1960, NBC broadcast the final episode of the *Howdy Doody* show, whose ratings had been in decline. "It was a graceful farewell that rang down the curtain on one of the last remnants of television's infancy. For that first TV generation, there was perhaps never a more poignant moment on television than the last moment of that last show when Clarabell the clown, silent through all thirteen years of the program, looked into the camera and quietly spoke, 'Goodbye kids.'"[33]

CHAPTER THREE

The Toddler Years
(the 1960s)

Life in the U.S.

The sixties were defined by tumultuous social, cultural, and political change, arguably the greatest cultural paradigm shift since the 1920s. The rigid conformist culture of the 1950s created a yearning for individual freedom, especially among the younger members of society, which erupted in the 1960s. This was the decade of the youth counter-culture and the "generation gap," when widely held beliefs and norms about authority, race relations, gender roles, sexuality, drug use, and many other areas of life were questioned and contested. As historian Steven Mintz sees it, "Although the word *revolution* strikes many as hyperbolic, the 1960s is a period in which the word seems apt. The young lived through turbulent times, including a sexual revolution, a cultural revolution, a student revolution, and a rights revolution."[1]

This all happened against a backdrop of global tensions which had been growing through the previous decade and continued to escalate into the 1960s. The Berlin Wall went up in 1961, bringing the U.S. and NATO into direct confrontation with the Soviet Union over the future of Europe. In 1962, the Cuban Missile Crisis, unfolding just miles offshore from Florida, brought the terrified nation to the brink of nuclear holocaust.

Domestic political violence seemed to surge along with fears of potential foreign conflict. President Kennedy was assassinated in November 1963 by a killer who had a history of strong pro–Soviet activities, plunging the country into a profound sense of shock and grief with not a little paranoia.

Only two months earlier, a bomb planted at a Baptist church in Alabama on the church's youth day killed four black girls, and in 1964 and 1965, urban riots broke out in Harlem and Watts. As racial tensions that had been simmering for years began to boil over, African American communities evolved a spectrum of political responses. At one end was the disciplined exercise of civil disobedience personified by Reverend Martin Luther King, Jr. At the other end of the spectrum were violent splinter groups of militants bent on terrorist acts, primarily aimed at police, for whom Eldridge Cleaver and Malcolm X were inspirational figures.[2] Between the extremes were groups which sought to promote Black empowerment both symbolically and through community activism. The symbolism of, for example, Black Panthers in military-like garb cradling (legal) firearms at demonstrations, which were presumably staged specifically to provide provocative images for mass media, enraged and frightened many white people while encouraging people of color to take pride in their heritage and actively resist racism.[3]

In 1965, the participation of American ground troops in the Vietnam War began, followed by enactment of the draft in 1966, generating antiwar protests on campuses which sometimes spread to violent street demonstrations around the country. Inspired by the pattern of Black militants, small extremist groups formed around the idea of stopping the war through violent attacks on institutions considered part of the war effort, like bombings of corporate offices. Such attacks were generally timed to avoid casualties, but they still became a part of the unpredictably violent texture of American life.[4] The assassinations of Martin Luther King, Jr., and Presidential candidate Attorney General Robert Kennedy in 1968 and the violence in the streets of Chicago during the 1968 Democratic National Convention intensified the feeling that the country was coming unglued.[5]

Yet somehow, despite the fact that the 60s were a decade full of turmoil, it was also a time of liberation and social progress. In the years following the assassination of President Kennedy, major efforts were made to realize some of his most cherished goals, including passage of a series of laws that made many forms of racial discrimination illegal. The Civil Rights Act of 1964 outlawed racial discrimination in schools, employment, and public places, while the Voting Rights Act of 1965 outlawed voting practices that discriminated against blacks. In 1968, the Fair Housing Act was passed, which banned racial discrimination in the sale or rental of housing.

Along with the movement against discrimination based on race, women's rights were also advanced during the 1960s. In 1961, John F. Kennedy's Presidential Commission on the Status of Women found widespread discrimination against women in employment and many other walks of life. The Commission's findings led to passage of the Equal Pay

Act in 1963, aimed at abolishing wage disparities between men and women employed in the same positions. The following year, Betty Friedan published *The Feminine Mystique*, calling on women to liberate themselves from the illusion that becoming a wife and mother was their only road to personal satisfaction.[6] "Consciousness-raising" sessions in which participants critically examined women's prescribed social roles were followed by marches and protests, and in 1966, the National Organization for Women was founded. By the end of the decade, women's liberation, or "women's lib," had become a household term.[7]

Perhaps "The Pill" was the wellspring of 60s liberation. The invention of the birth control pill and the IUD in 1960 produced a revolution in sexual norms and behavior and a profound transformation in family structure.[8] At the start of the decade, half of all women married between the ages of sixteen and nineteen and quickly gave birth to three or four children. Hardly any of these young mothers worked outside the home, while their husbands entered the workforce at an early age. By 1970, over half of married women with children under five were working outside the home.[9] Couples were marrying an average of six years later than at the start of the decade. As marriage age rose, college attendance soared even faster than the burgeoning college-age population cohort, and a larger number of better educated women sought work.

Changes in family structure led to changes in family values. The divorce rate shot up, doubling between 1960 and 1970. The number of men and women living together outside of marriage increased sixfold during the decade.[10] Abortion, formerly not a topic deemed proper for public discussion, became a political issue. Public opinion about these profound changes was deeply divided, with some seeing them as signs of social progress for women, while others saw them as signs of a dangerous breakdown in the family itself. These alternative ways to look at the social transformation taking place during the decade would contribute to the notion, later termed a culture war, that America was engaged in a crucial internal battle over the significance and implications of the enormous changes that were unfolding in this decade.[11]

The social and cultural revolution that played out in shifting family structures and values inevitably had an impact on children's lives. As the generation born during the postwar Baby Boom entered the 1960s, the number of teenagers in the country exploded. Unlike their parents, these young people grew up in a time of unprecedented prosperity, a time when their parents lavished them with attention, encouragement, and money. "Their parents' concern for their well-being became translated into their own search for personal fulfillment."[12] Yet, despite their comfortable lives and the attention and nurture they had received as children, many teenagers did not feel personally fulfilled. Instead, they felt alienated, disaffected, and estranged from society. They felt that their peers could understand their deepest passions and concerns in a way that their parents could not. The tumultuous events of the 1960s reinforced the sense shared by many of these young people that the norms and values of the older generation were not working and that they could find self-fulfillment not through conformity and materialism but by promoting social and moral change.

Many adults, including some child care experts, viewed the generation gap and the "counter-culture" attitudes and behavior of the young with dismay. They blamed the "permissive childrearing" practices promoted by experts like Dr. Benjamin Spock for creating what they saw as a generation of spoiled and defiant children. However, other social critics believed that the prior decade's emphasis on conformity and materialism had made it difficult for young people to find themselves. They argued that the postwar young had been raised to value independence and achievement, but schools and families gave them few avenues to express their independence or pursue meaningful accomplishments.[13]

Though every generation sees itself as different from their parents, the Baby Boomer generation had a particularly intense sense of itself as a distinct cohort, with similar interests, attitudes, and values that were not shared by the older generation. Having experienced the same TV shows, music, and fads, this generation of young people had an especially strong sense of peer group identity. This was no accident but the direct result of having been targeted as a distinct market by advertisers and the media. As two senior market research executives describe the industry take on the Boomer generation, "From infancy to maturity, they have been the driving economic force in the American economy, and thus the world, for the past sixty years. Even as they age, they will continue to dominate the marketplace.... There is no group now or ever before with the power of the Baby Boomers to move markets and spark change. Baby Boomers are a generational phenomenon unlike any other."[14] The postwar surge in new births had been catnip for commercial interests. The broadcasting and related entertainment and advertising industries enlisted innovative communication tools to provide all the elements needed for those 78 million or so young people to cohere as an audience that could be sold into. It was a massive but heady undertaking for those industries, which also grew powerful and more skillful with the experience.

The processes for addressing and cultivating youth markets matured with the Boomers. While continuing to market to the huge (and "dominant") Boomer generation, commercial interests prepared to focus as well on the next cohort of young children. They faced challenges, as society was evolving from the relatively uniform postwar ethos into a more diverse cultural landscape with disputed territories. Marketing in this changing world would require continued adaptation, but by now the communications industries possessed strategies that were proven and campaign-hardened. Children's television was a central, and favored, tool they would rely upon to reach emerging disparate audiences and attempt to create order within the increasingly fragmented youth market.

Television

The new fall season that began in 1961 saw the CBS debut of *The Defenders*, a legal drama series in the tradition of the anthologies that had aired during the "golden age of television." *The Defenders* was a courtroom drama that laid out the pros and cons of conflicting positions on serious and often controversial topics of the day, like entertainment blacklisting, the death penalty, and even abortion, which was then illegal and rarely acknowledged. To CBS' surprise, the show became an immediate hit.

For the most part, however, it was not until the latter half of the decade that the social and cultural conflicts and changes taking place in the sixties would begin to find their way into television entertainment shows. Instead, TV shows in the first half of the decade tried to give viewers a respite from an increasingly turbulent reality by generally avoiding any references to current events or relevant social issues, while continuing to present their audiences with familiar plots, characters, and settings. For example, *The Dick Van Dyke Show*, which premiered on CBS in 1961, was a family and workplace sitcom centered on the daily trials and tribulations of a TV comedy show writer, his wife, and his TV network colleagues. Though Rob and Laura Petrie, the central characters on the show, were depicted as smart, decent, and hard-working people who were true partners in life, Rob was the breadwinner and Laura was a housewife.[15] The show captured the ethos of white middle-class life in the early 1960s, much as *I Love Lucy* and *Leave It to Beaver* had done in the 1950s. Some popular sitcoms like *The Beverly Hillbillies* and *The Andy Griffith Show* glorified the homespun down-to-earth values of rural or small town America, while others like *Gilligan's Island, Bewitched, I Dream of Jeannie,* and *The Munsters* presented fantasy situations that bore little relationship to reality.

But as the decade progressed, life on television began to change. New attitudes toward African Americans and women, and the music and styles of the counterculture, if not its values and beliefs, started to find their way into television series.

Throughout the 1950s, television shows had largely mirrored the segregated nature of American society. African Americans were rarely seen on the air or were depicted in broadly stereotyped ways, as in shows like *Beulah* or *Amos 'n' Andy*, or cast in secondary parts. But as the Civil Rights movement made strides during the 1960s, socially-aware dramas like *The Defenders* and *East Side/West Side* began to tackle racially-charged themes and occasionally feature black performers in serious roles. A turning point in the depiction of blacks on TV took place in 1965, when comedian Bill Cosby was cast as the co-star of hit action-adventure espionage series *I Spy*.[16] Cosby played the role of a secret agent who traveled the world on exciting and dangerous espionage missions, together with his partner and friend, played by Robert Culp. Culp's cover identity was that of a professional tennis player, while the Cosby character's cover was that he was Culp's trainer. Besides being an expert at his job, Cosby's character was also a Rhodes Scholar who spoke seven languages. Later series like ABC's *Mod Squad* and NBC's *Julia* in 1968 also starred African Americans in serious, if not entirely realistic, roles.

I Spy was one of several shows in the mid–1960s influenced by the spy craze that followed on the heels of the popular James Bond movies that had made their debut a few years earlier. Other shows in this genre were *The Man from U.N.C.L.E*, *Secret Agent*, and spy show spoof *Get Smart*. This progression of the international intrigue genre—from serious, if formulaic and stylized, thriller to camp comedy—reveals how attitudes toward U.S.-Soviet relations softened during the decade. Gradually, the fear of nuclear war with Russia and the intensity of the Cold War rivalry that had been a constant backdrop to American life since the late 1940s lessened so much that it could be made the subject of light entertainment.

The depiction of women's roles on television programs also started to change in the sixties. *That Girl*, a sitcom on ABC which debuted in 1966, starred Marlo Thomas as a high-spirited single young woman living on her own in New York City while she pursued an acting career. Though Thomas' character had a steady boyfriend who soon became her fiancé, and her parents were shown as constantly worried about her independent lifestyle, the program nevertheless reflected changes in the American psyche that might have been too sensitive for the mass audience any sooner. *That Girl* was the first of several "independent woman" series, like the *Mary Tyler Moore Show*, that would follow in the next decade.[17]

The sounds and styles of the counterculture also began to enter middle-Americans' homes through television, as *The Ed Sullivan Show* presented the Beatles to a national American television audience for the first time in February 1964. The appearances on the show by the "Fab Four" (as they were often called in the press, without irony) generated huge ratings, and the *Sullivan* show quickly lined up other new rock and pop acts from Britain and the U.S.[18] Suddenly, the rather stiff and staid Ed Sullivan was hand-pumping the likes of Mick Jagger and Jim Morrison, and introducing the Dave Clark Five, the Beach Boys, the Animals, Petula Clark, and other artists from the top of the pop charts (Sullivan's decision to put Elvis Presley on camera in the 1950s did suggest his potential as a hitmaker, but he had not embraced the role to this extent before).[19] New music-based TV series like ABC's *Shindig* and NBC's *Hulabaloo* and *The Monkees* soon followed, in an effort to use the new sounds of rock 'n' roll to target a younger audience.[20]

Though the television landscape of the 1960s slowly began to reflect some of the changes in American society and culture, sitcoms and variety shows generally avoided direct references to the day's conflicts and controversies. The one glaring exception was *The Smothers Brothers Comedy Hour*, which premiered on CBS in 1967. Tom and Dick Smothers' irreverent variety show poked fun at virtually all the hallowed institutions of American society, like religion, government, and politics, and included references to current affairs and topical issues like protests against the Vietnam War. As the show became increasingly antiwar, it encountered a series of showdowns with CBS' Standards and Practices Department and was finally canceled in 1969.[21]

In contrast, NBC's *Laugh-In*, which also tried to reflect elements of the youth culture, never experienced any serious problems with the NBC censors. While incorporating many of the innovative elements used by Ernie Kovacs in his groundbreaking series of television specials earlier in the decade, like bizarre visuals, off-the-wall sketches, and short, unconnected interstitial segments, *Laugh-In* borrowed the look and style of the youth culture but studiously avoided any of its controversial substance. Its name alone, a take-off on the "sit-in" that was a form of non-violent political protest against the Vietnam War during the 60s, perfectly embodied the show's counter-cultural yet apolitical ethos. It used new editing tricks and techniques made possible by the use of videotape to present a fast-paced series of blackout sketches that squeezed together slapstick, vaudeville, satire, an air of hipness, and brief guest star appearances (including one by President Richard Nixon), all within a frantically-paced show whose psychedelic look set it apart from anything else on television when it debuted in 1967. By the end of its first season on the air, it had become a solid top ten hit.[22]

Children's Television

In the 1950s, most children's programs aired in the late afternoons or early evenings, while only a handful of shows were scheduled on Saturday mornings. But in the 1960s, local stations began replacing their late afternoon children's shows with programs for stay-at-home mothers, for which they could charge higher advertising rates, and they shifted more and more of their children's shows to Saturday morning. Saturday morning airtime, which had previously been characterized by small audiences and low advertising fees, began to become lucrative for the networks as it became the place for children's programs and advertising aimed at children. The proportion of total network programming for children airing on Saturdays grew from about 25 percent in 1958 to more than 50 percent by 1968.[23]

Like most entertainment television in the early part of the decade, shows for children generally avoided any acknowledgment of the social or cultural changes that were taking place across the country. Towards the end of the decade, however, a number of shows were created that were a direct product of these changes.

At the start of the decade, several new live-action shows for children debuted that were similar to many children's programs from the 1950s, in that they incorporated a mix of puppets, music, and fantasy. For example, *Pip the Piper*, which premiered in 1960, took place in the magic land of Pipertown high up in the clouds, where musical instruments grew on trees and everyone communicated by playing an instrument. The show revolved around the adventures of Pip, a medieval minstrel who played a magic flute. *The Magic Land of Allakazam*, which also debuted in 1960, starred a magician and his family, who used their magic tricks to outwit various villains. Later in the decade, there was *H.R.Pufnstuf*, a fantasy series centered on the adventures of a young boy with a magic flute, who ended up on a magical island after he was attacked by a witch while out sailing.

The Shari Lewis Show, which debuted on NBC in 1960, was a variety show that included live entertainers, puppets, and music. It starred an effervescent and multitalented ventriloquist who manipulated and provided the voices for a set of hand-puppets that she interacted with on the air. Lamb Chop, the starring puppet on the show, was essentially a sock puppet little lamb whose character was that of a shy, soft-spoken, but mischievous and wise-cracking six-year-old. Lamb Chop seemed to serve as a sassy alter-ego for Lewis. Dog puppet Hush Puppy was a sweet country bumpkin, and horse puppet Charlie Horse had the persona of a cocky buck-toothed ten-year-old. In addition to her skits with the puppets, Lewis also exhibited her song and dance talents on the show, often teaching moral lessons through her skits and performances. Lewis went on to host other versions of her show on NBC, PBS, and in syndication through the 1990s.

Some series that debuted in the early to mid-sixties, like *The Magic Ranch*, *Frontier Circus*, *Magic Midway*, and *Buckaroo 500*, continued the tradition of circus or rodeo-themed shows. There were also game shows, like *Shenanigans*, which aired on ABC from 1964 to 1965. Hosted by well-known performer/comic Stubby Kaye and sponsored by the Milton Bradley Company, producer of many popular board games, it featured a giant game board with large squares marked out on the studio floor. Two children would compete to progress along the board by answering questions or performing tasks, in order to reach "home" first.

Several new live-action dramatic series for children and families were also introduced during this decade. Like similar shows of the 1950s, these dramatic series had values-driven plots that taught moral lessons, while several also tried to introduce young viewers to different cultures. *Flipper*, which debuted in primetime in 1964, was similar to *Lassie* but took place in the ocean. It featured the adventures of the widowed chief ranger of a marine park in Florida and his son and daughter, but the real star of the show was Flipper, their pet dolphin. *Daniel Boone* revolved around the adventures of the great American folk hero, portrayed by actor Fess Parker, who had previously starred as Davy Crockett on the *Disneyland* show in the 1950s. Later in the decade, *Tarzan*, based on the earlier movie series, dealt with the adventures of the British Earl of Greystoke, who had returned to his native jungle home after years of formal schooling in England. *The Adventures of the Seaspray*, which was filmed in Australia, followed the wanderings of a free-lance writer and his three children on a boat in the South Pacific.

Most of the new shows for children that debuted in the 1960s, however, especially those that were added to the Saturday morning schedule, were cartoons rather than live-action shows. The shift to cartoons was driven largely by economics, and a new animation studio founded by for-

The Flintstones **was a parody of suburban living that first aired in primetime but became more successful once it was moved to Saturday mornings. Here (clockwise from upper left) pet Dino, Fred Flintstone, wife Wilma, and baby Pebbles enjoy an evening of Stone-Age television viewing.**

mer MGM studio animators William Hanna and Joseph Barbera was at the forefront of this trend. With the creation of *Ruff and Reddy* and *The Huckleberry Hound Show* in the late 1950s, Hanna-Barbera introduced a limited form of animation that featured pared down illustrations and minimal action scenes, with the characters sometimes moving only their mouths and eyes. These cartoons could be produced in much less time and, more importantly, at far lower cost than the more elaborately detailed cartoons that had previously been produced for theatrical showing. They also cost less to produce than many of the live-action shows that had been a staple of children's television since its inception.

In the early sixties, Hanna-Barbera created several cartoon series intended to air in primetime, with the goal of reaching an audience of both children and adults. *The Flintstones*, which premiered in 1960, made fun of modern suburban life by featuring a Stone Age family in a sitcom modeled after *The Honeymooners* show of the 1950s. Though the characters lived in the prehistoric city of Bedrock, they all behaved and spoke in a contemporary manner and dealt with the same kinds of situations that were typical in live-action sitcoms.[24] The following year, Hanna-Barbera debuted *Top Cat*, a primetime cartoon inspired by another popular 1950s series, *The Phil Silvers Show*. Top Cat, the animated star of the show, was a sly con artist who was the leader of a pack of Broadway alley cats always on the run from

© 1983 Hanna-Barbera Productions, Inc.

Scooby-Doo, the lovable cowardly Great Dane, first appeared in 1969 in *Scooby-Doo, Where Are You?*, where he helped solve criminal mysteries alongside his teenage sleuth friends. Seen here (from left to right) are Scrappy-Doo, Daphne Blake, Shaggy Rogers, and Scooby-Doo.

police officer Dibble, their avowed enemy. *Top Cat* was quickly followed by *The Jetsons*, which was a space-age version of *The Flintstones* set in the distant future rather than the distant past. Though they initially aired in primetime, all three series were later moved to Saturday morning, where they found greater success as strictly children's shows.

Hanna-Barbera soon became one of the most prolific producers of children's cartoons, and many of the cartoon characters they created became icons of popular culture. There was Yogi Bear, who first starred in the *Yogi Bear* show in 1961. Yogi, who liked to describe himself as "smarter than the average bear," and his diminutive pal Boo Boo lived in Jellystone Park, where they spent their days plotting different ways to pilfer park visitors' picnic baskets. *Quick Draw McGraw* was a comical western that starred a dim-witted horse marshal known as the "slowest gun in the West." Together with his Mexican burro sidekick, Baba Looey, Quick Draw valiantly but ineptly struggled to maintain law and order on the frontier. The show also featured segments starring other characters, like Snagglepuss, a trouble-prone lion; Snooper and Blabber, a cat and mouse; and Augie Doggie, a bright but impulsive dog. Scooby-Doo, the lovable cowardly Great Dane, first appeared in 1969 in *Scooby-Doo, Where Are You?*, where he helped solve criminal mysteries alongside teenage sleuths Daphne, Freddy, Shaggy, and Velma. Scooby continued to be featured in various cartoons on different networks through 1986.

The Adventures of Jonny Quest was a unique Hanna-Barbera production that differed from their usual output in both style and content. Premiering on ABC in 1964, the show played in primetime on Fridays, and later aired in reruns on other networks on Saturday mornings. *Jonny Quest* was an action-adventure series focused on the globe-trotting escapades of famous U.S. Government scientist Dr. Benton Quest, his 11-year-old son Jonny, his adopted Indian son Hadji, family bodyguard Roger "Race" Bannon, and pet bulldog Bandit. The Quests had a home compound on a remote island off the coast of Florida, but they spent most of their time flying around the world to investigate scientific mysteries that often had science fiction elements, from espionage robots to Egyptian mummies to pterosaurs come to life. These mysteries usually involved the work of various villains, like the evil recurring character Dr. Zin, an Asian criminal mastermind. The Jonny Quest team was entirely male (it was unclear if there was a mother in the family), and the show featured much more realistic violence than other children's cartoons of its day, which made it the target of parental complaints. It was cancelled after only one season, but it aired in reruns and syndication through the 1960s and 1970s, and

The Adventures of Jonny Quest was an action-adventure cartoon that featured more realistic violence than other children's cartoons of its day. Its all-male star-ring team consisted of (clockwise from left) Hadji (Jonny's adopted brother), Race Bannon (bodyguard), Dr. Benton Quest (Jonny and Hadji's father), Jonny, and dog Bandit.

Hanna-Barbera later produced a revival called *The Real Adventures of Jonny Quest*, which aired on the Cartoon Network in 1996–97.

Another popular Saturday morning cartoon was *Casper, the Friendly Ghost*, a Paramount Studios production that became a mainstay of ABC's

Saturday morning schedule in the sixties. Based on a series of Paramount movie shorts from the 1940s, the show's star was a childlike little ghost who tried to help people rather scare them. Though people were usually frightened by Casper, he didn't let that stop him from continuously seeking out human friendships.

In 1967, ABC added *George of the Jungle* to its Saturday morning lineup. Produced by Jay Ward, creator of *Rocky and His Friends*, the show was made up of three unrelated segments: George of the Jungle, a spoof of Tarzan; Super Chicken, a spoof of superhero shows; and Tom Slick, about the comical misadventures of a racecar driver. A revival of the show was produced in 2007 for the Cartoon Network.

Davey and Goliath, a syndicated cartoon first seen in 1961, bears mention as one of the few religious shows for children ever aired on television. Produced by the Lutheran Church and created by Art Clokey, the creator of the *Gumby* show, *Davey and Goliath* consisted of 15-minute episodes animated via claymation, the same technique used in *Gumby*. Each episode was a morality play that featured the adventures of young Davey Hansen and his talking dog Goliath, as they learned lessons about sharing, tolerance, respect for authority, and the love of God through dealing with everyday occurrences. The show dealt with such serious issues as racism, religious intolerance, and death.

The growing popularity of these Saturday morning cartoons and their relatively low cost spurred the networks to order even more. Trying to take advantage of the existing brand awareness associated with established TV or film properties, several of the new series were animated versions of popular live-action shows or movies, like *The New Three Stooges*, *The Abbot and Costello Show*, *King Kong*, *The Lone Ranger*, and *The New Adventures of Superman*.

Rock 'n' roll music increasingly found its way into children's television during this decade, in both live-action and animated programs. There was an animated series called *The Beatles*, which aired on CBS from 1965 to 1969. It starred cartoon versions of the "Fab Four," who performed two of their songs in each episode, with the songs' lyrics forming the basis for the show's plotlines. This series probably introduced many young children to the new sounds of the British rock invasion. *The Archies*, which debuted in 1968, was a cartoon series that featured the comical teenage characters of Riverdale High who had become staples of popular culture through comic books—Archie, Veronica, Jughead, Betty, and Reggie. In this incarnation, the group formed a rock band and performed a tune on each show. Despite the fact that they were fictional cartoon characters, several of their songs became hit records, including *Sugar Sugar, Jingle Jangle,* and *Who's My Baby?*. The show was so popular that it remained on the air in one form or another until 1988.[25]

Other children's shows that featured rock music included *Hollywood A Go-Go,* a syndicated dance participation show featuring children dancing to rock music, similar to *American Bandstand; The Beagles,* a cartoon parody of The Beatles, about a pair of rock 'n' rolling dogs; *Happening '68,* a musical variety show starring the leads from the Paul Revere's Raiders rock band; and *The Banana Splits Adventure Hour,* a combination of live action and cartoons, starring a rock 'n' roll band made up of four animals, performed by actors in animal costumes.[26]

The James Bond craze of the sixties also inspired several new animated children's shows. *Secret Squirrel,* which debuted in 1965, was modeled after the Bond film *Goldfinger.* It featured an undercover squirrel spy and his assistant, Morocco Mole, as they fought villain Yellow Pinky. The following year saw the premiere of *Cool McCool,* another animated James Bond parody about a secret agent who took orders from an unseen boss referred to as Number One. *King Kong,* which drew from two movie franchises, featured a friendly version of the titular ape, who helped Professor Bond and his family battle against evil villain Dr. Who. The show also included a short animated series about a secret agent called *Tom of T.H.U.M.B.,* modeled after *The Man from U.N.C.L.E.*

As the decade reached its mid-point and the move towards cartoon programming intensified, a particular kind of cartoon series for children began to predominate—the superhero cartoon. Early space adventures like *Captain Video* had sometimes featured characters with special superhuman powers, and the star character in *Superman* was a superhero. But animation removed the limits on depicting superhuman characters that had been inherent in the production of live-action shows, and animation programmers let their imaginations run free. Between 1965 and 1968, shows like *Roger Ramjet, Atom Ant, Marine Boy, Frankenstein Jr., and the Impossibles, Marvel Superheroes, Prince Planet, Space Kidettes, Moby Dick and the Mighty Mightor, The Super Six, Space Ghost and Dino Boy, The Amazing Three, Super President and Spy Shadow, Birdman and the Galaxy, The Herculoids, The Fantastic Four, Spiderman/The Incredible Hulk,* and *Batman* quickly became the most common type of children's shows on television. There was even an affectionate parody of the cartoon superhero genre, called *Underdog.*

In 1968, however, the superhero craze on Saturday morning network television abruptly came to an end, though these series continued in syndication and a later version of the genre would reappear in the following decade. What brought the trend to an end, at least temporarily, were the real-life events that took place that year. Though pressure on the networks to scale back television violence had been growing for some time, the assassinations of Robert F. Kennedy and Martin Luther King, Jr., and the urban riots that followed in Detroit, Los Angeles, Chicago, and Newark led to increased public outrage and revulsion over violent TV shows and more government hearings on violence on television. A convenient target for the public and the government were the new superhero shows, which were permeated with what the networks referred to as "action" but what critics of these shows called "violence," and the genre quickly came under fire as a potential contributor to the violence that seemed to be spreading through the country. In the harsh glare of this public outcry and government attention, all three networks announced that they would be dropping their superhero shows in favor of more benign Saturday morning programs. As a result, most of the new shows for children that debuted in the fall of 1968 and 1969 were still cartoons, like *The Go-Go Gophers*, *Wacky Races*, *The Archie Show*, *The Adventures of Gulliver*, *The Dudley Do-Right Show*, *Here Comes the Grump*, *The Perils of Penelope Pitstop*, and *Scooby-Doo, Where Are You?*, but they focused on comedy rather than conflict.[27]

These programming decisions were made not just in the context of the decade's violence but also in light of a public call earlier in the decade for television to pursue its unrealized potential for good, and especially to do better for children. The seed was planted in 1961 when Newton Minow, Chairman of the FCC, delivered a devastating and influential assessment of the state of television at the annual meeting of the National Association of Broadcasters. The official title of Minow's speech was *Television and the Public Interest*, but it has always been known by its single most resonant phrase, that television programming was a "vast wasteland." As the heads of the three broadcast networks listened in stunned silence, Minow challenged them to take a good long look at what their networks were regularly putting on the air: "I can assure you that you will observe a vast wasteland. You will see a procession of game shows, violence, audience participation shows, formula comedies about totally unbelievable families, blood and thunder, mayhem, violence, sadism, murder, Western badmen, Western goodmen, private eyes, gangsters, more violence, and cartoons, and, endlessly, commercials, many screaming, cajoling, and offending, and, most of all, boredom."[28]

Minow particularly took aim at children's programs, most of which he said were either too violent or "dull, gray, and insipid as dishwater, just as tasteless, just as nourishing…. There are some fine children's shows, but they are drowned out in the massive doses of cartoons, violence, and more violence. Must these be your trademarks? Search your consciences and see if you cannot offer more to your young beneficiaries, whose future you guide so many hours each and every day."[29] Commercial broadcasters were put on notice that the FCC would expect better of them, but it was in the public sector, not the commercial television industry, where Minow's challenge would soon bear fruit.

A key development took place towards the end of the decade that would result in the creation of a new crop of high quality children's shows and reshape the TV watched by generations of young viewers in the coming years. The Carnegie Corporation and its allied philanthropic trusts had for some time focused much study and funding on improving public education. In 1967, the Carnegie Commission on Educational Television released a report proposing a radical rethinking of educational television in the U.S., which at that point consisted primarily of dry instructional programming for adults on largely independent (but barely watched) noncommercial stations. The Commission's report outlined a completely new vision for these stations, rebranding them as "public television." The Carnegie vision was that the mission of public TV be reconceived as educational in the broadest possible terms, emphasizing entertainment, enlightenment, and education, not just instruction. Congress enacted and funded most of the report's recommendations,[30] creating what we now know as public television, in the form of the Public Broadcasting Service (PBS) for program distribution, and the Corporation for Public Broadcasting (CPB) for financing. The Carnegie philanthropies, along with other foundations, civic-minded and image-savvy businesses, and, in time, a multitude of "donors like you," would inject crucial funds into the production of programs for the new service.

In 1967, before the Carnegie innovations were enacted, however, PBS' precursor, the National Education Network, premiered a new show for preschoolers, one that was traditional in some ways but still very much a product of its times. *Mister Rogers' Neighborhood* was a gentle, thoughtful show that aimed at helping young children understand themselves better, accept themselves, and deal with their emotions. It was always a beautiful day in *Mister Rogers' Neighborhood*, as host Fred Rogers began each episode by entering his TV set house singing the show's theme song, "Won't You be My Neighbor?" He would hang up his coat and put on his cardigan sweater, take off his shoes and put on his sneakers, and settle in to talk directly to his young viewers, much as Miss Francis had done on *Ding Dong School* years earlier.

Like its host, the show was characterized by its quiet simplicity and gentle pace. Mister Rogers would talk to his viewers about all sorts of issues that might be on their minds, from fears about going to sleep or going to the doctor, to disappointment about not getting one's way, to experiencing the death of a loved one. He would sometimes take viewers on visits to shops and factories in his "neighborhood," demonstrate crafts or experiments, sing songs or listen to music, and interact with a cast of

It was always "a beautiful day in the neighborhood" on *Mister Rogers' Neighborhood,* a beloved educational show for preschoolers on PBS. Soft-spoken host and creator Fred Rogers would start the show singing the program's theme song as he changed into sneakers and put on his cardigan sweater.

guests and regular characters, including delivery man Mr. McFeely, Neighbor Aber, Lady Aberlin, Chef Brockett, Officer Clemmons, Mrs. McFeely, Handy Man Negri, and Emily the Poetry Lady.

At the start of each show, a little scale-model trolley was seen chugging along a track through a miniature neighborhood. The little trolley would reappear later in the show to indicate the transition from the realistic world to the fantasy world of the Neighborhood of Make-Believe, which was populated by puppet characters like King Friday the Thirteenth, Lady Elaine Fairchild, and Daniel Striped Tiger. Mister Rogers would usually talk explicitly about this transition, sometimes telling the audience what was going to happen and making it clear that it was all make-believe. This clear delineation between reality and fantasy contrasted with most other children's shows, where realistic and imaginary elements usually blended together.

Mister Rogers' Neighborhood addressed some difficult issues over the years, like divorce, illness, death, and war. The show's willingness to tackle such serious issues and its focus on helping preschoolers deal with difficult feelings like fear, anger, jealousy, and frustration, seemed to reflect the beginnings of a shift away from protecting young children from the harder realities of life to preparing them to deal with those realities. The show's emphasis on teaching self-acceptance was also a reflection of the ethos of the 1960s, which valued self-fulfillment over conformity.

With his gentle and calming manner, host Fred Rogers went on to entertain, educate, and reassure several generations of preschoolers, becoming one of the most beloved and iconic figures on television. *Mister Rogers' Neighborhood* continued to air original episodes on public television until 2001.[31] Perhaps Fred Rogers' most important performance, however, was in his testimony before the U.S. Senate Subcommittee on Communications in May of 1969, to argue for government funding for the newly-forming system of public television. His eloquent plainspoken words were credited by the Subcommittee Chairman himself, who was under pressure to cut the funding, with saving the $20 million allocation to launch the planned system.[32]

In November 1969, exactly one week after PBS was officially created,[33] a show debuted on public TV that ironically, given Fred Rogers' decisive advocacy of PBS, made Rogers' show and all other children's shows at the time look as ancient as the little trolley in *Mister Rogers' Neighborhood*. This new show was as fast as a race car. It had slick parts and funky parts, super cool and heartwarming parts, rough parts and beautifully honed precision parts, all blended into a perfect vehicle of seamless entertain-

ment that was also scientifically designed to educate preschool-age viewers. There had not been anything like it on TV, and it would become an
enduring classic. It had a huge two-year budget of over $8 million, as the
U.S. Department of Education, the Carnegie Corporation, the Ford Foundation, and the Corporation for Public Broadcasting had all contributed
funding to make it a success.[34] The world was welcomed to *Sesame Street*.

Inspired by the Head Start initiative, a mid-sixties government program to provide preschool education for disadvantaged urban children,
Sesame Street's main goal was to help preschoolers get a "head start" in
school by teaching them letter and number recognition and other simple
cognitive skills. The show's goals later evolved to also include more learning on affective topics like relationships, emotions, and ethics, but at its
roots, unlike *Ding Dong School, Romper Room, Mister Rogers' Neighborhood,* or *Captain Kangaroo*, it stressed cognitive development over emotional development or creativity.[35] *Sesame Street* was also unique in that
each episode of the show was written and produced to achieve specific
curriculum goals, and intensive research was conducted to help each show
achieve those goals and to measure whether the goals were being met.

Sesame Street **used techniques employed by TV commercials and by popular
shows like** *Laugh-In* **to teach preschoolers about letters, numbers, and other cognitive skills. The show depicted an integrated urban reality that had not been
seen before in television for children. The original** *Sesame Street* **cast included
(front row, from left to right) Big Bird (played by puppeteer Caroll Spinney),
Will Lee as Mr. Hooper, Matt Robinson as Gordon Robinson, Bob McGrath as
Bob Johnson, and Loretta Long as Susan Robinson.**

But what made *Sesame Street* truly revolutionary and the focus of considerable controversy was that the show's producers decided to use the techniques employed by TV commercials and by network TV shows like *Laugh-In* to engage and hold their young viewers' attention.[36] *New York Times* TV critic Jack Gould described the basic idea for the show in these terms: "If a spot commercial can arouse interest in an item of merchandise, the plan suggests, why can't a spot engender interest in the letter 'A,' the numeral '1' or the scientific phenomenon of a snowball?"[37] As Joan Ganz Cooney, the creator of *Sesame Street*, explained, "Children are conditioned to expect pow! wham! fast-action thrillers from television [as well as] ... highly visual, slickly and expensively produced material."[38] Cooney believed that *Sesame Street* needed to exploit this conditioning and employ the same techniques in order to compete successfully with network television. The resulting show was slick and fast-paced, with a mix of live-action and animated segments, "commercials" for letters and numbers, multi-dimensional human and puppet characters, clever and sophisticated comedy, cutting edge graphics, original music, and engaging plots.

Sesame Street's puppets, in the form of Jim Henson's Muppets, have been a crucial part of the show's appeal. One of the most popular Muppets is Big Bird, an eight-foot-tall bright yellow canary with a natural innocence and inquisitive nature, like a six-year-old child. Other Muppet regulars have included Elmo, a furry red mischievous little monster; Oscar, a lovable grouch who lives in a garbage can; Bert and Ernie, a pair of friends with opposite personalities, like a junior version of the movie and TV sitcom *The Odd Couple*; Cookie Monster and his cousins Telly, Grover, and Harry; the sardonic Kermit the Frog; Prairie Dawn, a precocious three-year-old daughter of hippie parents; Mr. Snuffleupagus, an elephantine creature with the personality of a five-year-old; and Count von Count, a Bela Lugosi-as-Dracula look-alike who loves to count things.

More than any other educational children's show, *Sesame Street* was a direct reflection of its times and illustrated how the country had changed since the 1950s. To attract the inner-city audience that it wanted to target, the show was set, not in a suburban middle-class environment or an imaginary land, but on an urban residential street with brownstones and garbage cans, and it featured a racially diverse cast, portraying a gritty integrated world that had not been seen before in television for children. Rather than having non-white characters in supporting roles, as was usually the case on TV shows at the time, two of the leading human characters on the show were Susan and Gordon, an African American married couple who owned the fictional brownstone row house in front of which much of the *Sesame Street* action took place. The casual mix of races on *Sesame Street* caused some controversy, and several public television stations in the South refused to carry the show initially.[39]

Like *Laugh-In*, *Sesame Street* used the latest forms of animation, special effects, and graphics to give the show a technologically and aesthetically modern look that evoked the youth counterculture. It featured frequent guest appearances by some of the most popular celebrities of the day and original music that included clever parodies of hit rock 'n' roll songs. These elements introduced preschoolers to some of the key aspects of modern popular culture. Together with clever jokes and contemporary references that only adults would understand or appreciate, they were also a way to entice parents to watch the show along with their children, which was another goal of the series.

Though *Sesame Street* quickly became a hit, it drew considerable criticism for its fast-paced delivery, "psychedelic" modern style, and appropriation of techniques used by TV commercials. Critics feared that the show would help children develop a taste for TV ads. They also worried that children would find school boring after becoming accustomed to *Sesame Street*'s fast delivery. Some conservative commentators disapproved of what they considered the show's embrace of liberal or counterculture values. Later research documented that children who had watched *Sesame Street* did better in school than similar children who had not watched the show, and as successive generations of children have continued to be entranced by the show, criticism of *Sesame Street* has largely abated.[40]

Advertising and Marketing to Children

As Saturday morning became the place where advertisers knew they could reach an audience almost entirely composed of children, it also became the place for a multitude of commercials for toys, candy, and sugared breakfast cereals. Building on the lessons learned by Mattel in creating and placing commercials on the *Mickey Mouse Club*, toy manufacturers and marketers of other children's products increasingly dealt with their products in terms of how they could be advertised to children on television.[41] Like the Barbie commercials that had proven so effective for Mattel, slickly-produced and quickly-edited commercials aimed at children proliferated.

Sales of licensed products based on children's shows also became a major growth market. For example, merchandising tie-ins from *The Flint-*

stones included toys, lunch boxes, comic books, soaps, and vitamins. In some cases, licensing involved using popular characters from children's shows as spokespersons for program advertisers. Both Yogi Bear and Huckleberry Hound became pitchmen for their sponsor, Kellogg's Corn Flakes,[42] while Fred Flintstone and his pal Barney became spokesmen for General Foods' Pebbles cereal.[43] Commercials featuring the stars of children's shows would often appear during the shows themselves, much as program hosts and characters on live children's shows in the late 1940s and 1950s had paused to advertise their sponsors' products during the show.

Another form of children's television that combined programming and advertising in a way that had been typical of some of the earliest children's shows appeared briefly again in the sixties. In 1964, *Linus the Lionhearted* debuted on CBS, and in 1969, *Hot Wheels* premiered on ABC. What these two cartoon series had in common was that both were based on children's products and were essentially program-length commercials. Linus was a character initially created to advertise General Mills breakfast cereals, and his show also featured other General Mills product symbols, like Sugar Bear and The Postman. Hot Wheels were a line of racing car toys from Mattel. With the public becoming more sensitive to the growing commercialization of children's television, *Hot Wheels* generated a public backlash and was cancelled when the FCC questioned its connection to a previously existing product. However, the practice of creating children's shows that were entirely centered on products marketed to children would arise again years later.

Stay Tuned...

The 1960s began with deep anxiety about nuclear annihilation, but by the end of the decade the nation's mood was changing. A sexual revolution liberated women and transformed families. The legal affirmation of Americans' civil rights, regardless of race, became a reality, even if cultural norms still lagged. These were changes in a single decade that might once have taken a century. While the war in Vietnam continued to provide an unavoidable nightmarish backdrop to everything going on in the U.S., the beat of psychedelic rock music and the flower-power euphoria of the Summer of Love worked its way into the nation's consciousness, and with it came a deep craving for peace. There would be no violent revolution. As the 60s drew to a close, the assassinations and riots that had traumatized the nation had begun to fade into history. The country's deep sense of inferiority to the Soviet Union in the space race turned to pride and jubilation on July 20, 1969, when over 300 million people around the world listened on the radio and watched on live television as American astronaut Neil Armstrong became the first person to set foot on the moon. One month later, 400,000 young people gathered at a dairy farm near Woodstock, New York, for what was billed as "An Aquarian Exposition: 3 Days of Peace & Music." Woodstock was not just a pivotal moment in popular music history but also a defining social and cultural moment that came to symbolize the counterculture generation that came of age in the sixties.[44]

By the end of the decade, children's television began to reflect some of the changes that the country had experienced during this time. Some children's shows adopted the youth culture's pop music and hippie spirit, while others embraced the values of diversity and self-acceptance. These trends in children's programming would intensify as the counterculture influences born of the 1960s took firmer root in the 1970s, with divergent outcomes.

CHAPTER FOUR

Early Childhood
(the 1970s)

Life in the U.S.

Streaking, mood rings, pet rocks, key parties—largely forgotten bizarre fads and outrageous behavior were some of the cultural touchstones of the 1970s, as the counterculture of the sixties percolated into the new decade. These admittedly silly, short-lived blips of nonsense were just the froth on a rising sea of new, experimental, improvised ways of thinking. Behavior considered shocking in, say, 1964, barely raised an eyebrow at the start of the 70s across wide swaths of the culture. "Doing your own thing" became the verbal shrug that excused, or even celebrated, almost any idiosyncrasy, whim, or impulse. Only now it wasn't just college students and hippies who were breaking the rules and flouting establishment norms in the name of self-expression. New attitudes penetrated into the heartland, disrupting conventional expectations in the mainstream of American culture. That the use of recreational drugs and sexual experimentation became more socially acceptable, even by residents of Main Street, was just the start. It seemed people of all sorts began to adopt a more expansive definition of what was possible and adapt to a wider sense of what was permissible. It was the dawning of the Age of Aquarius, at least in some people's minds, a time of liberation both political and spiritual, and this was the reality that came to dominate the youth-oriented popular media culture.

But just as in the 1960s, what many considered a liberating expansion of personal freedom and self-expression, others saw as a breakdown in traditional morality that constituted a serious threat to the established and proper order of things. In the 70s, the stakes grew until they encompassed a struggle for the essence of family, religion, community, and social cohesion in an increasingly complex and diverse American culture. Earlier threats to the country seemed to come mostly from outside enemies, real or imaginary; by the 70s, threats were felt as if they were bursting from within the national psyche.

There were many components to the danger perceived by constituent groups; a broad array of issues sparked controversy. They all hinged on who would have what rights in a nation that was once considered uniform but was now revealed to be a patchwork of disparate, potentially incompatible interests. Furthermore, the parts making up the whole did not fit together in a neat jigsaw puzzle where everyone had a place, nor did it form a symmetrical pattern with balance among the competing groups, and it certainly was not the melting pot that was still taught as the national norm for social assimilation in civics classes (there actually were civics classes at that time). The American social landscape in the 1970s looked more like the dynamic system of moving tectonic plates that had recently changed scientific knowledge of geology. Masses large and small had been set in motion, driven by poorly understood forces deep below the surface, some colliding to produce new landscapes, and some drawing apart, releasing ancient subterranean energy.

The central social dynamic of this decade was the growing division between newly empowered groups and those whose traditional authority would be eroded. Race was the most obvious flashpoint in many parts of the nation. Other stereotypes—of women's roles, of the rights of immigrants, of people whose sexual expression was considered immoral, and of particular note in this discussion, how children should behave and think—were suddenly open for debate, and not everyone thought that was a good thing at all. Many more people disagreed with the incremental outcomes as the debate went forward. All this divisive change would be played out against the background of a tragic and bloody war which not only lacked any general consensus as to its justification but would cost America both its prestige and its youth.

In 1971, ratification of the Twenty-Sixth Amendment to the Constitution lowered the voting age from twenty-one to eighteen. This was part of a general evolution of thinking about the rights and responsibilities of young people, whether they should be tightly supervised or trusted to grow naturally, and by the same token, the extent to which children had inherent rights or were under their parents' authority.[1]

The advances made in civil rights for minorities in the 1960s gained momentum in the 70s. Even without the leadership of Martin Luther King, Jr., cut down by a racist assassin's bullet in 1968, Jim Crow laws—which had created a robust system of legal racial discrimination especially in the South but also in many parts of the United States—were overturned one by one through civil rights legislation and hard-fought court battles. The focus for African Americans, who, as a people, had made important gains unprecedented since emancipation, now became how to overcome the heritage of systemic discrimination nationwide, which still perpetuated poverty, inequality, and injustice for minority communities. The nation responded unevenly to efforts to remedy persistent racist attitudes and more subtle and intractable forms of racist behavior. Efforts at desegregating public schools shifted from the South to the North, where court-ordered busing to integrate schools generated intense local conflicts. Responding to legal challenges, or to take a moral stand in the face of the legacy of slavery and racism, or just to reap benefits they felt would follow from increasing diversity in their makeup, employers and colleges instituted Affirmative Action programs, which critics fought and derided as "reverse discrimination."

Issues of race took on greater nuance and impact beyond urban centers in the 1970s, both due to internal migration of relatively affluent minorities and as a result of demographic shifts resulting from changes in the laws controlling immigration to the U.S. The Immigration and Naturalization Act of 1965 had abolished an earlier quota system based on national origin, which had favored immigrants from Europe, and established a new policy based on reuniting families and attracting skilled labor to the U.S. As the effects of the new law began to be felt, new immigrants came increasingly from Asia, Africa, and Latin America, rather than from Europe.[2] As a result, the new wave of immigrants was more diverse, and they did not follow the same pattern of congestion in cities that earlier groups had. Immigrants in the 1970s might just as easily settle in Tennessee or Iowa as in historical enclaves like New York or Boston.[3]

While racial and ethnic groups were gaining in their fight for equality, women's struggle for rights and protection against gender discrimination was also advancing, as the relationship between women's rights and civil rights became evident. In 1972, Congress approved the Equal Rights Amendment, which added language to the Constitution guaranteeing equal rights to women, though it was not ratified by all the states until 1977. In 1973, the Supreme Court's decision in Roe v. Wade struck down state laws barring abortion in the first trimester. Hailed by supporters and reviled by opponents, this decision and the abortion issue it supposedly settled would continue to be a matter of contentious debate far into the future, as it threw into high relief deep differences in American society along religious and class lines, which mirrored a split between traditional sexual mores versus the emerging views of liberated women's reproductive rights and gender rights in general.[4]

The impetus to expand women's rights also resulted in the passage of Title IX of the Educational Amendments of 1972, barring gender discrimination in public schools. Prior to its passage, differential treatment of girls and boys was the norm in most schools. High school vocational classes were divided by sex: girls took sewing or home economics; boys took wood shop or automotive mechanics. Pregnant girls were routinely expelled from school and, if they were even allowed back after giving birth, forced into non-academic courses. These practices began to change with the passage of Title IX, which prohibited sex discrimination in any educational program or activity. However, the most visible arena of change ushered in by the new legislation may have been school athletics, as high schools were now required to provide equal opportunities and funding for girls to participate in organized sports.[5] Women's health and fitness started to improve, along with a growing sense of self-confidence and empowerment, in tandem with rising expectations, fostered by a robust consciousness-raising movement, for equal treatment across gender lines. No more would everyone expect women to automatically acquiesce to sexist behavior, either from individual men or from institutions. Stereotypes of women's proper roles, challenged in the 60s, slowly began to crumble in the 70s.

The gay rights movement emerged naturally in the wake of the women's movement, as freedom from gender stereotypes and discrimination gained traction as a universal civil right. From a small number of activists to a widespread movement for equal rights, the symbolic moment of truth was probably when patrons of the Stonewall Inn, a gay bar in New York City's Greenwich Village, fought back during a police raid in June 1969, sparking three days of riots.[6] In vast numbers of families, a son or daughter or a parent came out of the closet. In 1973, the American Psychiatric Association removed homosexuality from its official list of mental disorders.

As much of the social and cultural liberalism of the 1960s flourished in the 70s, the movement engendered a backlash from those who believed it was of paramount importance to preserve what they saw as the true American culture and what they considered its traditional values. This reaction against the rising tide of change was particularly associated with some middle- and working-class whites, who were dubbed "the silent majority." They were outraged by the counterculture values that they believed were destroying the moral fabric of the country. As portrayed in news coverage of the time, they were tired of antiwar protests which they considered unpatriotic, of hippies and gays and others whom they cast as the spoiled results of parental and social indulgence, of government policies and programs that they thought coddled poor people, were lenient toward criminals, and favored black people at white taxpayers' expense. Whether because of this popular explanation or because of a myriad of other political forces at the time (not least of which was the assassination of the popular presidential candidate Bobby Kennedy), conservative Republican candidate Richard Nixon was elected President in 1968, promising to represent their interests. Nixon moved quickly to abolish many of Lyndon Johnson's War on Poverty programs, but his administration hardly slowed the momentum of the broad changes that were central to the fears of his supporters.[7]

As these social and cultural conflicts played out, a series of troubling and disillusioning events took place in the U.S. and around the world that added to the growing sense of threat and helplessness felt by much of the public. The country had begun the new decade still mired in the increasingly unpopular war in Vietnam. Public demonstrations against the war had been growing in intensity and size when, in May 1970, tensions boiled over. Spontaneous protests had erupted across the country when it was revealed that the Nixon administration, initially covertly and arguably illegally, had expanded the scope of the war by invading Cambodia.[8] On May 4, at a small nonviolent antiwar rally on the campus of Kent State University in Ohio, National Guard troops opened fire on unarmed student demonstrators, killing four young people and wounding nine. The photograph of an anguished young woman, looking straight toward the camera as she screamed, leaning over the body of a protester shot on the ground before her, ricocheted around the world, a jolt to even fervent supporters of the war.[9] Then, just ten days later, at Jackson State University in Mississippi, police shot and killed two black student protestors, uniting (at least symbolically in the news media) the antiwar and wider civil rights movements. Eventually, after mass demonstrations made clear the untenable political position of the Nixon administration, and as humiliating U.S. military losses continued to mount, public opinion turned decisively against the war. American troops finally pulled out of Vietnam in 1973. The nation's inability to prevail in this asymmetric war would forever dispel Americans' post–World War II sense of invulnerability. The deep divisions between those who felt betrayed by their government, either for prosecuting or for failing to win the war, and those who felt betrayed by their fellow citizens, either for failing to support the war or for failing to resist it, would shape the American political landscape for decades.

Adding to the country's sense of powerlessness, the major oil-producing countries imposed an embargo on exports of petroleum to the U.S. in 1973, in retaliation for the U.S. support given to the Israeli military in the 1973 Arab-Israeli War. Not only did the price of gas shoot up, but American motorists were forced to wait in hour-long lines to get their turns at the pump. The oil embargo added to the decline of the U.S. economy, which sputtered in the 1970s as high inflation plus slow growth and high unemployment rates—an insidious economic phenomenon called stagflation, which has no easy or quick solution—set in. After years of generally positive economic results, for the first time since the Great Depression, the country faced the possibility that its children might have a lower standard of living than their parents had experienced. This is the moment when the postwar economy changed, when the real income of blue-collar workers stalled and the very top earners began gathering an increasing portion of the nation's wealth, a long trend that would eventually produce a great schism of wealth inequality.[10]

Just as Vietnam forced Americans to confront the limits of their military power, the oil embargo brought home the idea that the Earth's, and America's, natural resources were limited, strengthening the emerging environmental movement. Efforts to protect the environment from man-made pollution became a popular social cause in the 1970s. The first Earth Day was celebrated in 1970; Congress passed the National Environmental Policy Act in 1971 and the Clean Air and Clean Water Acts in 1973. By the late 1970s, the U.S. Forest Service's mascot Woodsy the Owl was interrupting Saturday morning cartoons to remind kids to "Give a Hoot, Don't Pollute." But environmental consciousness was not all sunny skies. It led to awareness of the dark side of progress, driving yet another wedge between parts of an already riven society. Those who felt America's power and way of life threatened by those who wanted to reduce consumption in order to protect the environment mocked "tree-huggers," while those who believed a sustainable future would benefit everyone paid scant attention to, or openly disdained, the deep desires of the upwardly mobile for a better life today.[11]

And then there was the Watergate scandal. In May 1973, a Congressional committee began to hold hearings to determine whether the White House had been involved in the break-in at Democratic Party headquarters the previous year, during the presidential campaign that would overwhelmingly re-elect Nixon. The committee agreed to allow live television coverage of its hearings, which stretched on through the summer.[12] The country was riveted as viewers heard witnesses reveal a web of unethical and illegal acts that had been committed by White House staff. They learned that President Nixon himself had not only been fully aware of the break-in, of which he had publicly denied any knowledge, but had actually orchestrated it. Nixon had also ordered the FBI to stop investigating the break-in, and he had ordered his aides to cover up his involvement. In April 1974, the House of Representatives voted to impeach Nixon, but, with his reputation ruined and his popular support squandered, he resigned before a Senate vote could take place. It was a stunning fall for a president who had been reelected in a landslide of historic proportions less than two years earlier.[13]

Coming on the heels of the U.S. defeat in Vietnam, Watergate added to the national climate of disappointment and disillusionment. The resulting sense of cynicism and disgust with the political system caused many people to disengage from the political and social activism that had dominated the 1960s. What was left was still a culture divided. Those who felt most betrayed by the corruption of the Nixon administration retreated from politics or focused only on specific hot button issues of a primarily cultural nature, which would eventually form the core of a future conservative agenda. Others, perhaps to be free altogether of civic responsibilities with their taint of political engagement, turned to hedonism and sought personal freedom and pleasure, either through self-indulgence in the consumer culture or through the single-minded pursuit of self-actualization—a trend that caused writer and social observer Tom Wolfe to label the 1970s as "The 'Me' Decade."[14]

Inevitably, these changes in society had an impact on family life, which altered the lives of children. The 1970s were the start of what historian Steven Mintz sees as "a new phase in childhood's history," as the demographic and social changes that had begun in the 1960s led to new configurations of family life in the 70s.[15] The redefinition of women's roles had profound consequences, with more women seeking independence by getting jobs, postponing marriage, abandoning unfulfilling marriages, and postponing or avoiding childbirth. The divorce rate doubled between the mid–1960s and late 1970s, and by 1980, one out of every two marriages would end in divorce. Together with the increase in divorce came a steep increase in single-parent households, driving many newly-single women into the workforce.[16] The stagnant economy reinforced these trends, causing more women to look for work and to limit the size of their families. Even women with young children increasingly began to work outside the home. From the mid–1960s to the mid–1970s, the number of working mothers with children age five or under tripled.[17]

The most immediate and dramatic result of these trends was a steep decline in child bearing and the end of the Baby Boom. The birthrate among American women was cut in half, dropping from 120 births per 1,000 women in 1960 to 60 in 1975.[18] The trend to smaller families allowed parents to devote more attention and more money to each child. It also led to a sharp rise in parents' aspirations for the few children they had. Unlike parents of Baby Boomers in the 1950s, who wanted their children to fit in, middle-class parents of the 1970s saw their children as precious and "special" and wanted to give them every possible opportunity and competitive advantage in a world that no longer seemed benign, predictable or simple. Parents worried more about their children's safety and vulnerability to drugs. They focused more on academic achievement and the quality of schools. They began to reject the older ideal of a "protected childhood," which favored sheltering innocent children from adult realities, and to emphasize a "prepared" childhood, with the goal of inculcating independence and resourcefulness rather than emphasizing conformity and cooperation in their offspring.[19]

Among the public at large, many viewed the increase in the divorce rate, in the number of single-parent households, and in the number of working mothers as a breakdown of the family that would have dire consequences for society. Compounded by the troubling events in the country and around the world at the time, there was a growing sense that the country had entered a period of moral and economic decline, which only increased cultural anxieties about children. These anxieties took the form of a series of public panics about children's well-being, over issues like teen pregnancy, stranger abductions, child abuse, illicit drugs, juvenile crime, and flagging academic performance. These fears were further stoked during the 1970s and later years as both liberals and conservatives discovered that they could exploit the public's anxieties about child endangerment to mobilize political support for the causes they espoused.[20]

Television

Formats and themes that had proved successful in prime time television programs of the 50s were generally updated for the 60s, and this evolution continued into the 70s. But at each stage, the formulas were tweaked to adapt to changing social conditions and evolving audience appetites. One of the important characteristics in that evolution was a growing level of realism that reflected aspects of life in the world beyond the small screen.

For example, in 1973 alone, there were no fewer than ten new police dramas, or cop shows as they were known, added to the prime time schedule. On the one hand, these shows introduced a level of gritty action in contemporary settings, with heightened psychological conflicts not often seen before on TV. But structurally, as dramas, they shared much in common with the westerns that had been reliable standards since *The Lone Ranger*. Yet, as westerns yielded to cop shows and *Dragnet* yielded to *Kojak*, the details of how threat and authority were represented shifted. Threats were depicted as more specific and concrete—more real and less abstract than in the past. Actions to protect society had to be more direct and forceful. The danger was at the door, it was tangible, and its representation had to be just as convincing.

Realism increased in other genres as well. Consider the contrast between two rural family dramas, one an icon of the 60s, the other of the 70s. In the 1970s, *Little House on the Prairie*, a highly sentimental and nostalgic vision of an earlier America, was far more psychologically nuanced and realistic than the 1960s show *Bonanza*. *Bonanza*, set on a sprawling western ranch, was an idealized imaginary patrician world where conflicts ranged from the somewhat threatening (generally due to bad weather or the occasional cupidity of outsiders) to the mildly comic. Since the series featured a prosperous family made up only of men, emotional range was not a strong plot device. *Little House*, on the other hand, offered an emotional deep dive within a single isolated but large and loving family facing a tenuous existence in a sod house, where survival was dependent on family interactions and feelings drove the plot. While neither show would be considered particularly realistic, *Bonanza* relied on two-dimensional stereotypes which contrast sharply with the relatively rich emotional landscape of *Little House* a decade later. The change may have been incremental, but the evolution toward more realism was apparent on *Little House*, at least in its depiction of how relationships operate.

So, while television shows in the 1960s had only tentatively begun to acknowledge real-life issues and concerns, by the start of the 1970s they were gradually reflecting a greater awareness of the world beyond the screen and were poised to present stories and portrayals with more realistic elements and in a more realistic manner. Ironically, it was on sitcoms rather than dramas where a greater engagement with real-life issues began to fully blossom.

No show epitomized this new reality-based trend more than Norman Lear's *All in the Family*, which premiered on CBS in January 1971. Unlike anything seen on U.S. television before, *All in the Family* was a situation comedy that starred a bigoted working class character and dealt with such sensitive and controversial topics as Vietnam, racism, women's rights, homosexuality, impotence, menopause, rape, alcoholism, and many other issues. Audiences took some time to catch onto the nature of the show, as its willingness to wade into highly topical and divisive public issues, in essentially the authentic language of many American families, was such a radical departure from what was expected in the usual sitcom. The series' phenomenal popularity marked a turning point in television by making it easier for subsequent entertainment shows to address similar real-life concerns.

Lear went on to become arguably the most influential television producer of the 1970s, creating a number of socially-engaged sitcoms, like *Sanford and Son, Good Times, Maude, One Day at a Time*, and *The Jeffersons*.[21] These shows were also groundbreaking in their portrayals of blacks and women. As more writers and producers tried to emulate Lear's success, the world of TV comedies was quickly transformed from the all-white suburbia of the 1950s to the new racially-integrated ideal of the 1970s, perhaps a bit idealistic but more indicative of the situation in the real world, where minority groups were becoming increasingly visible and successful in seeking full participation in society.

Although a dominant force, Lear was not alone in breaking barriers through socially-engaged sitcoms. *The Mary Tyler Moore Show* debuted on CBS a few months before *All in the Family*. Though not as innovative as *All in the Family*, *Mary Tyler Moore* moved the TV needle in addressing the changing role of women by having a lead character who was an intelligent, unmarried career woman facing the same kinds of complications and situations in her daily life that real people often faced. Actress Mary Tyler Moore starred as Mary Richards, a small-town girl who came to the big city to make it on her own and landed a job as an associate producer for the evening news at a local TV station. The character's portrayal as an unmarried career woman with a responsible job other than secretary or teacher, who was not a widow, had no children, and was working because she wanted to build her own independent life and career, was a major break from television tradition.[22]

The new wave of socially-engaged series that combined comedy with drama continued with the 1972 premiere of *M*A*S*H* on CBS. Based on a popular 1970 Robert Altman film, *M*A*S*H* followed the adventures of two playboy military surgeons assigned to a field hospital during the Korean War. While the show somehow milked laughs from issues like military regimentation and the futility of war, it also showed citizen-soldiers in the best American tradition. The cynical surgeons mocked the system but treated their friends and patients with deep respect and affection, revealing that they really had hearts of gold. Their layered emotional world resonated strongly with viewers at the time the show debuted, near the end of the Vietnam War. After being scheduled between *All in the Family* and *The Mary Tyler Moore Show*, *M*A*S*H** quickly joined those blockbusters as a top-ten show, which it remained until the series ended in 1983.

In addition to these new-wave comedy series, television also dealt with controversial topics like rape, abortion, and homosexuality in mini-series and movie-of-the-week dramas. TV network Standards and Practices departments gave these controversial productions more leeway than continuing series since they only aired on a limited schedule, deftly side-stepping the potential downside of upsetting viewers on a continuing basis. But as audiences became more accustomed to watching shows that addressed controversial topics, ABC made the high-risk programming decision in 1977 to air a multi-part drama representing the history of slavery in America called *Roots*, by African American writer Alex Haley. In an unprecedented scheduling move, *Roots* ran on eight consecutive nights, rather than once a week, which was the usual practice with limited mini-series. The innovative scheduling strategy paid off, as the audience for the series grew each night, breaking every ratings record in TV history. *Roots* became a cultural and social phenomenon, as millions of people rearranged eight days of their lives to follow the show. The entire nation cheered for this portrayal of "The Triumph of an American Family," which was, for the first time on television, the triumph of black Americans.[23]

Children's Television

Similar to trends in TV shows for adults, children's shows in the early seventies initially continued to be characterized by escapist, fantasy fare that had little to do with children's daily lives or the actual world they lived in, though many shows incorporated or referenced pop culture trends like rock music, psychedelic graphics, and the continuing James Bond spy craze, as well as popular TV shows for adults. As the seventies progressed, however, children's shows began to reflect the changing demographics and social issues unfolding in plain sight throughout the decade.

Children's television in the 1970s was heavily influenced by the public criticism leveled against the networks in the wake of the urban riots and political assassinations of the late 1960s, which charged that violence on television, including on children's shows like superhero cartoons, was contributing to a culture of violence in the country. In 1968, these concerns had led a mother in a Boston suburb, Peggy Charren, to organize her neighbors into a grassroots organization called Action for Children's Television, which would become the most vocal and visible group campaigning to reform children's TV in the following decade. ACT focused most of their criticism on advertising practices in commercials aimed at children, but they also pushed the networks to reduce violence on children's TV shows, eliminate stereotyped portrayals, and generally improve the quality of children's programming.[24]

Faced with growing public criticism and activism about their children's programming, the networks responded by appointing executives to oversee their children's shows and imposing on producers strict mandatory internal guidelines designed to eliminate any hints of violence or conflict in children's programs. They dropped most of their superhero action-adventure shows and replaced them with more benign comedy series and fantasy shows as well as a veritable avalanche of new educational shows, all of which were closely monitored by network Standards and Practices departments and internal consultants. In an interview in *McCall's* magazine, NBC's head of daytime programming explained, "What we're dealing with is fantasy and imagination rather than action-adventure. We're trying to get the kids working with us to create their own reality and stay away from super characters, strong conflicts, and all kinds of action."[25] As one producer described the network's new guidelines for children's TV, "The program practices departments outlined four major 'don'ts.' No physical violence, no guns, no jeopardy, and no threats."[26]

With superhero cartoons largely banished from Saturday morning network TV, comical cartoons dominated the Saturday morning schedule in the seventies. Some featured classic cartoon characters from comic strips and the movies, like Bugs Bunny, Woody Woodpecker, and Sylvester and Tweety, while others were animated versions of popular primetime TV shows or movies, like *The Brady Kids*, *The Partridge Family: 2200 A.D.*, *The Addams Family*, *The New Adventures of Gilligan*, *Jeannie*, *Emergency +4*, and *Return to the Planet of the Apes*.

There were a handful of superhero shows among the cartoons on

Saturday mornings, but they avoided violence and depicted socially positive behavior. The new buzzword was "prosocial." For example, *Super Friends*, which debuted on ABC in 1973, was a Hanna-Barbera production that featured the adventures of the Justice League of America, from the DC comic book series. The Justice League was made up of Superman, Batman and Robin, Aquaman, and Wonder Woman. The TV series added to the team with new human characters Marvin and Wendy, who were supposed to be superheroes in training, and a pet mascot called Wonderdog. The show would usually begin with the heroes responding to an emergency detected by a huge computer in the Hall of Justice, the team's headquarters. The emergency was often a natural disaster caused by human or alien activity, and the series focused on environmental issues. The situation was usually resolved with the Justice League members convincing the antagonists to change their ways.

Rock music continued to be an element or theme of some of the new cartoons. *The Groovie Goolies*, which debuted in 1971 as a spin-off from *Sabrina the Teenage Witch*, featured a rock band made up of hip, now-friendly monsters from classic horror movies, like Drac (aka Dracula), Frankie (Frankenstein), and Wolfie (a hippie werewolf). The monsters lived in Horrible Hall, a haunted boarding house for monsters, on Horrible Drive. Each episode featured a couple of musical performances by the Goolies and by another resident band, like the Mummies and the Puppies or the Rolling Headstones. The show was structured like the immensely popular primetime show *Laugh-In*, with lots of short segments, jokes, and one-liners, including "Weird Windows Time," a take-off on the Joke Wall, one of *Laugh-In*'s signature elements.

Jabberjaw, which premiered in 1976, was a cartoon series from Hanna-Barbera about a rock band called The Neptunes, who lived in an underwater city in the year 2076. The group was made up of four teenagers—Biff, Shelly, Bubbles, and Clamhead—and a 15-foot great white shark called Jabberjaw. The recent debut of the movie *Jaws* inspired a shark mania, hence the shark character. The plotlines centered on the Neptunes' travels to other underwater cities, where they would encounter and battle against evil villains who wanted to conquer the undersea world. Despite the action-adventure premise, the show was a comedy in the mold of *The Flintstones* and *The Jetsons*, which used the underwater locale as the basis for jokes and parodies of modern life. Jabberjaw himself was modeled after the character Curly of The Three Stooges, though his catchphrase "No respect! I get no respect!" was borrowed from comedian Rodney Dangerfield.

Live-action shows also made a bit of a comeback, as the networks hurriedly looked for new non-controversial material to quickly and inexpensively fill the void left by the absence of superhero cartoons. A number of new live-action shows that aired during this decade were produced by brothers Sid and Marty Krofft. Building on their success with *H.R. Pufnstuf* in 1969, the Kroffts began turning out a series of similar shows that featured fantasy plots and settings, with casts made up of a combination of live performers, puppets, and actors in full-body puppet-like costumes. As described by brothers Timothy and Kevin Burke in their book *Saturday Morning Fever*, "The typical Krofft show was a surreal, dreamy affair in which weird giant puppet-people cavorted across the TV screen and got involved in marginally coherent shenanigans that managed to be vaguely disturbing and queerly entertaining at the same time."[27] Their show *The Bugaloos*, which premiered in 1970, starred an insect rock 'n' roll singing group who lived in a magical forest, where they were constantly menaced by an evil witch. In 1971, the Kroffts followed up with *Lidsville*, in which a teenage boy fell into a magician's hat and found himself in Lidsville, a mysterious world of living hats. On *Sigmund and the Sea Monsters*, which debuted in 1973, two brothers took in a gentle sea monster who was trying to escape from his more threatening family. In *Land of the Lost* in 1974, a forest ranger and his two children were caught in a time warp and found themselves in a prehistoric world. The following year saw the debut of *The Lost Saucer*, an outer space adventure/comedy in which aliens accidentally pick up a boy and his babysitter while visiting Earth. In 1976, the Kroffts tried their hand at a variety show called *The Krofft Supershow* (later retitled *The Krofft Superstar Hour*) which featured a mix of live-action segments, filmed segments, and pop music, and was hosted by a rock band created for the show.

Stylistically, Krofft shows had a true 1970s look and feel, with psychedelic graphics and hyperkinetic editing, similar to what was seen on *Laugh-In*. Combined with the fantasy settings and plots and suggestive titles of some of their series (e.g., *H.R. Pufnstuf, Lidsville*[28]), these qualities led some critics to charge that the Kroffts' shows included thinly-veiled allusions to drug use, though the Krofft brothers always denied any such allegations.[29]

When *Shazam!* premiered on CBS in 1974, it was the first time in almost ten years that a new live-action adventure series appeared on Saturday morning TV.[30] The show, which came from the Filmation production company, was loosely based on the comic book and movie series hero Captain Marvel, who could transform himself into a superhero by uttering the magic word "Shazam!" To distinguish itself from the controversial superhero shows of the 1960s, *Shazam!* featured very little violence and, in a throwback to children's action-adventure shows from the 1950s, a large dose of moralistic lessons, explicitly articulated at the end of each episode by the show's star speaking directly to the TV audience.

In 1975, *The Secrets of Isis* joined *Shazam!* to make up the *Shazam!/Isis Hour*. The star character in *Isis* was a female high school science teacher who acquired magical powers bestowed by the goddess Isis when she stumbled upon a sorcerer's amulet that had been given to the ancient queen of Egypt. Whenever she said the words "O Mighty Isis," the teacher would be transformed into a beautiful princess superhero dressed in a gold headband and cape, who could fly and control the land and sky. Like *Shazam!*, *The Secrets of Isis* had virtually no violence and incorporated explicit moral lessons as part of the show.

There were other new action-adventure series that featured animals, similar to shows from the 1950s like *Lassie* and *Fury*. These included *Run, Joe, Run* (which could best be described as a hybrid offspring of *Lassie* and *The Fugitive*), in which a German shepherd was on the run after being falsely accused of attacking his master; *McDuff, the Talking Dog*, about an invisible sheepdog and the veterinarian who is the only one who sees him; *Thunder*, about a wild stallion who rescues and helps humans; and *The Life and Times of Grizzly Adams*, an adventure series set around the end of the frontier era, in which the star character befriends a grizzly bear.

Recycling proven formulas, several new live-action space adventure series recalled 1950s shows like *Captain Video* and *Tom Corbett, Space Cadet*, but with bigger budgets, much better special effects, and the growing environmental movement as a popular theme. *Ark II*, which debuted on CBS in 1976, was set in the 25th century, after pollution, waste, and wars had destroyed the Earth. A small team of scientists had created a mobile storehouse of the world's scientific knowledge, called Ark II, and together with a crew of three young people they had trained, as well as a talking chimpanzee capable of abstract thought, they traveled the Earth searching for the remnants of humanity, with the goal of rebuilding human civilization. Each episode began and ended with a voiceover as the group's captain made a numbered entry in the Ark II's log, similar to the format of sci-fi space adventure show *Star Trek*, which had aired in the late 60s.

Premiering on CBS in 1977, the same year that the first *Star Wars* movie appeared in theaters, *Space Academy* was about a school that brought together young students from throughout the galaxy, some of whom had special powers, to explore the mysteries of space. Lessons and morals about social values like respecting diversity and learning from one's mistakes were conveyed in each episode. In 1979, CBS followed up with *Jason of Star Command*, a high-budget show with sophisticated special effects that attempted to recreate the fantasy fun of earlier space-adventure movie serials like *Flash Gordon* and *Buck Rogers*.[31]

The influence of the 1960s James Bond craze could still be found, in shows like NBC's *The Kids from C.A.P.E.R.*, which debuted in 1976. With a title clearly derived from 60s spy show *The Man from U.N.C.L.E.*, the live-action series followed the adventures of four teenage boys who worked as operatives for the Civilian Authority for Protection of Everyone Regardless and helped the police solve unusual cases. The series parodied different shows of the day, including *The Monkees, Shazam!*, and *Scooby-Doo, Where Are You?*

While most shows imitated or provided small variations on earlier children's programs, some new children's programming reflected greater racial and ethnic diversity. In 1970 and 1971, cartoon series *The Harlem Globetrotters* and *The Jackson Five* became the first commercial children's shows to feature non-white characters as stars. *The Harlem Globetrotters* show revolved around the adventures of the famous basketball team and showed how teamwork helped them solve problems and help others. The Globetrotters were also featured in two other children's series that aired later in the decade. *The Jackson Five* focused on the singing group's music, using the voices of the five Jackson brothers. Another cartoon with an African American celebrity star debuted in 1977. *I Am the Greatest: The Adventures of Muhammad Ali* featured an animated version of the heavyweight boxing star and was voiced by Ali.

Some shows had even more ethnically diverse casts of characters. Cartoon series *Kid Power*, which premiered in 1972, revolved around the Rainbow Club, a global organization of adolescents from a variety of cultures. It addressed issues like prejudice and encouraged teamwork, responsibility, and sharing.[32] In 1976, PBS aired a similar live-action show called *Rebop*, which consisted of filmed segments about children of different cultural and ethnic backgrounds.[33]

The rapidly changing role of women began to have an explicit impact on children's television in the 1970s with the appearance of several new shows starring female characters. The first of these were animated programs. Cartoon series *Sabrina, the Teenage Witch*, which debuted in 1970, was a spin-off from *The Archie Show*, where the Sabrina character had first appeared. Addressing common adolescent fears, the show's premise was that even though Sabrina had magical powers, she wanted to keep her powers secret from her peers, so that she could fit in with the group and avoid disbelief and ridicule. *Josie and the Pussycats,* a Hanna-Barbera cartoon which also premiered in 1970, featured the adventures of an all-girl rock band. One of the group's members, Valerie, was TV's first black female cartoon character. Other new children's shows that starred female characters included *Jeannie,* an animated version of popular primetime sitcom *I Dream of Jeannie,* and *Spider-Woman,* which featured a female version of Spiderman. As previously discussed, *The Secrets of Isis,* one of the first live-action programs with a female lead character, appeared in 1975, followed by *The Hardy Boys/Nancy Drew Mysteries,* a live-action series based on the classic children's novels. These shows are important not only because they starred female characters, significant as that is, but also for the ways in which their female characters were invested with power and skills equal to those of male characters of the time.

Another way the television networks responded to the growing public concern about children's television was with an onslaught of new educational series. Debuting on CBS in 1972, *Fat Albert and the Cosby Kids* was probably the most ground-breaking show of the bunch. Featuring Bill Cosby as host and co-producer,[34] this animated series revolved around a group of black inner-city kids as they helped each other deal with the challenges of modern life in their urban environment. The quirky characters were loosely based on Cosby's own childhood friends. Fat Albert was the rotund leader of the group. He faced life's challenges with determination and aplomb, making him a role model for his friends, Bill, Rudy, Old Weird Harold, Mush Mouth Leonard, and Dumb Donald, as well as for the show's viewers. While being funny and entertaining, the show dealt with such serious issues as prejudice, child abuse, and the death of loved ones. At the end of each segment, Bill Cosby himself would summarize that episode's events and life lessons, and then Fat Albert and the gang would present a musical interlude, performing on a variety of homemade instruments.[35]

CBS engaged noted educators as consultants to work with the *Fat Albert* writers on story details and character development. CBS continued the practice of using expert consultants to supervise the production of their other children's shows, like *Valley of the Dinosaurs, Shazam!, The Harlem Globetrotters Popcorn Machine, The Hudson Brothers Razzle Dazzle Show,* and *The U.S. of Archie,* and the other networks soon followed suit.[36]

Educational shows on NBC included *Hot Dog,* a live-action show that explained how things are made and featured guest stars like popular comics Jonathan Winters and Woody Allen; *Take a Giant Step/Talking*

Educational cartoon *Fat Albert* on CBS was based on the stories that comedian Bill Cosby told about his childhood friends. The star character and his pals performed a musical number with homemade instruments at the end of each show.

with a Giant, a discussion program for teens that focused on social, economic, and emotional issues important to them; *Go*, which explored different occupations; *The Fabulous Funnies*, in which comic strip characters like Alley Oop and the Katzenjammer Kids dealt with such issues as safety and healthcare; and *Hot Hero Sandwich*, an hour-long variety show for teens that included music, guest interviews, and skits on topics like friendship, family, grades, growth, and sex.[37]

On ABC, there was *The Curiosity Shop*, a variety show that explored the adult world through a mix of live action and filmed segments, cartoons, and interviews; *Make a Wish*, another variety show that stressed learning and growth through using one's imagination; *Kids Are People Too*, a Sunday morning magazine series; and the *ABC Afterschool Special*, an hour-long dramatic or documentary show occasionally broadcast in late afternoon. ABC also created a series of brief educational segments called *Schoolhouse Rock*, which aired between programs on Saturday mornings. *Schoolhouse Rock* used music and animation to educate viewers about math, grammar, history, and science.

In addition to *Fat Albert and the Cosby Kids*, CBS focused its other efforts in educational programming on providing news for children. The network produced *30 Minutes*, a junior version of their new hit news-magazine show *60 Minutes*, as well as brief interstitial segments called *In the News*.[38] CBS also recruited its popular evening news anchor, Walter Cronkite, to host a revival of *You Are There*, originally broadcast in the 1950s, which featured re-enactments of historical events.

A number of independently produced educational shows were syndicated to local stations. These included *Earthlab*, a live-action science show, and the *New Zoo Review*, which explored cultural and educational themes through musical numbers. There were syndicated magazine shows like *The Big Blue Marble*, with filmed segments about the daily lives of children around the world, and *Vegetable Soup*, with guest hosts like Bette Midler and James Earl Jones. *Hot Fudge* used a mix of live performers and puppets to explore pro-social themes. *Marlo and the Magic Movie Machine* gave viewers history lessons provided by a talking computer that displayed old newsreels and historical videotapes.[39]

PBS debuted two new educational series for older children who had graduated from watching *Sesame Street*. Premiering in 1971, *The Electric Company* was a variety show created by Children's Television Workshop, *Sesame Street*'s producer, which used a mix of musical numbers, animated segments, and comedy sketches to help elementary-school children improve their grammar and reading skills. Like *Sesame Street*, the show had a racially diverse cast that initially included Bill Cosby, Morgan Freeman, and Rita Moreno. It featured cutting edge graphics and computer animation, which gave it a hip, modern look.

A year later, PBS debuted *ZOOM*, a variety show hosted by an ethnically diverse group of seven children called ZOOMers. Wearing brightly colored striped rugby shirts and jeans and performing barefoot, the ZOOMers sang, danced, played games, told jokes, did science experiments, read viewer letters, and introduced filmed profiles of children with special talents. Viewers were encouraged to write in to the show with their questions and requests, which the ZOOMers would try to address, and much of the show was unscripted. The series was intended to encourage children to be active investigators, creators and problem-solvers. Responding to continued public concerns that watching TV made children passive, *ZOOM* ironically encouraged its viewers to "turn off the TV and do it!"

The increase in Hispanic immigration during the 1970s prompted PBS to air the first national bilingual show targeting Hispanic children, *Villa Alegre*, in 1973. The show was set in a fictional bilingual Spanish-English village and was aimed at helping Latino children learn English and Anglo children learn Spanish. It covered educational subjects like mathematics and science as well as information about Hispanic culture.[40]

Advertising and Marketing to Children

Television's early days had been marked by little oversight and few complaints about advertising to children. But as the public became more concerned about the impact of television on children in the 1960s and 1970s, children's advertising became a focus for criticism. Action for Children's Television was the prime instigator in what would become a movement. When ACT was formed in 1968, one of the group's key goals was to stop what they referred to as the "overcommercialization" of children's television, and in 1970 they petitioned the Federal Communications Commission for an outright ban on commercials during children's viewing hours. ACT's main argument against commercials targeting children was that children were more vulnerable than adults to being manipulated by commercials because they did not understand the "selling intent" behind commercials and could not distinguish between commercials and programs.[41] Throughout the 1970s, ACT continued to lobby the FCC, the FTC, and the networks for the reform of advertising practices in commercials aimed at children. They argued against the use of exaggeration and deception in ads, such as toy commercials that falsely represented the toys' capabilities. They pressured the networks not to accept commercials that advertised vitamins and drugs to children or commercials for candy and sugared cereals. They also urged the networks to reduce the number of ads aimed at children and to put "bumpers," short segments in which an announcer would say, "We'll be right back after these messages," between the ads and the programs.[42]

Though the FCC and FTC initially did not implement ACT's petitions, ACT persisted relentlessly. In time, their well-articulated criticisms and sustained efforts drew extensive news coverage and eventually built a base of public support. The networks and advertisers began to respond with voluntary guidelines, rules, and codes. The major drug companies agreed to end vitamin advertising on children's television. In 1973, the National Association of Broadcasters adopted new guidelines barring children's show hosts or animated characters from appearing in commercials during their shows and limiting the amount of commercials during children's viewing times to no more than twelve minutes per hour. In 1975, this limit was reduced to ten minutes per hour on weekdays and nine and a half minutes per hour on weekends. These voluntary guidelines were endorsed by the FCC.[43]

Even as the networks instituted a number of self-imposed limits in an attempt to respond to public criticism about the advertising that was driving much of their profits, their critics continued demanding that they do more. By 1975, the networks were complaining that the profitability of their children's programming was declining, in large part due to the measures they had taken to address the concerns raised by ACT and its allies.[44]

Stay Tuned...

As the TV networks struggled throughout the 1970s to maintain the profitability of their children's programming in the face of public criticism, a new force was gaining strength that would soon provide an even greater challenge to the broadcast networks' advertising coffers—cable TV. Cable television had originated as a method for extending the reach of broadcast television to remote areas which electronic signals could not reach, and had grown very slowly during the 1950s and 1960s. However, as the technology improved and FCC limitations on cable expansion were dropped, larger cities adopted cable as a way to provide better TV reception, and some cable channels began to originate their own programming.

Cable TV really began to take off in the 1970s, as new channels used a combination of cable and satellite transmission to expand their reach. Premium channel HBO debuted in 1972, and in 1976, Ted Turner's local Atlanta station WTBS became the first cable-fed superstation to reach a national audience. This was the start of an avalanche of new ways for television signals to reach the public. Broadcasters were beginning to imagine a future in which they might be forced to compete against hundreds of television channels. It was coming at them quickly. New channels of all kinds began to emerge, including USA in 1977 and ESPN in 1979. Then, in April 1979, Nickelodeon launched an entire cable network devoted to children's programming. It looked like a broadcaster's nightmare but a consumer's dream come true, and with it, a new era in children's television was about to dawn.[45]

CHAPTER FIVE

Middle Childhood
(the 1980s)

Life in the U.S.

As the new decade dawned, the American public was more than ready to leave the seventies behind. The late 1970s had been full of events that had undermined Americans' confidence in their country's institutions and sense of common purpose. In July 1979, in a televised address that the media called "the malaise speech," a weary President Jimmy Carter publicly acknowledged that the country was experiencing "a crisis of confidence."[1]

Then, as if to prove his point, a disheartening event occurred just a few months later that added even further to the public's feelings of helplessness and frustration. In November 1979, Iranian religious militants who had overthrown Iran's U.S.-supported government seized the U.S. embassy in Tehran and took fifty-two American embassy staff hostage. They demanded the return of the deposed monarch of Iran, Shah Mohammad Reza Pahlavi, then in the U.S. undergoing medical treatment and considered by the revolutionary government to be a fugitive criminal.[2] In what became an agonizing national ordeal, the news media daily reported the duration of the standoff. It took 444 days until the Carter administration finally negotiated an agreement for the release of the hostages, months after the death of the Shah from cancer.[3]

In reaction to the frustrations and anxieties of the prior years, and hoping for the return of traditional values in social, economic and political life, the public swept conservatives into elected positions in 1980. Ronald Reagan, a Hollywood actor who had gone on to become the governor of California, was elected president. He projected a genial disposition and optimistic style that many Americans found reassuring.

Conservatives blamed the country's economic woes on an undue tax burden, excessive government regulation, and large social spending programs, and they proceeded to cut all three. The effect was the worst recession the country had experienced since the Great Depression of the 1930s.[4] Factories shut down. Jobs disappeared. So did the social services that might have provided a safety net for the needy. Homeless people, some of whom had formerly been patients in now-shuttered mental health care facilities, soon became a fixture in American streets.[5]

After more than a year, Congress instituted reforms. A modest tax increase and higher deficits stimulated economic growth, and by the mid-eighties, the economy was improving. The recovery created the sense in the country that the good times were back, at least for those fortunate enough to win in the high-stakes, bare-knuckle game that was the deregulated American economy in the mid–80s. The hidden downside of this recovery was a widening economic rift, a long-term trend that would see American society increasingly split along an economic fault line.[6] Conspicuous growth at the top had for years been outpacing and eclipsing the decline of the middle and working classes, which were, in the words of one economic historian, starting to experience a "hollowing out."[7] At the time, however, with public attention focused on the success of the wealthy top tier, the sense of the nation was that things were on the right track again.

As the economy continued to expand, the mid- to late 1980s became synonymous with materialism and consumerism, best symbolized by the emergence of a new socioeconomic group termed young urban professionals, or "yuppies." Yuppies were Baby Boomers in their late twenties and thirties with college degrees, who lived in urban centers and had well-paying jobs and affluent lifestyles. Yuppies themselves, widely derided as being greedy, smug, shallow and superficial, often felt unfulfilled and full of self-doubt despite their affluence, as popular TV shows like *thirtysomething*, movies like *The Big Chill*, and novels like *Bright Lights, Big City* depicted. Yuppies were, after all, often the children of conservative parents still living agrarian, suburban, and small town lives. They shared similar normative images about what should constitute the "real" America. People on both sides of the widening social and economic divide felt unmoored by the shift that was becoming apparent, even if its causes and effects were not always well understood.[8]

As some segments of the public were enjoying the fruits of the economic recovery, a new source of anxiety arose in the form of a mysterious deadly disease that initially baffled healthcare workers and scientists. In its weekly journal of July 3, 1981, the Centers for Disease Control reported clusters of an extremely rare type of cancer, Kaposi's sarcoma, among forty-one homosexual men in New York and San Francisco. Soon more clusters of this cancer, as well as an unusual form of pneumonia and other opportunistic diseases, were identified among gay men across the country. The AIDS epidemic had begun. Some people feared that they could contract AIDS from any physical contact with gay men; others called the epidemic a sign of divine retribution.[9] Members of the gay community, who had been experiencing a degree of liberation and growing social acceptance, now felt a chilling backlash against them. The fact that doctors had no treatment or cure for this disease that was killing hundreds and then thousands of people added an undercurrent of fear to the national mood.

That mood was made even darker by another scourge, the so-called epidemic of crack cocaine. Crack, a highly potent, relatively inexpensive form of cocaine, primarily ravaged minority and poor urban communities. News reporting on crack, largely hyperbolic and light on facts, set off a multi-year panic. It painted a picture of a wave of crime by large numbers of desperate addicts and the violent, heavily armed gangs that competed to provide the drug.[10] The response was a national "war on drugs," leading to a huge spike in rates of incarceration, with enduring consequences for minority families in particular.[11]

Childhood in the U.S.

AIDS and the crack-inspired focus on crime added new sources of paranoia to the general anxieties and culture wars of the prior two decades, inevitably stoking anxieties about the safety and welfare of children, who often become the lightning rod for anxieties about society as a whole. Since the 1970s, such general anxieties have led to a series of publicized panics about children's well-being, usually crystallized by an event sensationalized by the mass media. A widespread panic over stranger abductions of children was set off by the unsolved disappearance of six-year-old Etan Patz in New York City in 1979 when he went to wait for the school bus by himself, and the abduction and murder of six-year-old Adam Walsh at a Florida shopping mall in 1981.[12] At the time, media reports claimed that as many as 50,000 children were being abducted and murdered by strangers annually. Pictures of missing children began to appear on milk cartons and billboards, as public concerns about an epidemic of child abductions quickly grew. But the FBI later reported that they had investigated only sixty-seven cases of children kidnapped by strangers in 1984.

The vast majority of missing children were runaways, and most murdered children were killed by their parents, not strangers.[13]

In 1983, a public panic about child abuse at daycare centers was set off by children's accusations of sexual molestation by staff at the McMartin preschool in California. These charges resulted in the longest and costliest criminal case in American history but concluded with no convictions. The McMartin case was followed by a series of forty similar cases against other daycare centers over the following two decades, but virtually none of the cases produced convictions, and it was eventually concluded that the preschoolers who testified about the incidents had been bribed and badgered by overzealous and poorly trained interviewers.[14]

These and other public panics about children's welfare were driven by the belief shared by many Americans that the growth in the divorce rate, single-parent households, and working mothers experienced by the country since the late 1960s were evidence of a "breakdown in the family" that would have serious negative consequences for children. The idea that placing children in daycare centers, sending them off alone to wait for the school bus, or momentarily losing sight of them at the mall would inevitably put them at risk was one of the ways that this vision of the breakdown of the traditional family and its dire consequences for children manifested itself. The American public increasingly began to see the world as a potentially dangerous place for children.[15] Parents felt more strongly than ever that they had to do everything in their power to help their children steer clear of avoidable hazards, be better able to face dangers that could not be anticipated, and become prepared to successfully navigate challenges in this world of risk.

Television

Given the national mood at the time, it is understandable that families would turn to the mass media for entertainment and diversion that they could enjoy from the safety and security of their homes, and that new media, including new forms of television, would arise to meet this demand. Cable TV continued to flourish during the 1980s, with the launch of more niche networks like CNN, BET, Cinemax, Bravo, the Weather Channel, and Lifetime. In April 1983, the Disney Channel debuted as a premium service competing with Nickelodeon in the children's cable TV arena. By 1988, more than half of U.S. households were subscribing to cable.[16]

MTV, a new cable channel that was launched in August 1981, had a profound impact on the music industry and popular culture. With its round-the-clock music videos, not only did MTV help in selling millions of record albums and making superstars out of artists like Michael Jackson and Madonna, it transformed the popular music industry, creating a greater emphasis on the music's visual aspects and turning it into a multimedia business. The unconventional fashions, hairstyles, and dance moves that MTV's videos disseminated became integral to selling the music and were imitated by young people around the world. The network's slogan, "I Want My MTV," became a national catch phrase, as teens around the country begged their parents to sign up for cable.[17]

A new broadcast channel was also launched during this decade. In 1985, British media mogul Rupert Murdoch purchased movie studio Twentieth Century–Fox as well as six independent U.S. TV stations, which he used to launch a scrappy and irreverent fourth U.S. broadcast network, Fox. Fox was soon airing edgy and ribald programs like *Married ... with Children*, and later debuted a new block of children's shows.

A key development in the regulation of video technology also took place during the eighties, one that would cause a sea change in how children and adults watch TV. Home video recorders had been introduced to the market in the mid–1960s, but they failed to gain much traction. The first recorders were technically complex, and there were open questions about whether home recording of network programming was even legal. When the Supreme Court issued a ruling in 1984 that home video recording of off-the-air television was permitted, sales of improved home video recorders took off. Videocassette recorders, now called VCRs, enabled viewers to time-shift TV programs and skip past commercials. The percentage of homes with VCR's exploded, growing from 10 percent at the time of the court's ruling to over 50 percent in less than three years.[18] Parents who wanted to control their children's television viewing and limit their exposure to commercials began recording children's shows for later viewing and buying or renting prerecorded videocassettes instead of letting their children watch off-the-air TV.

The television set was becoming a component in what was beginning to be called a home entertainment system. Another component that was soon added was the videogame system. There would now be even more competition for the time and attention that children might otherwise have given to over-the-air television viewing.

The videogame era that had begun in the 1970s approached critical mass in the 1980s. In the arcade game market, *Pac-Man* was introduced in 1980 and became one of the most popular videogames of all time. In 1985, the home videogame business was energized by the U.S. introduction of the Nintendo Entertainment System, bundled with its *Super Mario Brothers* game. Nintendo dominated the U.S. videogame market through the rest of the decade.[19]

The home computer also experienced explosive growth in the 1980s, evolving from a hobbyist pastime into a full-fledged consumer product. The IBM PC was launched in 1981 and soon became the preferred brand for professional users, while Commodore created the most popular home computers.[20] Apple introduced the Macintosh computer in 1984, which became the first commercially successful personal computer to feature a graphical user interface and a mouse.[21]

The potentially transformative nature of these new technologies was evident almost as soon as they hit the marketplace, but it was hard to predict with any confidence when or if they would pose a significant competitive threat to broadcasting. In the 1980s, the screen that mattered in most households was primarily used to receive programs in the traditional analog way. However, young children of this era would be the first digital generation, growing up knowing only a world with digital devices. The significance of this divide would eventually be recognized as comparable to the one between generations who grew up before and after the introduction of TV.

On primetime broadcast television in the 1980s, stylistic innovation and continuing efforts to stay current with changing social realities characterized new programming. Two noteworthy police dramas debuted at the start of the decade. *Hill Street Blues* on NBC was a different kind of cop show, mixing serious drama and violence with moments of humor, as *M*A*S*H** had done before. It also included occasional sex scenes that were considered very daring for network television at the time. The series was stylistically innovative, employing continuing storylines, overlapping dialogue, and hand-held camera work that gave the show a documentary look, features that became common in later dramatic series.

On CBS, there was *Cagney and Lacey*, another police drama that was innovative in its own way. *Cagney and Lacey* was TV's first female buddy show. The star characters were two women police detectives working closely together on high-profile cases. Cagney was single, ambitious and competitive, and determined to prove that she was as good as, or better than, any of the men on the force. Lacey was also dedicated to her career, but she had a husband and two children, and her home life was equally important to her. Along with solving crimes and catching criminals, the two detectives played out the work-life balance and gender discrimination issues that many women were facing in their own lives at the time.

September 1984 saw the debut of a new groundbreaking family sitcom, *The Cosby Show* on NBC, which became an immediate hit. Popular television personality Bill Cosby[22] starred as Cliff Huxtable, a successful African American obstetrician with an equally successful lawyer wife. The Huxtables had five children and lived in a comfortable Brooklyn brownstone. Without resorting to silly caricatures, stereotypes, or unrealistic plot points, the show captured the gentle humor of the family stories that formed the basis for Cosby's stand-up comedy routines. Though the Huxtable children were clever and funny and, like real children, constantly pushing the boundaries of parental rules and limits, Cliff and his wife Clair were firmly in charge of the household and always had the last word. The show not only played against social stereotypes about African American family life but captured the ethos of middle-class life in general in the 1980s.

The Cosby Show resonated across racial and ethnic lines, even though the series' depiction of upper-middle-class life in an African American family retained its ethnic style and character. The Huxtable family's race was not overtly stressed, but it was always present on the show in subtle ways. The children's rooms were decorated with pictures of black pop stars, anti-apartheid posters, and portraits of Martin Luther King, Jr., and Frederick Douglass. In family discussions about college, there were references to predominantly black schools. When the eldest Huxtable daughter gave birth to twins, she named them Winnie and Nelson, after South African anti-apartheid activists Winnie Madikizela and Nelson Mandela.

Children's Television

By the start of the 1980s, the business of children's television on the broadcast networks had become less profitable. Seismic social changes in the 70s, especially those which altered women's roles and expectations, produced a significant drop in the birthrate, so that by the 1980s there was a smaller audience for children's shows. Another reason the profitability of children's programming was falling at this time was the success of 70s activism, when groups like Action for Children's Television had convinced the networks to apply self-imposed limits on the amounts and kinds of advertising that could appear on children's TV.

The television industry proved resilient and creative in its response to these business challenges, however. A new hit children's show that debuted on NBC in the fall of 1981 not only turned that network's children's business around but energized the entire children's TV market. The hour-long cartoon series was called *The Smurfs*, and it chronicled the adventures of a cheerful, lovable group of little blue elf-like men (and one female Smurfette) who lived in a mushroom patch in the forest and whose happy existence was intermittently threatened by an evil sorcerer called Gargamel. The Smurf characters were adapted from a Belgian comic strip created in 1957, which had become a pop-culture fixture across Europe by the late 1970s and had generated a line of dolls that were beginning to enter the U.S. market.[23] Each of the Smurfs had a name that described their special character or attribute, like Jokey Smurf, Brainy Smurf, Greedy Smurf, Handy Smurf, or Vanity Smurf. The Smurf community was led by Papa Smurf, a wise and genial bearded elder.

The Smurfs was designed to be both entertaining and educational, and each episode conveyed prosocial lessons and values, like sharing, safety, responsibility, hard work, and staying in school. The show's content was shaped by input from NBC's Social Science Advisory Panel, a group of academic advisors whose role was to address such issues as gender and

The Smurfs **was an educational cartoon on NBC that chronicled the adventures of a cheerful, lovable group of little blue elf-like men (and one female Smurfette) who lived in a mushroom patch in the forest. In this scene, Jokey hands the Smurfette a gift which is really an exploding package, one of his favorite practical jokes.**

racial stereotyping and content and format appropriateness in the network's children's shows. The Panel thought that the show should have more female characters, but *The Smurfs'* Belgian creator, Peyo Culliford, refused to let NBC alter his initial concept to that degree. However, he did accept the Panel's recommendation that the female Smurfette be given a larger, less coquettish role, actively resisting villains herself rather than always being rescued by the other Smurfs. According to Horst Stipp, who worked in NBC's Social Science Research Department at the time and had helped to organize the Panel, "Smurfette became one of the most popular characters on Saturday morning, and ratings data indicated that both boys and girls liked the program. This experience helped to increase the number and status of female characters in Saturday morning programs and challenged the industry's conventional 'wisdom' that 'boys will only watch boys.'"[24] *The Smurfs'* success soon led to several similar children's cartoon shows, like *Monchikis*, *Snorks*, and *Wuzzles*, all of which starred adorable tiny fantasy creatures and conveyed prosocial lessons.

With *The Smurfs'* debut, a new trend in children's programming began that would come to characterize much of children's television in the 1980s. The trend had been briefly foreshadowed in 1969, when ABC had aired a new animated children's show called *Hot Wheels*, which had been funded by the Mattel toy company to promote sales of its Hot Wheels line of miniature toy cars. In response to an outcry from both the public and other toy manufacturers that the *Hot Wheels* show was essentially a thirty-minute commercial, the FCC issued a ruling prohibiting the airing of children's television programs based on licensed characters. *Hot Wheels* got the checkered flag and was off the air.

In the 1980s, with the FCC and the FTC now trending away from regulation of the communications industries, these kinds of limits were only reluctantly enforced. The result was a wave of new children's shows based on licensed characters and a shift in the business of licensing tie-ins, with children's products driving the development of TV shows rather than vice-versa. There were cartoons based on videogames (*Pac Man, Dungeons and Dragons, Saturday Supercade, Dragon's Lair, Pole Position, Super Mario Brothers Super Show*), cartoons based on children's toys (*He-Man and the Masters of the Universe, G.I. Joe, Thundercats, Transformers, Challenge of the Gobots, M.A.S.K., Jem, Pound Puppies, Strawberry Short-cake, My Little Pony and Friends, The Care Bears Family, Rainbow Brite*), and even cartoons based on TV commercials (*Hey Vern, It's Ernest!, The California Raisins Show*). According to one estimate, at least forty children's shows based on licensed characters were on the air by 1985.[25]

Though several of these shows appeared on the broadcast networks on Saturday mornings, most were syndicated series sold directly to local stations to help fill their weekday after-school time-slots. These shows harkened back to the earliest days of television, when programs were created specifically to serve as advertising vehicles for advertisers' products.

One of the toy-based shows, *Captain Power and the Soldiers of the Future*, included an interactive element, which hadn't been seen on television since the *Winky Dink and You* show in the 1950s. Premiering in 1987, *Captain Power* was a blend of live-action and animation that featured toy space jets from Mattel. The series was set in the 22nd century, after a war between intelligent machines and humans had resulted in the machines winning and subjugating the human race. In this post-apocalyptic world, robot soldiers called Bio-Mechs hunted down resisting humans and "digitized" them, turning them into virtual beings in OverMind, the supercomputer that ran everything. Captain Power was the leader of a human resistance group trying to regain control of the world.

The show included a five-minute segment in which children who owned one of the Mattel toy jets could play along and try to zap the villains on the TV screen. The toy jets responded to signals from the television, earning points when the target was hit and losing points when a sensor on the jet was "hit." When the jet reached zero points, the cockpit would automatically eject.

Captain Power was a controversial show and was cancelled after only one season. Critics condemned the high level of live-action violence on the show and the use of the interactive toy jets to shoot characters on the screen. To top it all off, the interactive game play actually didn't work very well.[26]

One of the more successful of the licensing-based shows was *Teenage Mutant Ninja Turtles*, a syndicated show based on a 1984 comic book and related set of action figures. *Turtles* was a goofy parody of the superhero genre that blended together aspects of four popular comics from the early 1980s—*Daredevil, New Mutants, Cerberus,* and *Ronin*. The premise was that four turtles that had been flushed down into the New York City sewers were exposed to radiation and transformed into half-turtle, half-human, pizza-loving teenagers. They were mentored by a Japanese mutant rat skilled in the martial arts, who trained them to become crime fighters. Each turtle had a name taken from the masters of Italian Renaissance art—Leonardo, Michelangelo, Donatello, and Raphael—and each had a favorite weapon.

One by-product of the trend in children's programming based on licensed characters was the creation of several new shows in the 1980s designed specifically for young girls. Despite *Smurfs'* success in appealing to both boys and girls, most children's programming executives still believed that boys would reject shows with female leading characters, while girls would readily watch shows with male stars.[27] As a result of this thinking, most children's shows were designed with boys in mind, and female characters were usually secondary or non-existent. Even *Fat Albert*, despite its prosocial and educational mission, had featured no significant female characters. Consistent with this industry assumption, many of the new shows in the eighties that were based on licensed characters were aimed at boys, like *He-Man*, *G.I. Joe*, *Transformers*, and *Teenage Mutant Ninja Turtles*, and they featured action, conflict, weapons, and superheroes vanquishing evil villains. But with the explosion of the licensed character market, toy manufacturers and TV producers realized that girls age three to seven were an untapped area for growth, and shows like *Strawberry Shortcake*, *The Care Bears*, *Rainbow Brite*, and *My Little Pony*, each designed to market a line of toys for little girls, were developed to target this newly recognized market segment.

On *Teenage Mutant Ninja Turtles*, four turtles that had been flushed down into the New York City sewers were exposed to radiation and emerged as half-turtle, half-human, pizza-loving crime-fighting teens. The group consisted of (from left to right) Donatello, Leonardo, Raphael, and Michelangelo.

These shows all featured cute little characters, bright pastel colors, and a focus on emotions and relationships. For example, in *Rainbow Brite*, the main character, a little girl named Wisp, was given the mission of bringing light and color to a bleak and gloomy world. With the help of a Sprite named Twink and a beautiful horse named Starlite, Wisp found the magical Color Belt and used it to free the seven Color Kids, who had been imprisoned by the evil King of Shadows. Wisp and the Color Kids then spread color across the land, working with like-colored Sprites who mined Color Crystals that they processed into Star Sprinkles, the essential components to coloring any object or place.

The Care Bears Family was designed to teach children about recognizing and managing their feelings. Each Care Bear represented a particular human emotion, and every week the Bears would leave their home in Care-a-Lot to help human children learn about their emotions and to battle against evil villain Dark Heart, who was trying to rid the world of feelings.[28]

My Little Pony was based on a line of toy ponies in bright and pastel colors manufactured by Hasbro, which became hugely popular with girls in the 1980s. The toy ponies had large blue eyes adorned with eye shadow, eyeliner, and thick lashes, and they had flowing manes and tails made of synthetic hair, which could be combed and brushed. Each pony had a different name and different decoration on its haunch, like a butterfly, star, or flower, representing its name.[29]

Though one might question the shows' origins as marketing tools to sell toys, they did portray worlds in which females were dominant, and girls could enjoy these shows without having to identify with male characters. Critics, however, denounced the new toy-based girls' shows as trashy, saccharine, and stereotyped. As one academic critic put it, "An endless stream of these happy little beings with their magical unicorns in their syrupy cloud-cuckoo lands have paraded across the screen demanding that they be snuggled, cuddled, nuzzled, loved, and adored, generally enticing children to lay bare their emotions so that they can be examined and made healthy."[30]

However, another academic analyst, Ellen Seiter, contends that much of the criticism aimed at these shows was actually a condemnation of their feminine values and appeal.[31] Like women's soap operas, these girls' cartoons were about the emotional lives and relationships among the characters. Rather than confronting problems or villains with weapons, combat, and conflict, the characters on the girls' cartoons solved them with teamwork, cooperation, and the shaming and rehabilitation of villains. While the bad guys on boys' cartoons were usually zapped away, imprisoned, or banished, the villains on girls' cartoons were usually reintegrated into the community. As Seiter notes, in girls' cartoons, "feelings rule the world," and villains can be redeemed through increased self-knowledge and emotional insight.[32]

One of the reasons that the girls' cartoons and other children's TV shows of the 1980s were so heavily criticized is that children's cartoons often portray aspects of adult culture in highly stylized, exaggerated versions that, to adults, range from embarrassing to repellant but are easily understood by children. In the case of gender roles, female characters were usually represented by cute little creatures with high-pitched voices, pastel colors, frilly clothing, long hair, and a large capacity for sympathy and emotional intelligence, while male characters were represented by superheroes with deep voices, big muscles, great physical strength, and a seemingly endless capacity for action and bravery.[33]

On the educational programming front, CBS launched an ambitious live-action variety show in 1986 that stood out among all the cartoons that dominated the airwaves—*Pee-Wee's Playhouse*. *Playhouse* starred performer Paul Reubens as Pee-Wee Herman, a high-voiced, bow-tied, child-like character who presided over a surreal playhouse filled with toys, puppets, talking furniture and appliances, a robot, and a host of supporting characters, like Miss Yvonne, Dixie, King Cartoon, Captain Carl, Cowboy Curtis, Reba the Mail Lady, and Jambie, a disembodied genie head that lived in a jewel-lined box. There was also a small group of children on the set. *Pee-Wee's Playhouse* combined live action, special effects, celebrity visits, and vintage cartoons. It had a retro look and feel that harkened back to classic shows like *Howdy Doody*, *Pinky Lee*, and *Captain Kangaroo*. The show was designed to be educational by conveying moral lessons to viewers about positive values like sharing and reciprocity. With its quirky, retro, surreal look, *Pee-Wee's Playhouse* attracted an audience of both children and adult fans and quickly achieved cult status. But the show was taken off the air in 1991, following Reubens' arrest for indecent exposure in an adult movie house.[34]

Programs like *The Smurfs* and *Pee-Wee's Playhouse* were educational in the sense that they taught good behavior and positive values. Few new shows dealing with cognitive subject matter, like English, history, science, or math, appeared on commercial networks in the eighties. However, CBS did add two new educational shows of this type to its schedule: *CBS Storybreak*, a series of cartoon adaptations of children's literature, in 1985, and *This Is America, Charlie Brown*, an animated miniseries featuring

Peanuts characters depicting key events in American history, in 1988.

Aside from those exceptions, educational programming with a curricular intent was generally left to PBS, where there were a number of new entries aimed at children beyond the preschool years. Most PBS shows for children continued to be live-action series, unlike the cartoons that characterized children's shows on commercial television at the time. Several PBS series dealt with science education, like *3-2-1 Contact*, *Newton's Apple*, *The Voyage of the Mimi*, and *Owl/TV*. *Reading Rainbow*, which premiered in 1983, focused on the encouragement of reading, while *Square One TV*, which debuted in 1987, focused on math. There were also shows that addressed

Pee-Wee's Playhouse was a postmodern take on classic children's variety shows of the 1950s. Pee-Wee (right) was played by comedian Paul Reubens. The King of Cartoons, played by Gilbert Lewis (left), was one of several quirky characters on the program.

prosocial topics, like *DeGrassi Junior High*, a dramatic series that depicted daily life with all its problems at an urban junior high school, and *Today's Special*, a live-action show with puppets, which was aimed at helping children deal with their feelings. *Wonderworks* and *Long Ago & Far Away* presented adaptations of children's books as well as original stories.

In 1989, PBS debuted *Shining Time Station*, a new show for preschoolers. A mix of live-action and animation, *Shining Time Station* was based on a five-minute British TV series called *Thomas the Tank Engine*, and each episode used the adventures of a little anthropomorphic train and his train friends to teach life lessons and values, like getting along with others. With its slow, gentle pace and focus on emotional intelligence and social understanding, *Shining Time Station* resembled *Mister Rogers' Neighborhood* more than it did *Sesame Street*. Former Beatle Ringo Starr was initially featured as an eighteen-inch-tall train conductor named Mr.

Conductor, who was later played by comedian George Carlin. Carlin would seem to have been a surprising choice for this role, given his reputation as a standup comic with a decidedly profane act, but Britt Allcroft, creator of the original British version of the show, was unfamiliar with Carlin's voice when co-creator Rick Sigglekow played her a tape. She must have agreed with comedian Jerry Seinfeld, who once said Carlin's voice had always sounded like he was speaking to a child, "like the naughtiest, most fun grown-up you ever met was reading you a bedtime story." Carlin embraced the role and brought to it a quality of warmth and kindness, completely separating himself from the persona he had created for his comedy act. Unused to performing without an audience, he brought a stuffed teddy bear into the sound booth to speak his lines to.[35]

Cable channel Nickelodeon had joined the broadcast networks in 1979 as a new source of children's television. Throughout the eighties, the programming on the new channel consisted primarily of live-action shows, mostly game shows, reality shows, and variety shows, along with a couple of dramatic series, aimed at older children and preteens. For example, *Double Dare* was an updated version of classic game show *Beat the Clock*, with two pairs of boy-girl teams competing for prizes by answering quiz questions. Teams could opt to either answer the questions or complete a physical challenge that usually involved making a big mess, like racing up a ramp covered with chocolate syrup, and the winning team took part in a messy obstacle course to win additional prizes. In one of the signature elements on the show, whenever a contestant or performer said the words "I don't know," he or she was "slimed," that is, a bucket of green slimy goo was poured on their head.

Green slime appeared again on another Nickelodeon show in the eighties, *You Can't Do That on Television*, a variety show with a sketch comedy format similar to *Laugh-In* and *Saturday Night Live*. The show starred pre-teen and teenage performers, who would also occasionally get slimed by the green goo, which later became a key part of Nickelodeon's brand image. Viewers at home could enter the Slime-In, a contest in which the winner was flown to the set to be slimed on the air.

As Nickelodeon began to position itself as a network where kids could be kids, without the oversight or influence of adults, the network embraced messiness and "gross" stuff as the key to the brand identity it wanted to convey. Nickelodeon's corporate handbook put it this way: "Mess, slime, and gak [a gooey, messy substance] are more than a gag or theme, they are Nickelodeon's mascots. Pretty much by accident, on shows like *You Can't Do That on Television* and *Double Dare*, we discovered that green

HBO's *Fraggle Rock* was a puppet show featuring Jim Henson's Muppets. Gobo (left) is holding a postcard he got from Uncle Traveling Matt (right).

slime and mess excite kids emotionally, symbolize their rebellion, and totally gross out adults."[36] Nickelodeon would run with that concept for a host of new original shows in the following decade.

Premium cable channels Showtime and HBO also ventured into children's programming with two original series in the 1980s. In 1982, Showtime debuted *Faerie Tale Theater*, an ambitious live-action anthology series created by actress Shelley Duvall, which presented adaptations of classic fairy tales. The episodes featured famous stars like Robin Williams and were directed by noted film directors like Tim Burton and Francis Ford Coppola. In 1983, HBO presented *Fraggle Rock*, a live-action puppet show from the Jim Henson Company, creators of the Muppets. The show was set in a rock underneath a scientist's house, where three groups of bizarre creatures lived—the Fraggles, the Doozers, and the Gorgs. A cartoon version of the show aired on NBC in 1987.

Advertising and Marketing to Children

The many children's shows based on licensed characters that proliferated during the 1980s were in themselves a form of advertising, one that had not been allowed since the 1950s but made a return during the dereg-ulatory atmosphere of the eighties. When it came to commercial spots aimed at children, TV networks and children's advertisers now felt free to ignore self-imposed rules that had barred unrealistic product portrayals and to use whatever techniques they thought would be effective in selling things to children.

Having learned from Mattel's success with TV ads for Barbie, most advertisers of children's products created commercials that didn't just show the product's attributes but dramatized its excitement and appeal. If the product was a toy, this was usually done by portraying a group of happy children playing with the product, sometimes in a fantasy setting. For food products, the commercials were often animated and used a mas-cot or licensed character to give the product a personality that would engage children's attention and emotions.

Regardless of what was being advertised, the world depicted in these commercials was one where "kids rule" and adult authority is absent or subverted, often by portraying adults as boring, clueless, or the butt of the commercials' jokes.[37] For example, a commercial for Nabisco's Teddy Gra-ham cookies showed a room full of school children eating Teddy Graham cookies and engaging in an impromptu rock concert while the teacher had his back turned. Another ad showed a boy finding relief from a boring family reunion by escaping to the kitchen and opening a bag of Starburst candy. Ads like these depicted the adult world as drab and self-restrained, celebrated the pleasures of playing and eating cookies or candy as forms of hedonism that only children could enjoy, and implicitly ridiculed adult disapproval of children's pleasures and values.

While the theme of rebellion against parental controls and against the regimentation of adult life has existed in children's literature and other forms of children's entertainment long before television came onto the scene, this theme may have been particularly resonant for children in the eighties, when parents, fearful about their children's well-being and future success, ramped up efforts to supervise and control their children's lives. Advertisers must have picked up on the idea that rebellion would strongly appeal to children of over-attentive parents.

Like the licensed-character toys and the TV shows based on them that proliferated during the eighties, TV commercials were also very gender-specific. If the commercial showed children engaged with the product, advertisers believed that it was crucial to show the right peer group for that particular target audience. Ads for toys aimed at boys showed only boys playing with the toy, and ads for toys aimed at girls were similarly gender-exclusive. Ads also employed different aesthetic styles that were assumed to appeal to the targeted gender. For boys, commercials tended to use intense upbeat music, bold colors, and rapidly-edited action scenes, while those aimed at girls were more sedate, with calm soundtracks backing images washed in pastel hues.[38]

Though TV shows for children became more racially-integrated in the eighties, commercials aimed at children were slow to follow. When they were set in realistic environments, commercials generally represented a generic suburban middle-class world. If any non-white children were included, they were shown in non-leading roles or on the periphery of the action. Often, a single African American child would be the token minority in a group of children.[39]

Stay Tuned...

In December 1989, as the eighties drew to a close, the recently launched Fox broadcast network premiered an innovative new primetime show. Though it wasn't really aimed at children, *The Simpsons* would usher in a shift in depictions of children and families that would come to permeate popular culture, including shows for children, in the decade to come.

CHAPTER SIX

The Tweens
(the 1990s)

Life in the U.S.

It was "The Best Decade Ever," according to author Kurt Andersen, and in many ways, the 1990s were indeed an upbeat, hopeful time for much of the country.[1] The decade began promisingly with a previously unimaginable development: the Cold War and its attendant threat of global nuclear Armageddon suddenly came to an end, as the Soviet Union collapsed, East and West Germany were reunited, and the nations of Eastern Europe became largely independent. The fact that in 1990, a U.S.-led military coalition successfully drove the invading Iraqi army out of Kuwait in just four days, ending the Persian Gulf War, boosted Americans' military pride and helped dissipate the lingering "Vietnam syndrome."

The country's economic system was also firing on all cylinders. It is true that the nation's budget deficit at the start of the decade was massive, but this was erased in a financial turnaround of historic magnitude. The 90s economic boom was a continual economic expansion unprecedented in American history during peacetime. Between 1992 and 1999, the U.S. economy grew by an average of 4 percent per year, an average of 1.7 million jobs were added annually, and the unemployment rate dropped from nearly 8 percent to 4 percent (effectively full employment) by the end of the decade. The median American household income grew by 10 percent during this time, while stocks quadrupled in value.[2]

The good news just kept coming. Violent crime rates fell precipitously and the murder rate declined by 41 percent. The lethal grip of HIV/AIDS started to loosen when a treatment for this scourge was finally developed.[3]

There were some clouds on the horizon. The country's newfound sense of safety and security was briefly shaken when a jihadist truck bomb detonated in the parking garage below the north tower of the World Trade

Center in 1993 and when a car bomb set by domestic anti-government terrorists blew up the federal building in Oklahoma City in 1995. At the time, however, these horrific events seemed like the isolated actions of deranged individuals rather than harbingers of more terrorist acts to come.

As important as these developments were, however, the nineties may best be remembered as the decade when the digital age got fully underway, presaging a new order of things that would emerge more clearly at the beginning of the 21st century. At the dawn of the 1990s, a few scientists, engineers and academic researchers were mulling the need for a better way to share data on the Internet ("Internet" was itself a recently coined term for the network that had incrementally emerged as separate large computer networks became compatible with each other, essentially evolving into one).[4] They imagined a graphical point-and-click interface to the Internet with the ability to easily jump back and forth between different remote computers, where users could find content waiting for them—no one would have to send the data because it would already be waiting for anyone who wanted to access it.

Once this vision existed, a handful of computer scientists quickly devised the code and protocols that made it possible, expanding existing software paradigms (especially hypertext) to work across the Internet and to trigger the much more complex software elements that would render a web page. In essence, thinking they were making a robust online database that would resemble an encyclopedia, they opened the lid of a toy box called the World Wide Web, where data could take the form of text, pictures, animations, videos, and everything else we now take for granted in the digital universe.

The first web server, with a single website, launched in December 1990, and the concept was gradually refined and circulated among scientific communities starting in 1991.[5] By the middle of the decade, there were a quarter of a million sites. People needed a tool to help find anything, so the browser was invented. When AOL bundled an early browser with their popular e-mail service, suddenly everyone wanted a personal computer.

By the end of the decade, with the number of websites rocketing past 17 million and something like a hundred million personal computers being sold annually,[6] people could barely remember a world without computers. The computer, the Internet, and the Web became virtually indistinguishable, and indispensable, in people's daily lives and in the popular consciousness.

Hot on the heels of the Internet-fueled computer revolution was a second transformative technology that made the decade of the 90s a point of inflection. Previously, mobile phones were the size of bricks and the battery was pitiful. They were barely a step up from the shoe-phone used by the hapless spy in the 1960s comedy series *Get Smart*. Cell phone calls cost a dollar a minute and dropped calls were the norm. But the second-generation cell phones that hit the market at the end of 1989 were more like the communicators featured in the sci-fi series *Star Trek*. The North American market penetration of cell phones grew from 6 percent in 1993 to 37 percent by the end of the decade.[7] Everyone knows where that trend would lead.

On the popular culture front, hip-hop music achieved mass market appeal and dominance in the nineties and quickly spread throughout the globe via the World Wide Web. The first three *Harry Potter* novels appeared during this decade, becoming a sensation among both children and adults and reigniting an interest in reading among children. In the movies, *Titanic* became one of the most successful films of all time, while traditional Disney animation continued its comeback with *The Lion King* and *Aladdin*, and Pixar raised computer-generated animation to a new level with its *Toy Story* movies.

Childhood

Overall, U.S. birthrates had been falling since 1957, with an especially large drop after 1970 as women delayed having children and had smaller families.[8] However, there were so many Boomers that even with a decline in the birthrate, the absolute number of their children and grandchildren constituted a substantially large cohort of their own.[9] The children born in the 80s and 90s were initially called Echo Boomers until the more evocative term Millennials caught on, and the parameters of this group were extended to include births until 2004. This new cohort would go on to outnumber their Boomer ancestors, becoming the largest living generation in the country by 2016.[10] Like Boomers, Millennials were born during a time of economic expansion and growing prosperity, but there were profound ways in which their lives were different from what their forbearers had experienced as children.

About half of Millennial children would spend at least part of their childhood in a single-parent home, in part because of the increase in the divorce rate that had begun in the 1970s, and in part because an unprecedented number of them were born to unmarried mothers.[11] With many mothers working outside the home and childcare too expensive for most, the term "latchkey children" was coined to describe how children of this generation were often left unsupervised after the school day ended, until their parents returned home from work. Without having a mother at home to monitor their activities, Millennial children spent less of their free time playing outside with other neighborhood children and roaming freely on foot, scooter, or bicycle until supper time, as their parents had done when they were children. When not in school, Millennials spent more of their growing years alone at home or in organized supervised activities, where parents would not have to worry about their safety.

Millennials' parents differed significantly from earlier parents, including parents of Boomers. Parents in the 90s tended to be older and better educated than their own mothers and fathers had been. They worried intensely about their children's safety, psychological well-being, and academic performance. Parental anxiety about their children had become the norm among middle-class parents, and parents of Millennials ratcheted up the level of concern. Their anxiety was exemplified, and stoked, by now-familiar but still potent media-driven public panics about children's safety-panics about stranger abductions, poisoned Halloween candies, childhood obesity, and now the specter of children being exposed to pornography or pedophiles over the Internet.[12]

Concerned parents became more involved in children's day-to-day lives, in ways that their own parents had never been. The term "helicopter parent" was coined in 1990 to describe the new parenting style. These were parents who paid extremely close attention to their child's experiences and problems and tried to oversee every aspect of their child's life.[13] With so much seemingly at stake for their child's future success and happiness, Millennials' parents felt that it was their responsibility to constantly supervise, mediate, and intervene in their children's lives to ensure that they had every possible advantage. In addition to monitoring and supervising their children's activities, more affluent parents tried to enhance their children's education with special tutoring and a myriad of extracurricular activities like sports, music, dance, and gymnastics, while less well-to-do parents compensated with intense protectiveness against dangerous or illegal activities that would threaten their children's future. If their children didn't have the self-discipline to sit still in a classroom or concentrate on their homework, helicopter parents would never accept this behavior as natural vitality or spunky independence, nor would they just resign themselves, as their own parents might have done, to the likelihood that their children were not going to be very successful in school. Millennials' parents, possessing a culturally-legitimized belief that it was their duty to take whatever steps were necessary to help their offspring win in the battle for success, and being no strangers to psychoactive drugs, readily resorted to medicating their children with drugs like Ritalin to get them to settle down.[14]

Television

Several primetime TV shows defined the evolution of entertainment programming in the 1990s. Two of these shows were primetime cartoons that depicted children and families, but they were a world away from earlier primetime cartoons like *The Flintstones* that had been intended as wholesome family viewing. *The Simpsons*, which first aired on the still-novel Fox network as a Christmas special in the last days of 1989, was a full-fledged situation comedy that just happened to be animated. Set in the generic U.S. town of Springfield, it depicted the everyday life of a typical middle-class family consisting of dad Homer, a dim-witted, lazy, and overweight safety control engineer at the town's nuclear plant; his much smarter, well-intentioned but often hapless wife Marge, a stay-at-home-mom; their ten-year-old son Bart, a proudly underachieving and misbehaving smart-aleck fourth-grader; daughter Lisa, a sweet, precocious and sensitive second-grader; and baby Maggie, constantly sucking on a pacifier, a silent observer of the absurd world around her. All the characters, but especially Bart and Lisa, pilloried assumptions about family life and flouted many of the norms for behavior and conventions for gender roles at the time. Bart was a bad boy who was good at heart but always rebelling against authority, whether that of his parents or his teachers, and part of that rebellion consisted of not caring about doing well in school. By contrast, his younger sister Lisa was an excellent and disciplined student, but also an independent thinker who refused to conform to sexual stereotypes. Aimed at a broad audience, not just at children, the series parodied American culture, society, institutions, television, and the human condition itself.[15] *The Simpsons* struck a chord with audiences, and it began its 28th season on the air in September 2016, becoming the longest-running scripted primetime TV series in American history.[16]

South Park, which debuted on little-known cable network Comedy Central in 1997, took the irreverent satirical tone and content of *The Simpsons* and considerably upped the ante. The "outrageous cartoon about four foul-mouthed third-graders and their twisted little Rocky Mountain town"[17] carries a TV-MA content rating, which means it is intended for adult audiences only. The show even lampoons its content rating, preceding each episode with this disclaimer: "All characters and events in this show—even those based on real people—are entirely fictional. All celebrity voices are impersonated ... poorly. The following program contains coarse language and due to its content it should not be viewed by anyone." The TV-MA classification, however, relies on parental enforcement, which is notoriously lax. Needless to say, lots of children do watch the show.

Many of *South Park's* plotlines revolve around the kids' relationships with eccentric, hapless members of their own families and occasionally with aliens, maniacs, unhinged celebrities, world leaders, or agents of corrupt corporate and government interests, whom the boys meet with a mixture of idealism, cynicism, and childish befuddlement. No aspect of life has been immune to the series' merciless, profanity-laden, and frequently obscene parodies. No ethnic group or nationality has been spared as the program has careened through a repertoire of topical current events and imagined crises. While the show does seem to have a particular comical animus towards Canadians, *South Park* is an equal opportunity offender, eviscerating every sacred cow with biting sarcasm. Religion, politics, race, gender—all are fair game and are remorselessly mocked. Manners, fads, traditions, conventions, social norms— all are exposed as hypocritical to varying degrees. In the end, the characters usually find an imperfect but essentially ethical, rational or forgiving response to the impossible challenges posed by their morally compromised world. The series was an immediate hit, forcing more cable systems around the country to begin carrying the Comedy Central network. Despite, or because of, its controversial nature, *South Park* became an enduring pop culture phenomenon and remains one of Comedy Central's most popular shows.

By contrast, single adults were the main focus of NBC's *Seinfeld*, which would become the defining TV show of the 1990s. The premise of this sitcom, which made its debut in May 1990, was that it was about the everyday life of stand-up comedian Jerry Seinfeld, the series' real-life creator, and his friends. Though ostensibly "about nothing," the show's success was driven by its satirical and ironic view of life among a group of neurotic, wordy, upper-middle-class singles in uptown Manhattan. In 1994, NBC followed up on *Seinfeld's* success with *Friends*, another sitcom about the day-to-day lives of a group of twenty-somethings living in Manhattan.

Cable television increasingly drew audiences away from broadcast TV throughout the decade, and in 1998, premium cable channel HBO produced two hit series that illustrated the differences between broadcast television, with its government-imposed restrictions on content, and cable, which had no such restraints. In the summer of 1998, HBO began airing *Sex and the City*, a sophisticated sitcom about a group of stylish upper-middle-class women friends, which pushed the boundaries of sexual content on TV with frank language, nudity, and a focus on sex as recreational fun. The show presented all these elements in the form of an accessible "female buddy" sitcom that made it all seem familiar, acceptable, and almost mainstream. Later that year, HBO created another hit with *The Sopranos*, a serial drama about the life of Tony Soprano, a New Jersey mobster. *The Sopranos* juxtaposed Tony's gangster business life with quotidian matters of typical family conflicts and issues in an affluent suburban setting, using the premise of Tony's regular psychotherapy sessions to advance the plot. The result was a world of complex characters trying to sustain their own internal contradictions, which held audiences in a state of ambivalent fascination.

A major transformation in television news programming also occurred in the nineties, driven by the O.J. Simpson case. Simpson, a famous athlete-turned-actor, was accused of murdering his wife and her male friend in 1994. Beginning with live coverage of a freeway chase with the police in pursuit of Simpson, the case was made-to-order for new 24-hour cable news services like CNN and Court TV, which continually televised every aspect of the story to which they could get access. With the broadcast networks joining the media frenzy, Simpson's arrest and trial became a lurid tabloid mega-event, as much entertainment as news, which consumed the public's attention for over a year. The announcement of a not-guilty verdict in Simpson's trial was covered by 10 different TV networks and attracted nearly 60 million viewers, becoming one of the most-watched TV events of the decade.[18] Having discovered the ratings bonanza that tabloid-style coverage of celebrity-driven crime and controversy could fuel, television news was changed forever and television itself would never be quite the same.

Children's Television

The deregulatory free-for-all in children's television that had characterized the 1980s created a public backlash, led by the grassroots activist group Action for Children's Television. ACT's efforts culminated in passage of the Children's Television Act of 1990, which required broadcast stations to carry more educational programming for children and formally imposed limits on the number of commercial minutes that could air during children's shows, as the networks had voluntarily agreed to previously.[19] The Act was revised in 1996, with the stipulation that stations carrying any children's shows had to include at least three hours per week of programs that were explicitly informational or educational. As a result, television networks began airing more children's shows that they thought would pass muster with the FCC while still being sufficiently entertaining to draw large audiences. Most of these shows claimed to be educational simply because they conveyed positive social messages in their stories, a definition of "educational" that many critics considered overly broad.

While the three major commercial broadcast networks struggled with the challenge of meeting these new FCC requirements, they also confronted growing competition in the children's television market. New sources for children's programming became available in the nineties that greatly expanded the number of viewing options available to the children's audience and transformed the competitive landscape. In 1990, upstart broadcast network Fox launched a block of children's programming called the Fox Children's Network, later renamed Fox Kids, that aired on Saturday mornings and weekday afternoons. In January 1995, two additional broadcast networks, UPN and The WB, began operations, and both soon debuted their own children's programming blocks.

The biggest change in children's television in the nineties, however, was the growing shift in viewing from broadcasting to cable television. Nickelodeon had held a predominant position with the children's cable audience since 1979, but in the 1990s, new cable networks eager for their share of the children's market joined the competitive fray. First out of the gate was the Cartoon Network, launched in 1992. Soon, as other cable networks added their own children's blocks or found themselves partnering with broadcast networks through corporate mergers, it became increasingly difficult to keep track of all the players without a program. Take the year 1996 as an example. In this one year alone, the Discovery Channel, which had been launched a decade earlier, added its own block of children's shows called Discovery Kids, which was later spun off as a separate channel; Animal Planet debuted, another cable channel with family-friendly shows that would appeal to children; and Disney bought the ABC Network, with Disney studios providing much of ABC's children's programming from that point on. Then, in 1997, The Disney Channel, which had been launched in 1983 as a premium cable channel[20] with family-friendly programming, began transitioning to a basic cable service with more programs oriented specifically to children. And in 1998, Fox purchased cable network The Family Channel from The Christian Broadcasting Network, renamed it the Fox Family Channel, and reprogrammed it with children's shows in the daytime and family-oriented shows in the evenings. Cable channels USA Network and Black Entertainment Television also began airing some children's shows. By the end of the decade, both CBS and Nickelodeon were owned by Viacom, and Nickelodeon supplied much of the programming for CBS' Saturday morning block.

It was a crowded field throughout the 90s, and NBC was the first broadcast network to see the writing on the wall. In 1991, NBC decided to drop its Saturday morning cartoons altogether and replace them with a combination of news programs and a few live-action shows for teens, like *California Dreams* and *Running the Halls*, a spin-off from *Saved by the Bell*. *California Dreams* was about a multi-ethnic group of high schoolers who form a rock band, while *Running the Halls* focused on the hijinks of students at a private school. NBC's strategic retreat from a children's television market that was becoming increasingly dominated by cable was a harbinger of things to come.

As the first cable network for children, Nickelodeon obviously had had a head start in gaining traction with child viewers and was determined to hold its position as these new sources of competition emerged. Nick truly came into its own during the 1990s under the leadership of new network head Geraldine Laybourne. Nickelodeon had done extensive market research with children, learning that in an age of latchkey kids with working mothers and helicopter parents who organized and monitored every moment of their children's lives, children felt constantly under pressure and had little time to just play and goof around. Nickelodeon decided to actively embrace the idea that their channel should not only be a place that treated children with respect, meaning that their programs would be non-violent, non-sexist, and not primarily aimed at selling toys, but also a place where kids could be kids, free of parental demands and interference, and where programs would reflect a child's point of view. As its employee handbook put it: "It's an adult world out there where kids get talked down to and everybody older has authority over them. For kids, it's 'Us vs. Them' in the grown-up world: you're either for kids or against them.... We were on the kids' side, and we wanted them to know it."[21] Nickelodeon's branding and programming reversed the historical distinction between children as naïve and innocent, and adults as all-knowing, worldly, and sophisticated. In Nick's world, kids were "cool," while adults "just didn't get it"; kids were interesting, while adults were boring; kids were spontaneous, while adults were predictable; kids were wacky, while adults were uptight.[22]

A good example of how Nickelodeon's focus on presenting things from a child's point of view translated into new programming was *Clarissa Explains It All*, which debuted in 1991. *Clarissa* was Nick's first entry in what would become a string of "tween"-oriented shows starring strong, independent, and often unruly (or just willful, depending on your attitude toward traditional social norms) adolescent girls—a market that Nickelodeon believed had been underserved. The live-action series was about the day-to-day life of a smart, self-reliant teenager, Clarissa Darling, as seen through her own eyes. Clarissa's family and friends presented a picture of demographics, lifestyles and attitudes that were typical of the 1990s. Clarissa was a sarcastic, funny teenager with a wild imagination, wild clothes, a wildly-decorated bedroom, and a pet alligator named Elvis. In a reversal of prior generational dynamics, her parents were former hippies who retained a strong sense of social responsibility and gave Clarissa a lot of freedom. Clarissa's younger brother, Ferguson, with whom Clarissa was always fighting, was a self-avowed Young Republican who idolized Ronald Reagan and was always coming up with get-rich schemes. Clarissa also had a platonic friend, Sam, who enjoyed skateboarding and whose parents were divorced.

Clarissa narrated her life's ups and downs directly to the audience, beginning each episode with an often sarcastic and self-reflexive opening monologue that laid out the theme for that episode. Each episode also tapped into one of teenagers' new obsessions by showing Clarissa tackling the episode's issues through playing a fictional videogame. Together with Clarissa's commentary, the show's plots and storylines often presented a critique of social norms and conventions about girls, boys, romance, and families. Defying industry assumptions that boys would not watch shows starring girls, *Clarissa* attracted a large audience of both genders, and its success motivated Nickelodeon to continue producing shows starring strong, independent girls, like *The Secret World of Alex Mack* in 1994, *The Mystery Files of Shelby Woo* in 1996, *The Wild Thornberrys* in 1998, *The Amanda Show* in 1999, and *As Told by Ginger* in 2000.[23]

The success of *Clarissa Explains it All* was a turning point for Nickelodeon, as was its foray into animation with the 1991 debut of *Nicktoons*, a block of three original animated shows: *Rugrats, Doug,* and *The Ren & Stimpy Show*. Rather than licensing these shows from a limited number of outside producers, which was standard practice among the broadcast networks, Nickelodeon created an in-house animation department where program creators could produce their own shows with an unusual degree of creative freedom.[24] *Nicktoons* became very popular and led to a growing emphasis on animated programming at Nickelodeon in the years to come.

Rugrats was the preeminent *Nicktoons* series, becoming the number one children's show on television by 1995.[25] The series centered on the day-to-day lives of a group of toddlers—adventurous Tommy Pickles, his more cautious friend Chuckie, his younger brother Dil, twins Phil and Lil, and Tommy's spoiled three-year-old cousin Angelica—as seen through the toddlers' own eyes. In the babies' minds, common life experiences became surprising adventures, and challenges often arose due to the babies' misinterpretation of their parents, who could be inattentive and were often oblivious to what the babies were up to. Angelica, whose catch-phrase was "You dumb babies!," further complicated matters by trying to mislead, manipulate, or even bully the babies, but she usually got her comeuppance by the end of the show. The series had a unique look, with a rough, squiggly animation style that made the babies look a little ugly and not a little demented. It incorporated frequent cultural references that only adults would understand, and it projected a jaded view of family life and consumer culture, but each episode managed to convey a moral lesson that the babies learned through their adventures.[26]

The second entry in the *Nicktoons* block was *Doug*, a show about the life of eleven-year-old Doug Funnie, his pal Skeeter, and dog Porkchop. Doug was an intensely insecure daydreamer coping with the common

Rugrats was Nickelodeon's first hit cartoon. It depicted the world as seen through the eyes of a group of toddlers. Starring characters included (clockwise from top left) Stu, Tommy, Didi, Chuckie, Angelica, Phil, Lil, and Spike.

predicaments of adolescence, like self-esteem, peer-pressure, bullying, romantic and platonic relationships, gossip and rumors. Doug would narrate each episode as he wrote about it in his journal, and the show incorporated many imaginary scenes that played out Doug's fears and fantasies. Like *Rugrats*, every episode of *Doug* had an implicit moral lesson that arose out of what Doug had experienced and learned in that episode.[27]

Completing the Nicktoons block was *The Ren & Stimpy Show*. *Ren & Stimpy* was wildly creative and difficult to describe. As one source put it: "An intense, hyperactive Chihuahua (Is there any other kind?) and a happy-go-lucky, empty-brained cat share bizarre and often repulsive adventures. Their experiences usually involve hairballs, filthy litterboxes, 'magic nose goblins,' sentient farts, jars of spit, outhouses, eating dirt, monkey vermin and any other imaginable disgusting substance."[28] Unlike *Rugrats* and *Doug*, *Ren & Stimpy* didn't try to be educational or moralistic, though it did embody Nickelodeon's mission to "just let kids be kids." As the show's creator, John Krikfalusi, explained, "I'm on the kids' side.... You poor kids! You have to go to school during the week, you have to go to church on Sunday, you have to listen to your parents give you rules after school, you have to do your goddamn homework.... You don't want to get morals in your televisions shows, movies and cartoons. Yet, everyone wants to give them to you. There are non-stop authority figures. My idea was to give kids at least a half hour off every week, when they don't have somebody telling them what to do."[29] *Ren & Stimpy*'s absurdist and scatological humor, sexual innuendo, and violence quickly made it controversial and generated frequent internal clashes at Nickelodeon that eventually led to Krikfalusi's departure, but it ran for five seasons, received critical acclaim, and developed a cult following among adolescents and young adults.[30]

Nickelodeon's *Ren & Stimpy* was a wildly creative show about a nervous, hyperactive Chihuahua and his trusting feline sidekick. The show's scatological humor, sexual innuendo, and violence made it controversial and generated frequent internal clashes at Nickelodeon.

Premiering in 1993, *Rocko's Modern Life* was the fourth show added to the Nicktoons block. *Rocko* was a very edgy, absurdist cartoon in the mold of *Ren & Stimpy*, centering on the surreal life of an anthropomorphic Australian-immigrant wallaby named Rocko, who was constantly overwhelmed by the complexities of life, and his friends: Heffer, a gluttonous steer; Filburt, a neurotic turtle; and Spunky, Rocko's faithful dog. With lots of cartoon violence, sexual allusions, double-entendres, satirical social commentary, and other forms of adult humor, the show was criticized by some as inappropriate for children.

Hey Arnold, a Nick cartoon which debuted in 1996, was a more conventional child-focused series. The show centered on the day-to-day life of Arnold, a fourth grader living with his eccentric but loving grandparents, who owned a boarding house in the city, and Arnold's friends and school classmates, like street-smart Gerald, and Helga, who was always bullying Arnold as a cover-up for the secret crush she had on him. Plotlines often involved Arnold trying to help a schoolmate or boarding house tenant deal with a personal problem or dealing with a predicament of his own.

Among other popular Nickelodeon shows were several live-action series that were aimed at older children and tweens. *Are You Afraid of the Dark?* was an anthology series that dramatized the scary stories a group of teens called "The Midnight Society" would tell each other every week, when they met at a secret location in the woods after dark. In a nod to 60s sci-fi show *The Twilight Zone*, each story teller would start their tale with the phrase "Submitted for the approval of the Midnight Society..." The stories usually involved paranormal phenomena, like demons, ghosts, haunted houses, aliens, magical curses, witches, and so on, and centered on what happened when unsuspecting young people encountered one of these forces. But there was almost always a happy ending, with the potential victim safely escaping from danger.

The Adventures of Pete & Pete, which debuted in 1993, was a surreal sitcom about the hilarious exploits of two brothers, teenager Pete Wrigley and preteen "Little Pete," who lived in a peaceful suburban neighborhood which, in Little Pete's eyes, seemed very strange and illogical (as the adult world can sometimes look to children). The series earned hipster cachet for its music and frequent cameos by non-mainstream celebrity guest stars, like Iggy Pop, Steve Buscemi, Janeane Garofalo, Patty Hearst, and Debbie Harry.

Nickelodeon also built on its success with its earlier show, *You Can't Do That on Television*, by producing another sketch comedy-variety show,

All That, in 1994. Like a junior version of *Saturday Night Live*, *All That* featured a mix of short comedy sketches and performances by musical guests. The sketches parodied various aspects of contemporary culture and were performed by a racially diverse cast of child and teen performers, several of whom went on to star in other Nickelodeon series.

Two performers from *All That*, Kenan Thompson and Kel Mitchell, became the stars of teen sitcom *Kenan and Kel*, which debuted in 1996. The two played a pair of teenage friends who were constantly getting into and out of trouble as they pursued various schemes that were meant to improve their lives or solve problems they encountered but only ended up creating unexpected complications. Kel was the more dim-witted of the two, who usually dreamed up the various schemes and strategies that went awry, while Kenan was the (slightly) more cerebral character who tried to foil Kel's misguided plans or dealt with their consequences. Kenan and Kel were both African American, and the show's theme song was performed by Coolio, a popular hip-hop singer at the time, putting the viewer on notice that the show had an urban sensibility.[31]

Having begun to carve out a programming niche aimed at adolescents with series like *Clarissa Explains It All*, Nickelodeon turned to the opposite end of the children's market with an initiative to broaden its slate of educational programs for preschoolers. In 1988, Nickelodeon had created a programming block for preschoolers called Nick Jr., which ran from 9 a.m. to 3 p.m. on weekdays, but the block initially had a relatively low profile. In 1994, the network decided to strengthen the block by adding several new original shows. *Gullah Gullah Island* was a live-action show with sing-along music, revolving around an African American family living on the fictional Gullah Gullah Island. The first preschool series on a commercial network to star a black family, the show was inspired by the Gullah culture and language of the Sea Islands off the coast of South Carolina and Georgia, which were populated by descendants of former slaves. Each episode featured singing, dancing, and lessons about telling the truth, social skills, problem solving, and cross-cultural understanding and cooperation.[32]

Gullah Gullah Island was infused with music, and music also played a prominent role in *Allegra's Window*, which dealt with the daily life of a precocious little girl puppet named Allegra. The show depicted Allegra's daily life, as she and her big brother Rondo, best friend Lindi, and pesky neighborhood cat Riff tried to learn about the world around them. At the end of each episode, Allegra would sit at her window and reflect on the lessons she had learned. The series' format was a blend of live actors, puppets, and animation, along the lines of *Sesame Street*. Music was a central element of the show, and many characters' names were musically inspired, like Allegra herself, Lindi, Rondo, Riff, Reed, Ms. Melody, Ellington, Sonata, Clef, Woofer, Aria, and Tweeter. The series included numerous original songs, and there were also segments that featured talking musical instruments that hung on the wall of a music shop.

The show that really put Nickelodeon on the map for innovative and successful preschool programming was *Blue's Clues*, which premiered in 1996 and soon became the highest-rated preschool show on commercial television, remaining in production for a decade. The series was a combination of live action and animation, following an animated dog named Blue as she left behind clues in a problem-solving game played with the host and viewers. Following the *Sesame Street* model, *Blue's Clues* was explicitly developed to be both educational and entertaining, with each

Nickelodeon used extensive research to create *Blue's Clues*, an educational show designed to encourage active engagement by preschoolers. Seen here is animated canine star Blue surrounded by (clockwise from left) Shovel and Pail, Mailbox, and Tickety Tock.

episode designed to meet specific cognitive curriculum goals. As with *Sesame Street*, research with preschoolers was integrated into all stages of the show's creative and production process. Where the two programs differed, however, was that *Blue's Clues* made no attempt to appeal to parents. Instead, *Blue's Clues* only employed formats and content specifically aimed at addressing preschoolers' tastes, preferences, and cognitive abilities.

Blue's Clues was designed around a growing body of research that provided convincing empirical evidence that preschool children are intellectually active while watching television. It totally rejected the commonly-held misconception that television viewing is inherently passive. The series was therefore structured to provide opportunities for active participation from its viewers. Like *Ding Dong School*'s Miss Francis and *Mister Rogers' Neighborhood*'s Fred Rogers before him, the series host would talk directly to home viewers, asking for their assistance in solving the puzzle and posing questions to guide them through the problem-solving process. He would then wait, patiently giving them time to think and respond. To help preschool viewers reach higher levels of cognitive involvement and gain greater mastery of the show's curriculum, each episode of the show was initially repeated daily for five consecutive days, taking advantage of preschoolers' love of repetition.[33]

Blue's Clues did not look like anything else on television at the time. The animation team for the show combined high-tech and low-tech methods by creating and photographing three-dimensional objects made from simple materials like paper, fabric, or pipe-cleaners, then cutting out the photographs and scanning the images into a Macintosh computer, where they could be quickly and easily animated for each scene. This cutout animation technique and the use of primary colors made the show look childlike and simplistic, like a storybook that had been freshly cut and glued together.

Nickelodeon became synonymous with children's television in the 1990s, but the decade was also dominated by a couple of other megahits on the newer broadcast networks, Fox and The WB. Fox entered the children's television market in 1990 with the launch of a programming block called The Fox Children's Network, later changed to simply Fox Kids. Fox Kids mostly consisted of animated shows that aired on Saturday mornings and weekday afternoons, like *Bobby's World, Taz-mania, Batman: The Animated Series, Eek! The Cat, X-Men*, and *Steven Spielberg Presents Animaniacs*.

Animaniacs, which later moved to The WB network, was an animated variety show produced by Steven Spielberg and Warner Brothers. It fea-

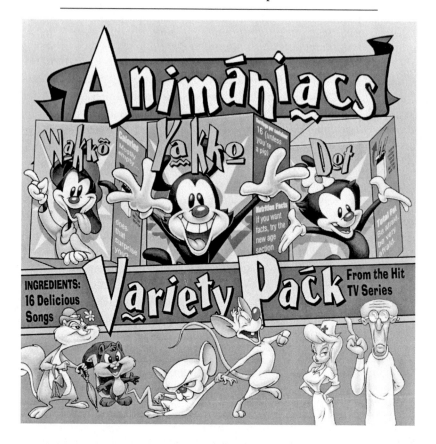

Animaniacs starred the fictional Warner siblings Wakko, Yakko, and Dot, and included (bottom row, left to right) Slappy Squirrel and Skippy Squirrel; the Brain and Pinky, who later got their own spin-off series *Pinky and the Brain*; and Hello Nurse and Dr. Otto Scratchansniff.

tured the supposed Warner brothers, Yakko and Wakko, and their sister Dot, who created mayhem and wreaked havoc in the lives of everyone they encountered. The show was a mix of rapid-fire witty dialogue, slapstick, pop culture references, and cartoon violence, all presented in Warner Bros.' classic animation style. It also included comical educational segments on subjects like history, geography, math, astronomy, science, and social studies, often in musical form.

These shows did well, but Fox struck children's programming gold with another new entry in 1993, *Mighty Morphin Power Rangers. Power Rangers* was a live-action show produced by Haim Saban and Shuki Levy, about a group of teenagers who had been chosen to protect the world from alien invaders. Their main adversary was Rita Repulsa, a space villainess who had been captured 10,000 years earlier by the wise sage Zordon and imprisoned in an extraterrestrial container but inadvertently freed by U.S. astronauts. Zordon recruited the teens to help him recapture Rita and battle against other villains like Lord Zedd, Rito Revolto, and Master Vile, all of whom wanted to conquer Earth. Thanks to Zordon, the teens could "morph" into spandex-clad superheroes with special powers, and they had the ability to summon the Zords, huge robotic dinosaur-like creatures. The Zords functioned as both vehicles and fighting machines, and each Power Ranger had his or her personal Zord, which they could enter and control. The Zords could also meld together into a giant Megazord that the Power Rangers could pilot in battles against the invaders.

The series was adapted from a popular Japanese TV show and used stock action footage from the show, with American voices dubbed in, whenever the Power Rangers were in their superhero forms. Since the Power Rangers wore helmets with visors that covered their faces, the voice dubbing was not apparent. To appeal to girls in the audience, there was at least one female Ranger included in the group, usually cast as the Pink Ranger or some other "feminine" color, and they were just as adept as the male Rangers in using their martial arts skills and superhero powers to battle the invaders.

Power Rangers generated considerable controversy and parent complaints about its level of violence. Nevertheless, the show and the vast array of licensed products that it generated were immediate hits, and *Power Rangers* went on to become an icon of 1990s pop culture. Naturally, a host of copy-cat shows soon followed, all of them live-action series with adapted Japanese stock footage, featuring teams of teenage superheroes with special powers fighting alien or fantasy villains, like *Superhuman Samurai Syber-Squad, V.R. Troopers, Tattooed Teenage Alien Fighters from Beverly Hills, Masked Rider,* and *Big Bad Beetleborgs.* An updated version of *Power Rangers* began airing on the ABC Kids block in 2010. The series also generated two feature films, one released in 1995 and another in 2017.

Mighty Morphin Power Rangers was one of two hit children's shows in the 1990s that intensified the trend toward what Mark I. West has referred to as "the Japanification of children's popular culture" in the U.S,[34] a case in point of the historic trend toward globalization in the 90s. The development of home videogames produced by Japanese companies in the 1980s introduced many children to elements of Japanese beliefs and culture, which gave different meaning to some of the elements of classic Western children's stories and themes. For example, Japanese culture differs from Western culture in its conception of monsters. While monsters in Western culture are powerful creatures that are usually evil and a threat to society, Japanese monsters are imaginary or fantasy creatures which may be powerful but are not inherently "bad." Humans can have positive relationships with these creatures, which seem to more closely resemble elves or fairies in traditional Western culture than what is conjured up by the term "monster." In *Mighty Morphin Power Rangers*, the teenage superheroes' symbiosis with their unambiguously "good" Zords empowered the Rangers, and home viewers could experience that positive force vicariously.[35]

A similar dynamic was one of the factors behind the popularity of *Pokémon*, another television show originating in Japan, which debuted on The WB network in February 1999 and quickly became a national craze. *Pokémon*, which is short for "pocket monsters," began life as a Nintendo Game Boy videogame but grew into a multi-billion-dollar franchise that included TV shows, feature films, a trading-card game, and endless licensed toys. The show's premise, like that of the videogame and trading card game, was that there were little wild monster creatures with various powers that roamed the countryside and could be caught with special Poké Balls by Pokémon trainers, who kept them as pets and trained them to fight battles. In the Pokémon universe, a Pokémon trainer would usually begin to collect these creatures at the age of ten. Trainers would travel to Pokémon Gyms to compete and earn badges by winning, and ten badges would qualify a trainer to enter the Pokémon League, a kind of Pokémon Olympics, where a Pokémon Master would be anointed.

In the animated *Pokémon* TV show, the main character was a ten-year-old boy named Ash, a Pokémon trainer who aspired to become a Pokémon Master. Together with his friends, ten-year-old Misty and twelve-year-old Brock, and his own Pokémon, Pikachu, Ash searched the world for all 150 Pokémon, while trying to avoid or outwit his evil rivals, teenagers Jessie and James of Team Rocket, and their Pokémon, Meowth, who were always trying to capture and steal Pikachu.

A central element in the Pokémon world was the idea of collecting as many Pokémon as possible, learning all there was to know about the Pokémon monsters' various powers at their different evolutionary stages, and then using that knowledge to control them. "In the same way that memorizing dinosaur names gives kids a feeling of authority over powerful creatures, viewers and players of *Pokémon* memorize hundreds of creature names, powers, and statistics.... The motto 'Gotta catch 'em all!' appeals to kids' need to collect things, to gain power in a world where they have little voice, and to 'learn the way to take command.'"[36]

A huge hit on The WB, *Pokémon* was an entire world and body of knowledge where children were the experts and from which adults were excluded. The show's star characters were (from left to right) Misty, Ash, Pikachu, and Brock.

Pokémon was an entire world and body of knowledge where children were the experts and from which adults were excluded. It gave viewers and players a feeling of mastery, control, and independence. In the fictional *Pokémon* universe, children who wanted to become Pokémon trainers were expected to leave home at the age of ten and travel the world on their own, where they could explore, have adventures, and possibly face danger every day, with no adult authority figures telling them what to do. For American children in the late nineties, who were increasingly forbidden from playing outside unsupervised or exploring their neighborhoods on their own, the Pokémon universe must have seemed very appealing, giving them a virtual world they could explore and master independently.

In *Pokémon*, power and status were derived from competition based on knowledge and expertise rather than physical strength, so any child, regardless of age or size, had a chance for respect, fame, and glory. Gender was also not a factor. Ash, the lead character, was a boy, but his friend Misty, another Pokémon trainer, was portrayed as very much his equal.

Girls were as likely to be Pokémon trainers as boys, and they, too, had to leave home at age ten to pursue their quest.

Though there had been a handful of Japanese cartoon shows on American television previously, *Pokémon's* enormous success generated an increase in such shows over the next few years. For example, there was *Dragonball Z*, originally derived from a Japanese manga, or comic book as they are sometimes called, although "graphic novel" would be a better term for this type of serial publication. A successful manga was often made into an anime (for animated) series, and this was the evolution of *Dragonball Z*, which debuted on the Cartoon Network in 1999 and later moved to The WB. The show followed the adventures of lead character Goku and his friends as they battled to defend the Earth against various intergalactic villains, powerful androids, and other evil magical creatures.

Digimon, which began airing on Fox Kids in 1999, was an almost perfect clone of *Pokémon*. It, too, was a Japanese media franchise that included virtual pet toys, anime, manga, videogames, films, and a trading card game. The franchise was built around Digimon creatures, which were little monsters living in a digital parallel universe spawned by the Earth's various communication networks. Digimon were raised by humans called "Digidestined" or "Tamers," and they would team up to try to defeat evil Digimon and human villains trying to destroy their digital world.

One of the more controversial pre–*Pokémon* anime was *Sailor Moon*. Popular in Japan as both manga and anime, *Sailor Moon* appeared in syndication on various channels in the U.S. as early as 1995, but it struggled to find an audience until it was picked up by Cartoon Network in 1998. The series followed the adventures of a young schoolgirl named Usagi, who could transform into Sailor Moon, a guardian who must fight to save the Earth from the forces of evil. Usagi assembles a team of fellow female Sailor Guardians, and they discover that in their previous lives they were members of an ancient moon kingdom which was destroyed in a war with the Dark Kingdom. The moon kingdom's ruler, Queen Serenity, sent her daughter Princess Serenity, together with her protectors the Sailor Guardians, into the future to be reborn through the power of a magical Silver Crystal. Usagi and her comrades set out to find the Silver Crystal and keep it from being stolen by the forces of the Dark Kingdom, who want to use it to destroy the solar system.

Sailor Moon was one of the first anime series to star a girl heroine, and it was seen as empowering to girls and women. But the show generated some controversy because, even though Sailor Moon and her accompanying Sailor Guardians were strong, aggressive, independent fighters who thwarted evil, they were drawn with exaggerated, hyper-feminine features—sexy schoolgirl outfits with very short pleated skirts emphasizing extremely long legs, and very large round orb-like eyes. These stylizations of the female form are typical in representations of girls and women in Japanese manga, especially those which, intended for adults, are explicitly erotic.

Sailor Moon would seem to have had a strong influence on *The Powerpuff Girls*, an American anime-like series that also debuted on the Cartoon Network in 1998. In fact, *The Powerpuff Girls* seemed like a playful parody of *Sailor Moon*, only without the sexual innuendo perceived by Western sensibilities. The series featured Blossom, Bubbles, and Buttercup, three little girls with superpowers, and their father, Professor Utonium, who had created them from a mixture of "sugar, spice, and everything nice." The girls were frequently called upon to defend their town from villains and giant monsters, but they also had to deal with normal issues in young children's lives, like sibling rivalry, loose teeth, bed wetting, or reliance on a security blanket. Unlike the animation style of *Sailor Moon*,

On the Cartoon Network's *Powerpuff Girls*, Bubbles, Blossom, and Buttercup (seen here from left to right) were frequently called upon to defend their town from villains and giant monsters, but they also had to deal with annoying issues like sibling rivalry, loose teeth, bed wetting, or reliance on a security blanket.

the *Powerpuff Girls* were drawn with large heads, only the slightest a hint of a torso, and stubby arms and legs, wearing white tights with little black Mary Jane shoes. They did have enormous round eyes, but on their childlike little faces, their eyes just seemed to enhance their innocent appearance. The show was praised for its mix of low-brow and adult-level humor and frequent pop culture references, and it became one of the Cartoon Network's most successful shows, attracting both boys and girls as well as older viewers.

Cartoon Network had launched in 1992 as a potential programming destination for children and a rival to Nickelodeon, but it would be some years until they could mount a true challenge to the cable leader in children's TV. They began to hit their stride with original cartoons, like *Dexter's Laboratory* in 1996. Dexter was a boy genius who was always creating inventions in the science laboratory in his basement, which he somehow kept secret from his cheerful but oblivious parents. He was constantly tormented by his air-head sister Dee Dee, who managed to get into his lab despite Dexter's best efforts to keep her out, and he engaged in a bitter rivalry with his neighbor, evil fellow-genius Mandark.

With its portrayal of Dexter's clueless parents, the Cartoon Network seemed to take a page from Nickelodeon. Other original Cartoon Network shows emulated the surreal and gross style of Nick's *Ren & Stimpy*, a style really more suited to Cartoon Network, which presented itself as a network for both adults and children, than to Nickelodeon. For example, *Cow and Chicken*, which debuted in 1997, followed the adventures of a cow named Cow and her chicken brother named (you guessed it) Chicken. In an exaggerated parody of typical cartoon clichés, the series featured repulsive comedy, grotesque animation, and frequent cartoon violence, with plotlines often centered on common childhood fears and anxieties. Cow and Chicken's parents were portrayed as nutty, dimwitted humans seen only from their legs down.

Courage the Cowardly Dog, which first aired on the Cartoon Network in 1999, was about an anxiety-ridden but resourceful dog that lived with an elderly farming couple, Muriel and Eustace, out in "The Middle of Nowhere." Eustace barely tolerated Courage, while Muriel doted on him. Courage and his owners were frequently thrown into strange misadventures involving bizarre supernatural villains, with Muriel and Eustace usually oblivious to the monsters' existence. Courage frantically tried to protect them, not overcoming his fear so much as fighting through it to earn his seemingly ironic name. The show was known for its surreal, disturbing humor and its dark, often mature themes, combining elements of comedy, horror, and science fantasy.

Ed, Edd, 'n' Eddy, which debuted on the Cartoon Network in 1999, revolved around the lives and misadventures of three preteen boys living on a suburban cul-de-sac. The trio was constantly coming up with schemes to scam the other kids on the cul-de-sac out of their money, so they could buy their favorite candy, jawbreakers, but their schemes usually fell through. The neighbor kids, who understandably didn't like the Eds, were a diverse group made up of a mix of oddballs, like Jonny 2x4, a loner with an imaginary friend that was a wooden board named Plank, and the dreaded Kanker sisters, three teenagers who lived in a nearby trailer park and were in love with the three Eds. The series depicted a world populated only by children, though adults were occasionally seen in partial view.

The WB's children's shows were mostly cartoons, like *Animaniacs*, which moved to The WB from an earlier run on the Cartoon Network, and *Pinky & the Brain*, a spin-off from *Animaniacs*. Like *Animaniacs*, *Pinky & the Brain* was produced by Steven Spielberg. The show was about two lab mice living in a cage at the fictional Acme Labs research facility, who were always unsuccessfully plotting to take over the world. The mice had been genetically altered, so they could think (sort of) and talk. Brain, who looked and sounded a lot like Orson Welles, was the arrogant, scheming member of the duo, while Pinky was rather feebleminded but ever optimistic and good-natured. Brain would constantly belittle, insult, and smack Pinky around, especially when Pinky's stupidity caused Brain's schemes to fail, but ever-loyal Pinky didn't seem to mind, even laughing when Brain would hit him. As on *Animaniacs*, much of the humor on *Pinky and the Brain* was aimed at adult viewers. Parodies of pop culture icons were common, and movies were a frequent subject of the spoofs, not surprising given Spielberg's role as producer.

As more networks got into the children's television business, another prominent trend that emerged during the 1990s was a wave of new educational shows for children on the commercial television networks, generated by the requirements of the Children's Television Act. While some of these shows stretched the meaning of the term "educational," others were legitimately educational in focus. Together with the growing number of PBS shows for children, the 1990s offered the largest array of educational shows that the television industry had ever provided for children.

PBS had long been the unchallenged leader in educational programming for preschoolers since it began airing long-lived hits *Mister Rogers' Neighborhood* and *Sesame Street*. They now had another preschool blockbuster in *Barney & Friends*, which premiered in 1992. *Barney*, which had started out as a series of home videos, was a live-action show that starred a giant purple dinosaur and his dinosaur friends Baby Bop, B.J., and Riff, played by actors in full-body costumes. Like many other successful children's shows, *Barney & Friends* took a large, powerful, and dangerous creature, in this case a Tyrannosaurus Rex, and turned him into a cheerful, helpful, and loving companion. As Barney and his friends engaged in games, songs and dance routines with a group of young children, the show conveyed prosocial educational messages about love, kindness, sharing, friendship, and using your imagination.

Each episode would begin with the children engaged in an activity, and as they used their imaginations, the plush purple Barney doll on the set would come to life as the "real" full-size Barney. At the end of the episode, Barney would turn back into his small plush doll form, and the children would briefly discuss what they had done that day. This was followed by a photo montage recapping the episode, with voice-over narration by Barney summarizing the day's lessons. In later seasons, Barney would reappear at the end of the show, telling viewers, "And remember, I love you!" before finally waving good-bye.

Barney & Friends was a simple, sweet (some might say cloying), gently-paced show that used frequent repetition and an uncomplicated structure designed for preschoolers' tastes, preferences, and cognitive abilities. As with Nickelodeon's s *Blue's Clues*, no attempt was made to appeal to adult sensibilities. Though critics complained that it was too simplistic, too repetitive, and too relentlessly upbeat and saccharine, and many parents found it unwatchable, the show was enormously successful with its intended viewers and became a licensing phenomenon.

Having expanded the preschool market with *Barney* at the start of the decade, in 1998 PBS launched another show aimed at even younger viewers. *Teletubbies* was a surreal British import aimed at babies as young as one year old and designed to hold a baby's attention, while encouraging exploration and helping toddlers handle transitions from one activity to another. The show was a candy-colored combination of live action and animation, starring four baby-like fuzzy little creatures with television sets embedded in their tummies, on which they could watch video images of real children, and TV antennas sprouting from their heads. The Teletubbies, named Tinky-Winky, Dipsy, Laa Laa, and Po, together with their friend Noo-Noo, an anthropomorphic vacuum cleaner, lived in idyllic grassy Teletubbyland, where they would have fun laughing, running around, rolling on the ground, and doing other toddler activities. The Teletubbies cooed, babbled, and talked baby-talk, while an off-screen Narrator, mysterious Voice Trumpets that emerged from the ground, and a

Many parents found PBS' *Barney* repetitive and simplistic, but children adored the big purple dinosaur. Seen here (from left to right) are Baby Bop, Barney, Miss Etta Kette, Scooter McNutty and BJ.

Magic Windmill helped direct the Teletubbies' activities. A bright sun with a real baby's face superimposed on it would rise and set at the beginning and end of the show, and laugh when funny things happened, while Talking Flowers provided commentary and rabbits ran about below. At the end of every episode, a soothing male voice would say: "The sun is setting in the sky. Teletubbies say goodbye." Reluctantly, the Teletubbies would wave and vanish down a hole in the grass.

Teletubbies generated a degree of criticism for its use of babbling and baby-talk, which some child development experts thought would slow toddlers' language learning. Other critics questioned the show's entire premise, asserting that children under the age of two should not be watching television at all. But the series' producers contended that babies already sit in front of the television set, and this was a show they could understand and enjoy.[37]

Teletubbies was a surreal British import aimed at babies as young as one year old and designed to hold a baby's attention. The Teletubbies consisted of (clockwise from top) Tinky Winky, Dipsy, Po, and Laa-Laa.

A bizarre controversy arose around *Teletubbies* in 1999, when conservative pundit and televangelist Jerry Falwell claimed that Tinky-Winky was homosexual and a bad role model for children.[38] Falwell based his claim on Tinky-Winky's purple color, triangle-shaped antenna, and the red handbag that he sometimes carried. Each of the Teletubbies had a personal prop that helped them explore the world; Tinky-Winky's handbag allowed him to demonstrate the concept of volume. The absurdity of this kerfuffle only makes sense in the context of the toxic political environment of the 90s, when a "culture war" raged in Washington and there were sustained efforts to delegitimize many public institutions which were seen by some to reflect an unacceptable moral or political bias. Public television was a frequent target.

This political sideshow and the essential weirdness (to adult eyes) of the show notwithstanding, *Teletubbies* was very popular. It competed against home videos claiming to stimulate infant cognitive abilities, like the *Baby Einstein* series, which were being snapped up by parents eager to help their children gain an educational advantage, and the sooner, the better. There was clearly a demand for this kind of media for babies, and despite the controversies and complaints that surrounded *Teletubbies*, it drew a large audience. Its surreal setting and characters, bright colors and psychedelic patterns, and occasional physical comedy also gained it a cult following among young adults. *Teletubbies* aired on PBS for ten years, and it was acquired by Nickelodeon in 2016.

PBS launched another long-lasting hit a few years later with *Arthur*, an animated show aimed at young elementary-school children. *Arthur* debuted in 1996 and is still in production, having become one of the longest-running children's shows on PBS. Based on a popular book series, the show revolves around the lives of Arthur, an eight-year-old anthropomorphic aardvark, and his family and friends. According to PBS' *Arthur* website, "*Arthur*'s goal is to help foster an interest in reading and writing, and to encourage positive social skills … through engaging, emotional stories that explore issues faced by real kids. It is a comedy that tells these stories from a kid's point of view without moralizing or talking down. Situations on *Arthur* develop in realistic ways, and don't always turn out as we—or Arthur and his friends—might expect." Although ostensibly a comedy, the show regularly deals with the characteristic issues faced by school-age children, like jealousy, peer pressure, bullying, and homework, and has even addressed such serious topics as dyslexia, Asperger's Syndrome, and cancer. Arthur's parents and those of his friends are shown struggling with the demands of parenting and the stress from working hard at middle-class jobs, though they cheerfully maintain a positive atti-tude. Like *Sesame Street, Arthur* has featured many celebrity guest stars, each providing the voice for his or her anthropomorphic animal counter-part, and it regularly includes references to popular culture and satirical parodies that are probably over the heads of its younger viewers. As a result, in addition to its large audience of children, *Arthur* has also attracted an active adult fan base.

Throughout the course of the nineties, PBS continued to premiere other new innovative and substantive educational shows for children. These included *Where in the World Is Carmen Sandiego?*, a game show based on a popular computer game, that taught geography while it engaged viewers in tracking down an international thief; *Ghostwriter*, a mystery series aimed at teaching reading and writing skills; *The Puzzle Place*, a Muppet show designed to promote respect for others; and *Wishbone*, a live-action series starring a Jack Russell terrier who acted out classic chil-dren's stories.

Besides PBS and Nickelodeon, other new commercial networks also contended for market share among television's tiniest viewers, creating blocks of educational programming for the preschool audience. The Fox Cubhouse, which debuted in 1994, featured several educational shows, including *Rimba's Island*, where puppets representing animals from Native American folklore sang, danced, and told stories. The series was intended to introduce children to shapes, colors, and letters, as well as prosocial values like self-esteem, cultural diversity, and respect for the environment.

The Disney Channel's preschool block was originally called Play-house Disney and later renamed Disney Jr. *Bear in the Big Blue House*, one of its most popular programs, first went on the air in 1997. A puppet show produced by the Jim Henson Company, creators of the Muppets, the show's main character was a singing seven-foot-tall bear, who lived in the Big Blue House with his animal friends Ojo, Tutter, Treelo, Pip, Pop, and Shadow. In each episode, Bear and his pals would have adven-tures that conveyed lessons about problem-solving, sharing, cooperation, and other social skills.

The Cartoon Network's preschool entry, premiering in 1996, was a live-action show called *Big Bag*, produced by Children's Television Work-shop, the creator of *Sesame Street*, and also featuring Muppets from the Jim Henson Company. Like many other educational series for preschool-ers, *Big Bag* was designed to convey social lessons through the adventures of the characters on the show. The central Muppet characters were a dog named Chelli and his best friend Bag (an anthropomorphic paper bag), who interacted with a large cast of human characters, including an assortment of child friends. Like *Sesame Street*, the show also featured a number of regular animated segments.

Several new science education shows for school-age children premiered in the nineties. *Beakman's World*, syndicated to CBS and then to The Learning Channel on cable, followed a live-action format somewhat in the style of the old *Soupy Sales* show. Debuting in 1992, it starred Paul Zaloom as Beakman, a wild-haired, manic, eccentric scientist who performed wacky experiments and demonstrations in response to viewer mail asking about scientific concepts like density, electricity, and even flatulence. When his experiments went well, he would exclaim, "Zaloom!" Other characters on the show were Beakman's female assistant, whose name changed throughout the show's run, and Beakman's lab rat, Lester the Rat, initially a puppet but later played by a man in a tattered rat costume. In a brief segment that appeared at various points in the show, two puppet penguins named Don and Herb would be seen watching *Beakman's World* on their TV at the South Pole, in homage to Don Herbert, star of the show that established the genre for popularizing and teaching about science concepts, *Watch Mr. Wizard*.

Like *Beakman's World*, *Bill Nye the Science Guy*, which premiered on PBS a year later, was another update of the *Mr. Wizard* approach. Nye, as a scientist in a blue lab coat and bow tie, starred in a fast-paced show that used comedy and demonstrations with everyday objects to illustrate scientific processes and concepts. Music was an important element in the show, and there were parodies of popular songs or

Bill Nye the Science Guy was a fast-paced show on PBS that used comedy, pop music parodies, and demonstrations with everyday objects to illustrate scientific processes and concepts.

music videos in many episodes, with Nye replacing the song's lyrics with his explanation of the topic covered in that episode. Outtakes and bloopers were often shown, adding to the comedy.

The Magic School Bus took a different approach to science education. Based on the eponymous popular book series, *The Magic School Bus* was the first fully animated show to air on PBS when it debuted in 1994. Comedian Lily Tomlin provided the voice of the show's lead character, elementary school science teacher Ms. Frizzle, breaking the gender stereotype that science was a male domain. Ms. Frizzle took her students on field trips in a magical school bus, which transformed into a plane, a submarine, a spaceship, or even a miniaturized vehicle small enough to travel through the human body, going anywhere to give her students and home viewers a close-up view of the world of nature and science.

The ABC network also presented two animated science shows for children, *Cro* in 1993 and *Science Court* in 1997. Inspired by author David Macaulay's book, *The Way Things Work*, *Cro* was intended to teach children about the basic concepts of physics, engineering, and technology. The title character was an orphaned Cro-Magnon cave boy who lived with a family of Neanderthals and used his superior knowledge and intelligence (then an accepted paleo-anthropological paradigm) to help his community address problems and needs by applying the principles of physics. *Science Court* (later renamed *Squigglevision*, for its unique animation style) used a courtroom trial format to teach scientific principles and debunk scientific misconceptions. In each episode, two opposing lawyers would argue a case involving a point of science, like gravity, flight, energy, or matter. As the case unfolded, humor and music would be used to highlight and enliven the proceedings and help illustrate scientific concepts. As in *The Magic School Bus*, the science experts on this show were women. The female trial lawyer, Alison Krempel, was portrayed as modest, intelligent, and kind, and her logical arguments would explain the scientific points being made, while her opponent, Doug Savage, who was arrogant, ignorant, and unscrupulous, inevitably exposed his own scientific misconceptions as he attempted to make his case. The presiding judge, also a woman, was voiced by comic Paula Poundstone.

Science was not the only subject of substantive educational shows on the commercial networks. *Where in the World Is Carmen Sandiego?*, which debuted on Fox in 1994, was an animated version of the similarly-titled live-action show on PBS. It took place inside a home computer, where a teen detective duo, Ivy and Zack, followed clues as they pursued an international thief around the globe, providing lessons about world geography along the way. On Kids' WB, animated series *Histeria!*, which premiered in 1998, taught history through satirical skits and song parodies, along with generous doses of slapstick comedy. *Gladiators 2000*, first syndicated in 1994, was a children's version of popular game show *American Gladiators*. The show featured two pairs of children competing in physical challenges and answering questions about health, fitness, and nutrition.

Nickelodeon had one of the few news shows for children, *Nick News with Linda Ellerbee*, which debuted in 1992. Intended for tweens and teens, the weekly live-action show covered important current events and social issues, and provided a forum for teens to discuss and give their opinions about often sensitive and controversial topics.

On the TBS and Kids' WB channels, a new show which premiered in 1990, *Captain Planet and the Planeteers*, promoted activism to save the planet from pollution and other environmental ills. By this time, environmentalism had become a national and global movement, and organizations like Greenpeace and the World Wildlife Fund had become well-known to the public. Adapting the *Power Rangers* concept, *Captain Planet* was an animated space adventure about superhero Captain Planet and his force of five teen Planeteers from around the world, who battled environmental villains destroying the planet through pollution, deforestation, and poaching. The Planeteers each had a magical ring given to them by Gaia, the spirit of the Earth, which granted them power over a specific realm— Earth, Fire, Wind, Water, and Heart. When they encountered situations in which their indi-

Captain Planet and the Planeteers was an animated eco-action-adventure show about superhero Captain Planet and his force of five teen Planeteers from around the world who protected the Earth from pollution, deforestation, and poaching. The show promoted environmental responsibility.

vidual powers were not enough to stop the villains, they would call on superhero Captain Planet by shouting, "Let our powers combine!" and then activating all their powers one after the other. Once Captain Planet appeared, he would absorb all the Planeteers' powers in magnified form, and the Planeteers would shout, "Go Planet!" as Captain Planet flew off to fight the villains. On his triumphant return, he would restore the Planeteers' powers with his catchphrase, "The power is yours!" Each episode would end with a "Planeteer Alert" in which an environmental issue was discussed and viewers were told how they could contribute and become "part of the solution, not the pollution." The series tried to illustrate to young viewers that they were not powerless to stop the destruction of the ecosystem and that group action was more effective than individual efforts.

Most of the other new educational shows aimed at children that were added to the networks' schedules during this decade dealt with providing life lessons or enhancing social skills. On Fox Kids, there was *Life with Louie*, a cartoon series based on the childhood of comic Louie Anderson; *C-Bear and Jamal*, an animated series about a ten-year-old African American boy and his rap-singing teddy bear, who showed Jamal imaginary scenarios to help him make good choices in life; and *Angela Anaconda*, a series produced in clip-art animation, about an imaginative eight-year-old girl who rejects common female role stereotypes. ABC had *Pepper Ann*, a cartoon based on a popular comic strip, which followed the daily ups and downs in the lives of Pepper Ann and her friends in middle-school. Fox Kids also had *Recess*, a cartoon about a group of elementary school children who had formed their own social structure during recess. Their social system was a microcosm of society, complete with government, class system, and set of unwritten laws, and it was ruled by sixth-grader King Bob, who deployed a team of classmate enforcers to make sure his decrees were carried out. The series addressed issues of balancing individual freedom against conformity to social rules and norms. Its depiction of the playground hierarchy and the school administration, together with its introductory music and overall style, made it seem like a parody of classic prison movies.

The WB's contribution to this programming category was *Detention*, a short-lived animated series about a group of misfit rebellious seventh-graders at the fictional Benedict Arnold Middle School, who regularly ended up in detention. The show's premise was similar to that of *The Breakfast Club*, a popular 1985 John Hughes movie. The series' educational goal was to convey lessons about how to make responsible decisions.

In a trend that was just starting to make itself felt, the digital revolution that was underway and permeating life, especially among children and teens, was now beginning to have an impact on programs' style and substance. For example, videogames were used as plot devices in shows like *Clarissa Explains It All* and *Where in the World Is Carmen Sandiego?*, and the animation technique that gave *Blue's Clues* its unique look was made possible by the new Mac computer's graphic capabilities.

Reboot, an animated show that premiered on ABC in 1994, was the first completely computer-animated half-hour series on television. But *Reboot* was not just digitally created, it was about *being* digital. The show's setting was the inner world of a computer system known to its inhabitants as Mainframe. The premise was that there were "Guardians" whose job it was to keep Mainframe working properly, and the series followed the adventures of one of these Guardians, named Bob, and his pals Enzo and Dot Matrix as they fought to protect Mainframe from evil viruses Megabyte and Hexadecimal.

Another early show completely produced by computer animation was *Rolie Polie Olie*, a series for preschoolers which debuted on the Disney Channel in 1998. The show revolved around the adventures of Olie, a young little robot living with his family The Polies in a geometric world called Planet Polie. The show followed Olie as he had various adventures and learned important life lessons while growing up. Olie and his family were all drawn using spheres, while his best friend Billy Bevel and his family, who came from the Planet Cubey, were drawn with cubes.

With all the rapid advances made in computer-generated animation since these early efforts, both these shows looked rather primitive within just a year or two. But they were groundbreaking in their use of computer imagery with which children were becoming familiar through playing games on computers and videogame systems. In short, as one would expect, the key technology of the age found its way into children's lives, both in real life and on television.

Television Advertising and Marketing to Children

The primary focus of the Children's Television Act of 1990 was to improve the quality of children's television by requiring commercial networks to air more informational and educational programming for children. The act also confirmed the FCC's support for enforcement of time limits on commercials during children's shows, to 10.5 minutes per hour on weekends and 12 minutes per hour on weekdays, and it required distinct transitions to be inserted before and after commercial breaks.

Though "program-length commercials" had previously been banned, it was not clear if this ban applied to TV shows that were one element in a multi-faceted media and licensing franchise that usually included licensed toys. In the 1990s, a growing number of shows began to fit this description, from *Rugrats* to *Power Rangers* to *Pokémon*. In fact, it was rare that a successful children's TV show did not try to generate additional profits from licensing and merchandising, and most shows were developed with these opportunities in mind. Even non-commercial shows on PBS engaged in licensing their brands in order to raise more money to support their programming efforts. *Barney* began life as a series of home videos before becoming a major licensing franchise. Children's Television Workshop, which had developed a large and very successful *Sesame Street* licensing arm, unexpectedly created a national craze in 1996 when its interactive Tickle Me Elmo doll, produced by Tyco Preschool, sold out before Christmas, leading to a shopping frenzy as consumers desperately tried to find one of the toys to buy for their children.

Stay Tuned...

As the 1990s were coming to an end and a new century was about to dawn, the world suffered a case of what might be called millennium madness. The computer industry, which by now was a huge driver of the economy, was unnerved by reports that the internal clocks integral to all computers would be unable to cope with the changeover to the year 2000, that somehow the digits would not compute. Well-respected computer scientists thought the danger was real and that even a few malfunctioning computer calendars might bring down the Internet, crash the electrical grid, and paralyze communications and the stock market. Things had been going so well—the economy had been booming for years, the country was at peace—that Americans had become unused to the crisis mentality, and now it seemed that The Machines might turn against us in a world-ending act of self-destruction. In retrospect, we must classify this as a collective folly, a wave of irrational thinking set off by apocalyptic superstition in the guise of modern technology. Nevertheless, it had just enough plausibility that a significant number of computer programmers in the waning years of the 1990s were busily employed making fixes for the "Millennium Bug." The rest of the population waited nervously, their computers unplugged and shut down before midnight on December 31. Not a few had restocked their bunkers and old bomb shelters.[39]

In this loopy, nervous world, everyone needed a break, preferably one that offered a return to more innocent times in a paradise under the sea. Otherwise, what could explain the immediate success of a new animated show on Nickelodeon in July 1999, featuring a sweet, innocent, always cheerful, bright yellow sea sponge? By that fall, *SpongeBob SquarePants* had displaced megahit *Pokémon* as the number one children's show on television, ushering in a new stage in the evolution of children's television as it entered the 21st century.

CHAPTER SEVEN

The Postmodern Child
(2000–Present)

Life in the U.S.

The birth of a new millennium could have been a moment of forward-looking optimism for the country. Following a decade of record-breaking economic growth and peace, many Americans were basking in a reaffirmation of their economic and political systems. But there would be only brief millennial euphoria. The years following the millennial celebrations came to be defined by a shocking act of terrorism on U.S. soil—the events of September 11, 2001—which plunged the country into grief, fear, and anger. A stunned public struggled to understand why and how 9/11 could have happened.

Subsequent episodic terrorist attacks in the U.S. and around the world contributed to on-going global turmoil radiating from its epicenter in the Middle East. Uprisings toppled governments or forced major reforms (nearly all of which proved temporary) in some dozen Arab countries, and radical jihadist organizations diversified and spread.[1] In the U.S., two brothers associated with radical Islam planted bombs at the Boston marathon in 2013, killing three and injuring hundreds. Similarly-inspired attacks in San Bernardino, California, in 2015, and Orlando, Florida, in 2016, left dozens dead and wounded, a pattern repeated in a tragically long list of places around the world where terrorism spread its dark seeds: Ankara and Istanbul, Paris and Nice, Belgium, Germany, India, Thailand, and more.

The new decade was also marked by two economic crises. In 2000, the "Dot.com bubble" burst, as many companies in the first wave of new Internet-based enterprises failed to prosper, defaulted on $70 billion in debt, laid off 500,000 employees, and in many cases went out of business.[2] Then, deregulation allowing banks and Wall Street speculators to trade home mortgage debt in unorthodox ways created a bubble in the housing market, which finally burst in 2007. Almost $8 trillion of home equity disappeared. The mortgage market crashed, as thousands of homeowners defaulted on loans that had been thought to be among the most secure of investments, and with it the stock market tanked, precipitating a financial panic that soon spread across the globe. Eight million Americans lost their jobs. The U.S. financial system, along with that of much of the world, teetered on the brink of collapse as the specter of global economic meltdown seemed a terrifying possibility.[3]

The mood was understandably troubled before the 2008 Presidential election, when Americans responded to a campaign of hope and change, electing Barack Obama as the first African American president of the United States. Obama's administration quickly enacted legislation to rescue the sinking U.S. auto industry, help debt-ridden homeowners, and shore up failing banks. The recession began to abate, but the damage was so extensive that economic recovery was slow and uneven. Income inequality and the resulting decline of the American middle class, longstanding trends, became pivotal political issues around which other unresolved social problems, like those of race and diversity, for example, revolved.[4]

Obama's presidency was a milestone in the U.S. population's continuing demographic shift toward greater racial and ethnic diversity. By 2000, more than a quarter of the U.S. population was non-white, increasing to more than one-third by 2014.[5] Obama's campaign and election galvanized African Americans and young people, and raised hopes for a new chapter in American race relations. Whether these hopes will be realized remains to be seen. The start of 2017 saw a conservative party in control of all three branches of government, with its own agenda for change that shared little with that of the previous administration.

The digital revolution, another systemic influence on American culture, accelerated in the 2000s. Virtually every business, if it had not already, experienced a wrenching reboot. None were more changed than those in the communications sector, which, by its nature, touched everyone's daily life. Even a seemingly minor innovation, like the integration of video cameras into cell phones, or the growth of social media, once derided as a trivial time-waster, would have unforeseen consequences, allowing individuals to document and share their lives, organize social movements, and even instigate popular uprisings.[6]

Wireless Internet became widely available, co-evolving with new generations of ever more powerful devices running increasingly sophisticated software, until the boundary between phone and computer blurred and ultimately disappeared. By 2015, 68 percent of U.S. adults owned a smartphone. The result was a digital universe in which "digital natives" like Millennials and younger children were particularly comfortable. It all happened rather quickly, the transformation of life into something largely experienced through an interactive screen.[7]

The videogame industry, which had contributed to this evolution from the beginning, continued to advance, with industry leaders Sony, Microsoft, and Nintendo releasing more advanced gaming consoles on a regular basis. As the new consoles allowed for more interactivity and better special effects, violent videogames like those in the *Grand Theft Auto* series, first released in 1997, became very popular in the 2000s. Newer versions[8] sharpened the first-person nature of the hyperviolent game, in which the player, in the role of a sociopathic criminal, roams through realistically rendered dystopias stealing cars and fighting and killing police, gang members, and anyone else who shows up. The games sparked public controversy about their potential psychological harm to young players—an issue that seems to have arisen in some form with every advance in children's media.[9]

While the earliest computer games depended on low-resolution graphics, the ambition of most designers from the beginning of gaming had been to strive for realism, offering higher resolution and providing more life-like interactivity without sacrificing game play. With the introduction of commercially viable virtual reality technology to the market after 2015,[10] a new level of immersive experience started to become part of the gamer's world.[11]

There were also a number of advancements in television and video technology that enhanced user control and interactivity. DVD's had first come out in the late 1990s and superseded videocassettes as the standard in prerecorded video by the early 2000s, enjoying a hegemony they would not hold long as technology advanced. Next up was the digital video recorder, or DVR. DVR devices like TiVo made it possible to digitally record TV broadcasts without degrading the quality of the picture (something no VCR had managed) and with unprecedented control, allowing users to watch TV shows on their own timetable and easily skip commercials. Cable TV operators began offering cable set-top boxes with built-in DVR's, making VCR's so obsolete they became grist for comedians. In addition, Video on Demand from cable providers gave viewers a library of video content stored on a central server, which they could access and view at any time. High-definition television became available to consumers in the early 2000s and grew in popularity after the government-mandated "digital transition" in 2009, when television broadcasting switched from analog to digital signals.[12]

As Internet speed and bandwidth inexorably continued to improve, online streaming of television and other video content became a reality, giving consumers yet another way to watch television content whenever they wanted to. By fall 2005, 40 percent of U.S. households had high-speed internet access, prompting the broadcast networks to begin testing online streaming of some of their shows.[13] From YouTube in 2006, to Netflix and Apple TV in 2007, to Hulu and Roku in 2008, viewers had a growing number of different services that let them watch TV content on their computers, on their videogame consoles, and in short order, on their cell phones and tablets. The diverse varieties of interfaces available to consume content proliferated so rapidly that by 2010 or so they began being referred to simply as "devices" or "screens." The interface became incidental, and while television remained a relevant experience and type of content, people slowly dropped obsolete terms like "TV sets" or "the TV" as they had years earlier stopped listening to "records on the stereo."

Childhood in the U.S.

Two events occurred on the cusp of the millennium that marked a turning point in the country's sense of itself and its children. On April 20, 1999, two students at Columbine High School in Colorado shot and killed twelve of their classmates and a teacher, and wounded twenty-three others before killing themselves.[14] The events of 9/11 occurred a little over two years later. Both of these tragedies drew a dark line marking a loss of innocence and an increased sense of vulnerability for the nation and its youth.

These events reinforced a shift in our views of children and childhood that, seen in retrospect, had been underway for some time. Historian Steven Mintz is among a number of theorists who have referred to our current perceptions and attitudes toward children as the era of postmodern childhood, a time of questioning and reevaluation of formerly dominant norms about the family, gender roles, age, and sex.[15] The notion of childhood as a protected sphere in which the young are kept isolated from adult realities has broken down. Children are no longer seen as naïve and innocent creatures, unaware of the realities of the adult world. Instead, they are considered junior citizens who are all too familiar with violence and wise in the ways of the world and the media. With the Internet providing virtually equal access to all information (and in many ways favoring digitally native youth), the boundaries between children and adults seem to have become even more permeable.[16] Children and adults now dress similarly, behave similarly, and enjoy the same books (e.g., *Harry Potter*), movies, and TV shows. Media theorist Neil Postman primarily credits (or blames) television's accessibility for breaking down the distinctions between children and adults, which the invention of print had fostered. In Postman's view, unlike print, no special instruction is needed to watch or understand TV; unlike print, TV doesn't make any complex demands on its viewers' minds; and, unlike print, TV doesn't segregate its audience by age or other demographic categories.[17]

The progression toward the era of postmodern childhood has had several benchmarks. One that was key was when children were first seen as consumers and became a market segment. That process began earlier in the 20th century but grew in intensity and sophistication with the development of children's television and in tandem with the emergence of the Boomer generation. Still evolving, postmodern childhood is deeply enmeshed with market-driven consumer media. As Buckingham sees it, children as consumers are no longer considered innocents in need of protection but rather sophisticated and discriminating independent agents in the commercial marketplace: "Children have become 'kids'; and kids, we are told, are 'smart,' 'savvy,' and 'street-wise.' Above all, they are 'media literate.' They are hard to please; they see through attempts at deception and manipulation; and they refuse to be patronized. Kids know what they want from the media—and it is the job of adults to provide them with this, rather than falling back on their own beliefs about what is good for them."[18]

As a postmodern childhood has been constructed, so has a postmodern adulthood. Adults have long yearned to return to the supposedly innocent, carefree days of their youth. But those longings were tempered by the realization that childhood was also a time of limited autonomy and deferred pleasure, which adults were happy to trade for the traditional authority, rewards, and control over their lives that came with growing up. Increasingly, however, that negative side of childhood has begun to fade. Children's TV shows and ads have treated children as cool, smart, fun-loving, and able to manage their own lives without adult supervision, and adults as boring, clueless, and unnecessary. Generations have matured with that meme. A.O. Scott argues in his *New York Times* essay on "The Death of Adulthood in American Culture," "It is now possible to conceive of adulthood as the state of being forever young. Childhood ... is now a zone of perpetual freedom and delight. Grown people feel no compulsion to put away childish things: We can live with our parents, go to summer camp, play dodge ball, collect dolls and action figures and watch cartoons to our hearts' content. These symptoms of arrested development will also be signs that we are freer, more honest, and happier than the uptight fools who let go of such pastimes."[19]

At the same time that the boundaries between childhood and adulthood have become less distinct, postmodern children increasingly live in their own semi-autonomous youth culture, sharing interests, norms, and knowledge from which adults are excluded. Television has a played a key role in this evolution as well. It stands to reason that, the more that adults try to share in children's culture, the more that children try to keep them out. Having their own obscure vocabulary and their own cultural touch points of which adults are unaware and, even if perceived by adults, would not be comprehensible to them, gives children a degree of power.

Youth culture has given postmodern children an arena in which they can be in charge, momentarily free from the demands of "helicopter parents." As historian Paula S. Fass has noted, parents have become fixated on supervising and managing their children's lives, not because they are bad parents but because they believe their hovering and supervision is needed, given the risks and demands of modern-day life.[20] The pressure on parents to try to micromanage and control their children's lives, which became common in the nineties, grew even stronger in the new post–9/11 millennium, articulated in books like *Battle Hymn of the Tiger Mother*, which became a best-seller in 2012.[21] In this memoir, author Amy Chua described her own success in training and disciplining her children to meet their mother's goals and expectations rather than pursue their own desires or make their own decisions, which she saw as an indulgence that would doom children to less-than-perfect lives. However, Chua's book generated considerable controversy, as a backlash against the over-controlling approach to parenting had begun to develop. This counter-vailing view was expressed in books like Lenore Skenazy's *Free-Range Kids: Giving Our Children the Freedom We Had Without Going Nuts with Worry*,[22] and Jennifer Senior's *All Joy and No Fun*,[23] in which Senior lamented the sense of inadequacy shared by many modern parents as a result of the unrealistic demands for high performance that they made on themselves and on their children.

Television

A key trend in TV programming in the 2000s was the growing popularity of reality shows, like *Big Brother* and *Survivor* on CBS, *Temptation Island* on Fox, and *Fear Factor* on NBC. Programs like these took the exhibitionists and publicity seekers that had previously been seen only on syndicated daytime talk shows and gave them a primetime spotlight. Beginning with *American Idol*, which debuted on Fox in the summer of 2002, competition reality shows in the tradition of the talent shows that flourished on television decades earlier also drew large audiences. In their modern incarnation, these shows now allowed viewers to vote for the winner by texting in votes with their smartphones.

By 2001, more than ⅔ of U.S. homes had a cable subscription, and the combined audience for cable shows began to surpass those for the broadcast networks.[24] Reaching this audience size set the stage for the flourishing of critically acclaimed edgy dramas on cable networks, continuing a trend that had begun with *The Sopranos* on HBO. Shows like *Mad Men* and *Breaking Bad*, which debuted on cable channel AMC in 2002, were heralded as the start of a new golden age of television drama, and AMC's zombie apocalypse series *The Walking Dead*, which premiered in 2010, became a huge hit. HBO produced another mega-hit drama in 2011 with *Game of Thrones*, a dark historical fantasy with generous amounts of violence and sex, and, as fans consistently pointed out, dragons.

On the broadcast networks, mainstream shows like crime procedurals *CSI* and *NCIS* and sitcoms like *The Big Bang Theory* still drew large audiences. Popular series *Modern Family*, which premiered on ABC in 2009, was a classic sitcom with a couple of twists. Filmed in mockumentary style, it sympathetically depicted an unconventional extended family that included a committed gay couple with an adopted Asian baby and an older white man happily married to a much younger sexy Hispanic woman. *Glee*, which debuted on FOX the same year, was another unconventional sitcom, revolving around the members of a high-school glee club competing for prizes but also dealing with social issues like sex, homosexuality, teenage pregnancy, disabilities, and acceptance of diversity.

Children's Television

The children's television landscape continued to change in the 2000s, as advertising time limits and growing competition from cable made children's programming increasingly less profitable for the broadcast networks. These were challenges familiar from past business cycles, but with audience share continuing to shift increasingly to cable, the broadcast networks' responses were now more defensive than proactive, as they sought to cut their growing losses. In 2001, The WB network discontinued its weekday morning children's block, giving the time back to their affiliates, and replaced their afternoon children's block with Cartoon Network shows like *Sailor Moon* and *The Powerpuff Girls.* The following year, CBS turned over its three-hour block of Saturday morning children's shows to sister channel Nickelodeon, which filled the time with reruns of Nick shows, and NBC replaced its three-hour block of live-action shows for teens with FCC-friendly programs from the new Discovery Kids Channel. In 2006, The CW inherited the afternoon Kids' WB block when the channel was created through the merger of The WB and UPN, but dropped the block the following year. In 2008, The CW decided to outsource its Saturday morning cartoon block to children's TV producer 4Kids Entertainment. That same year, Fox gave up its Saturday morning cartoons and replaced them with two hours of paid infomercials.

As the traditional broadcast networks were cutting back or outsourcing their children's shows, other companies were systematically launching new cable channels to try to capture their piece of the children's television pie. While this may sound like the 90s redux, the television business had evolved through mergers, acquisitions, and partnerships into an even more complex cast of characters. In 2000, Time Warner launched Boomerang, a digital cable and satellite TV channel specializing in classic cartoons and repeats of Cartoon Network shows. In 2005, Sprout (initially called PBS Kids Sprout), a new cable channel targeting preschoolers, was created through a partnership among PBS, Comcast, HIT Entertainment, and Children's Television Workshop. Comcast took full ownership of the channel in 2012, adding it to their stable of NBC Universal properties, and the NBC broadcast network replaced its Discovery Kids block of Saturday morning shows with a block of shows from Sprout called NBC Kids. In 2006, a partnership among NBC, Ion Media Networks, Corus Entertainment, and Scholastic Corporation launched Qubo, a digital cable channel and multi-media brand aimed at providing educational, values-oriented programming for children age four to eight. Qubo was also intended to be a bilingual brand that would appeal to the growing Hispanic population, and its programming initially consisted of reruns of children's shows from NBC, Telemundo, and Ion Television. In 2012, Disney spun off its Disney Jr. preschool programming block as a new digital cable and satellite channel.

Discovery Communications and the Hasbro toy company joined forces in 2010 to relaunch Discovery Kids as The Hub network, another new children's channel, whose shows included programs based on Hasbro products, like *G.I. Joe, Transformers,* and *My Little Pony.* To forestall expected criticism about its focus on toy-based programs promoting Hasbro products, The Hub had a policy of not airing ads for the toys featured in their shows either within or adjacent to those shows. Nevertheless, other toy manufacturers were reluctant to advertise on the channel and it failed to become profitable. In 2014, Discovery bought out Hasbro's share of the channel and relaunched it as the Discovery Family channel, with a new slate of family-friendly shows from the Discovery Channel.

As these realignments were reshaping the children's television industry, the shows themselves reached new heights of creativity. One animated series which had made its debut on Nickelodeon in 1999 emerged as arguably the most iconic children's show of the new millennium. *Sponge-Bob SquarePants* revolves around the adventures of the title character, a bright yellow sponge, and his various friends in the underwater city of Bikini Bottom. SpongeBob lives in a pineapple, has a pet snail named Gary who meows like a cat, and works as a fry cook at the Krusty Krab restaurant. His best friend is Patrick, a cheerful but dim-witted starfish, and his next-door neighbor and nemesis is Squidward, an arrogant and cranky octopus who plays the clarinet, likes to paint self-portraits, and hates SpongeBob and his friends because of their juvenile behavior. There are a host of other characters, including another good friend of SpongeBob's, Sandy Cheeks, a female squirrel from Texas who is a scientist and an expert in karate. Sandy wears an underwater diver's suit when she is outside of her airtight home, since she can't breathe underwater.

Within its first month on the air, *SpongeBob* overtook The WB's hugely popular *Pokémon* as the highest-rated Saturday morning TV show, and it was soon garnering high ratings among adults as well as children. What accounted for *SpongeBob's* enormous success? Unlike other children's shows that have held appeal for adults, *SpongeBob* is not filled with sophisticated dialogue, ironic humor, or parody. The show does include sly jokes and allusions that younger children are unlikely to notice or understand, but it delivers these references in an atmosphere of straightforward sincerity and innocence.[25] As one journalist noted, "The tenor of *SpongeBob SquarePants* is distinctly sweet and silly. It lacks most of the blatant scatology of recent crossover hits like *Ren & Stimpy,* and avoids the acerbic social commentary of adults-only cartoons like *The Simpsons* and *South Park*… That apparent lack of sardonic self-awareness in a culture defined by wiseguy knowingness may be exactly what works for *SpongeBob.* Adults—and even kids—know the wink-and-nudge routine all too well."[26] So, in the context of *SpongeBob's* overall sense of innocence,

SpongeBob SquarePants revolves around the adventures of its sweet and silly title character, a bright yellow sponge, and his friends in the underwater city of Bikini Bottom. Much of the show's appeal derives from its lack of sardonic self-awareness.

setting the show in Bikini Bottom and naming a female character Sandy Cheeks caused no great controversy.

SpongeBob SquarePants was one of several new children's shows that have aired since the early days of television that might be characterized as postmodern. In the realms of aesthetics and culture, postmodernism is a term that has been widely debated but often used to refer to works that include the appropriation of earlier styles and elements from both popular culture and "art" and their reconfiguration into contemporary creations, outside of their original context and meaning. Just as postmodern childhood entails a blurring of the boundaries between childhood and adulthood, postmodern art involves the blurring of boundaries between different genres, different types of content and even different forms of media, like television, computers, and videogames. Postmodernist work is often self-referential in nature, using accepted conventions of older cultural genres in playful or distorted ways as a form of ironic meta-commentary on these conventions. Pastiche, homage, parody, and irony are key elements of postmodernism. It can also incorporate aspects of surrealism and magical realism.[27]

If children in the new millennium are increasingly living out a postmodern childhood, it is not surprising that more of their television shows have also taken on some of the characteristics of postmodernism as well. Earlier shows like *Rocky and Bullwinkle*, *Pee-Wee's Playhouse*, *Animaniacs*, and *Ren & Stimpy* have all used the classic conventions of their genres in ironic, self-referential, playful, and sometimes surreal ways. The appeal of such shows is based on the assumption that viewers are sufficiently familiar with television conventions that they would recognize and enjoy seeing them exaggerated, distorted or ironically misapplied. *SpongeBob SquarePants* took the postmodern approach even further by playing it straight, even as its inclusion of realistic contemporary allusions in an absurd setting made it seem both retro and surreal. These kinds of shows are popular with both adults and children, another feature that makes them postmodern, since a blurring of the boundaries between childhood and adulthood is a central condition of postmodern childhood.

Several other new children's shows with postmodern elements have been introduced in the last decade and a half. On the Disney Channel, *Phineas and Ferb*, which premiered in 2008, became one of Disney's most popular and long-running shows before it ended production in 2015. The animated series followed the escapades of two tween stepbrothers, Phineas and Ferb, during their summer vacation. In each episode, the boys embarked on a crazy new project, like building a full-size rollercoaster or inventing a shrinking submarine, while their controlling older sister Candace tried to thwart their fun by reporting on them to her mother. There was also a secondary plot featuring the boys' pet platypus, Perry, who secretly worked as a spy for OWCA (the Organization without a Cool Acronym) in order to defeat the schemes of mad scientist Dr. Heinz Doofenshmirtz. At the end of each episode the two plots would intersect, erasing all evidence of the boys' project before Candace could show it to her mother.

Phineas and Ferb included frequent pop-culture references, clever word play and other forms of adult humor that would not have been recognized or appreciated by most young children, earning it a large adult audience. For example, in one episode, after Phineas and Ferb created robot doubles of themselves, Phineas exclaimed, "Look! They've started their own overpriced coffee franchise! (pauses) That's so nineties."[28] *The New York Times* described the show as "*Family Guy* with an espionage subplot and a big dose of magical realism."[29] *Variety* deemed it "a latter-day *Scooby-Doo* ... albeit with a sly, self-knowing air considerably more sophisticated than the simple animation and character design would suggest."[30]

The Cartoon Network embraced the postmodernist approach to children's programming most fully, probably because it did not define itself as just a network for children but one that would also appeal to adults. In 2000, the Cartoon Network premiered *Sheep in the Big City*, a series about a runaway sheep named Sheep. The show's premise was that Sheep had been living happily on a farm when evil General Specific, the leader of a secret military organization, tried to capture Sheep to activate his new Sheep-Powered Ray Gun. Sheep was forced to flee the farm and take up life in The Big City, where he was constantly on the run from General Specific and his henchmen, Private Public, the Angry Scientist, and the Plot Device, while romancing his new love interest, Swanky the Poodle.

Each episode of *Sheep in the Big City* was a mashup of various unrelated short sketches and interstitial segments, many of which were comical references to television genres and conventions. For example, the show would begin with video from an apparently random TV show, which would turn out to be a show that Sheep was watching. Sheep would then press a button on his remote to change the channel, and the theme music from his own show would begin. Fake advertisements would appear between the show's segments, usually for bizarre products from the Oxymoron Company. A key feature of the show was its frequent breaking of the fourth wall, with characters talking to the viewer about the show's structure, its script, and even its entire premise. For example, in one episode the Angry Scientist admitted that he didn't actually have a working Sheep-Powered Ray Gun ready, because he assumed they would never capture Sheep since that would be "so contrary to the set-up of the show." The Narrator, who was a key character on the show, would frequently provide commentary about the show itself, telling viewers to "just go with it" when the script made no sense.

One of the most creative and surreal postmodern shows of the new millennium is *Adventure Time*, which debuted on the Cartoon Network in 2010. The animated series follows the adventures of a boy, Finn the Human, and his best friend and adoptive brother Jake the Dog, who can change shape and size at will. Finn and Jake live in the post-apocalyptic Land of Ooo, which had been ravaged a thousand years earlier by the Mushroom War, a nuclear cataclysm. Like SpongeBob, Finn is an innocent, good-hearted, selfless character, always ready to help others in need. When he makes mistakes, they result from the best of intentions, and he works hard to fix them. The series also includes a large number of supporting characters, chief among them Princess Bubblegum, the ruler of the Candy Kingdom; the Ice King, an evil but misunderstood wizard; and Marceline the Vampire Queen, a thousand-year-old vampire and rock music fan.

Adventure Time's creator, Pendleton Ward, describes the series as a dark comedy, inspired by the fantasy role-playing videogame *Dungeons & Dragons* but also by the "beautiful moments" in the films of Japanese animator Hayao Miyazaki. He has noted that, even though the show's premise includes magic and fantasy, its world has an internal consistency and logic in how the characters deal with its fantasy elements.[31]

A summary of the show's premise, however, inevitably fails to capture its strangeness and multi-layered complexity. *Rolling Stone* has described *Adventure Time* as "the trippiest show on television" and "rapturously surreal."[32] Critic Emily Nussbaum of *The New Yorker* has noted that, on one level, *Adventure Time* can be seen "as a cartoon about a hero who fights villains, with fun violence, the occasional fart joke, and a slight edge of Bushwick [a gritty but arty neighborhood in Brooklyn] cool-kid hipness," but its dark back-story also makes it "one of the most philosophically risky and, often, emotionally affecting shows on TV."[33] It is hard to imagine that a children's show of earlier decades could have been set in a hallucinatory post-apocalyptic environment after a devastating nuclear war, but *Adventure Time* was created after 9/11, which seems to have reset expectations so much that this view of the world in a TV show for children is neither

From the Cartoon Network's surreal, post-apocalyptic series *Adventure Time*, Finn the Human is surrounded by (clockwise from bottom center) his best friend Jake the Dog, Lumpy Space Princess, Princess Bubblegum, Orgalorg, Finn's videogame console BMO, a Candy Person, and Marceline the Vampire Queen.

unacceptable nor particularly shocking. For younger viewers, its depiction of Finn's comical escapades provides a fantastical, fun diversion from the show's tragic premise. Describing the series as dreamlike, Nussbaum concludes, "But that's part of the show's most freeing quality: childlike, nonlinear, poetic, and just outside all the categories that the world considers serious...."[34]

Adventure Time has been a solid ratings success for the Cartoon Network, where it still airs. Like other postmodern shows, it has attracted a large audience of young adults as well as children. The same can be said for two other postmodern Cartoon Network series—*Regular Show* and *The Amazing World of Gumball*. Premiering in 2010, *Regular Show* revolved around the lives of two twenty-something friends, a blue jay named Mordecai and a raccoon named Rigby, who worked as groundskeepers at a local park. The two spent their days slacking off and trying to entertain themselves in any way possible, a habit which usually led to surreal misadventures. Other main characters included Mordecai and Rigby's two bosses, Benson, a gumball machine, and Pops, who had a lollipop for a head; their coworker Skips, a yeti; a large lumpy green person called Muscle Man; and an entity called Hi-Five Ghost. The show has been described as zany, absurd, bizarre, and anything but "regular."

The Amazing World of Gumball debuted on the Cartoon Network in 2011 and is still on the air. The series follows the life and adventures of Gumball Watterson, a twelve-year-old cat, who attends middle school in the fictional city of Elmore. Gumball constantly finds himself in trouble as a result of various harebrained schemes he cooks up, but he remains ever optimistic. Gumball's best friend is his adopted brother Darwin, a goldfish who was the family pet until he grew legs and became a part of the Watterson family. Gumball's mother is the family breadwinner, working long hours at a rainbow factory, while his father is a stay-at-home dad who spends his time watching TV and playing videogames. Gumball resents his brainy sister Anais because she is the smartest one in the family. Gumball's sister and father are both rabbits, while his mother, like Gumball, is a cat. Though plots often feature supernatural and surreal elements, Gumball and his family and friends seem like normal suburbanites, except for their appearance, and many of the plots revolve around Gumball coping with the usual issues faced by most middle-school children.

The characters on *Gumball*, who are drawn in a highly stylized manner, are set against photo-realistic backdrops, a clash of animation styles that enhances the surreal atmosphere produced by having its bizarre-looking characters acting like normal people dealing with normal everyday issues. As *Wired* magazine concluded, "In a lineup alongside surreal heavy-hitters like *Adventure Time* and *Regular Show*, *Gumball* manages to be every bit as strange, and quite possibly a tiny bit more earnest.... The show manages to have genuine heart even as the plots themselves transition from well-worn TV tropes to all-out madness."[35]

Not all Cartoon Network series that have debuted in the new millennium could be described as postmodern. Cartoon Network also continued to air new Japanese anime series, like *Hamtaro* and *Naruto*, as well as superhero shows like *Teen Titans, Justice League* and *Ben 10*. There were also two new shows based on the Star Wars franchise—*Star Wars: Clone Wars* in 2003, followed by *Star Wars: The Clone Wars* in 2008. The latter version, produced in full 3-D computer animation, was the first weekly TV series from Lucasfilm.

Samurai Jack, which debuted on the Cartoon Network in 2001, bears mention for its unusual animation style. The series followed the trials and adventures of a samurai warrior who had been sent into the distant future, as he tried to find a portal to take him back in time so he could defeat the demonic wizard Aku. In a classic battle of good versus evil, Jack had to face constant obstacles set by Aku, but each time he overcame an obstacle, a new challenge would arise that would keep him from completing his quest. *Entertainment Weekly* described *Samurai Jack* as "a meditative epic starring a laconic hero owing more to Homer's 'Odyssey' than Hanna-Barbera, featuring minimal comedy and a near-complete absence of dialogue."[36] Its unique style and storytelling helped to make *Samurai Jack* an early breakout hit for the Cartoon Network.

Foster's Home for Imaginary Friends, which debuted on the Cartoon Network in 2004, was a funny but also poignant cartoon that dealt with one of the more fraught transitions faced by children in the process of growing up. The show was set in an orphanage for imaginary friends that children had outgrown, where they would stay until a new child came to adopt them. The central storyline revolved around an eight-year-old boy who reluctantly gave up his imaginary friend Bloo, an anthropomorphic security blanket. But he couldn't bear to make a complete break with Bloo, so he made a deal with the orphanage to keep Bloo from being put up for adoption as long as he continued to visit Bloo regularly at the home.

Another key trend in children's television in the new millennium, reflecting demographic changes in the U.S. population and the television audience, has been an increase in shows starring characters of diverse ethnicity, especially many of Hispanic heritages. A key example of this trend was the debut of animated educational preschool series *Dora the Explorer* on Nickelodeon in 2000. The series' star character is a bilingual little Latina girl named Dora, who has a talking purple backpack and an anthropomorphic monkey companion called Boots, for the red boots he wears. Dora, Boots, and the other characters on the show use occasional Spanish words or short phrases as they talk.

In every episode, Dora is on a quest to reach a destination, like a gymnastics event at the school, but encounters obstacles along the way that she and Boots have to overcome and puzzles that they have to solve before they can reach their destination. As in *Blue's Clues*, Dora and Boots talk directly to the audience and solicit their help by asking them to shout out the answers to the questions or puzzles they encounter, then pause to give the viewer time to respond. Each episode ends with Dora and Boots successfully reaching their destination and singing the "We Did It!" song.

Dora the Explorer was a huge hit for Nickelodeon and has also aired on CBS, Telemundo, and Univision. In 2005, Nickelodeon created an animated spin-off series, *Go, Diego, Go!*, an educational show designed to teach preschoolers about science and nature. The show's main character is Dora's eight-year-old cousin Diego, a bilingual adventurer who rescues animals in trouble. Like Dora, Diego directly elicits the viewer's help in finding and rescuing animals in peril, asking the audience questions and pausing for their responses. Like Dora, Diego's dialogue is sprinkled with Spanish words and phrases.

In 2014, with *Dora the Explorer* still on its schedule and still ranking among the top ten preschool shows on television, Nickelodeon took the risky step of creating a new version of the show, called *Dora and Friends: Into the City*. Designed to appeal to older children who might be outgrowing *Dora the Explorer*, the new series stars Dora as a preteen, with longer hair, more detailed facial features, and a less child-like wardrobe. While the younger Dora's adventures take place in the rain forest, the older Dora attends school in the city of Playa Verde, where she has human friends who join her in doing volunteer community service work and help her in her adventures. In a sign of the changing times, Dora's trusty map has been replaced by a map app on her smartphone. She still enlists the participation of viewers in her adventures and continues to mix in Spanish words as she speaks, but the focus of the series' curriculum is tilted more toward the development of social rather than cognitive skills.

Nickelodeon also featured Hispanic stars in two live-action sitcoms aimed at preteens that debuted in the new millennium. *The Brothers Garcia* premiered in 2000 as the first English-language sitcom with an all-Latino cast and creative team.[37] It revolved around the everyday life of a middle-class Mexican American family living in San Antonio, Texas. *Taina*, which first aired in 2001, was about the typical teenage trials and tribulations of a fourteen-year-old Latina girl attending the Manhattan High School of the Performing Arts and aspiring to become a singer and actress. Like the 1980s musical TV series *Fame*, the show's multicultural cast would periodically break out their instruments and stage elaborate production numbers in the school hallways.

The WB also debuted a Hispanic-focused children's program in 2002, *¡Mucha Lucha!*. This animated series followed the lives of three children who were training to become masked free-style wrestlers in the Mexican lucha libre tradition. The lead characters, who called themselves Rikochet, The Flea, and Buena Girl, attended school at the Foremost World-Renowned International School of Lucha, in a lucha-obsessed town where everyone had a mask, a costume, and a signature wrestling move.

PBS had been one of the first networks to air Hispanic-based children's programming, and in 2004, it added to its earlier initiatives with animated sitcom *Maya and Miguel*. The series followed the daily life and adventures of fraternal twins Maya and Miguel Santos and their family and friends. The twins' mother was from Mexico, while their father came from Puerto Rico, and they lived in a culturally diverse town in the U.S. The storylines usually dealt with Maya's well-intentioned meddling in other people's lives, which would inevitably result in misunderstandings and problems that Maya and her brother and friends would have to fix. With its inclusion of Spanish words and phrases in the characters' dialogue, the show presented a positive, rich portrayal of Latino family life, language, and culture, while encouraging bilingualism and cultural diversity.

On the Disney Channel, *The Wizards of Waverly Place*, which began its run in 2007, was one of several popular live-action sitcoms aimed at tweens and teens. *Wizards* did not specifically focus on Hispanic life or culture, but it had a Hispanic angle in that it depicted a family in which the mother was Mexican and the lead character, Alex, was played by Latina actress Selena Gomez. The series chronicled the adventures of three teenage wizard siblings in the Russo family, who lived on Waverly Place in Manhattan's Greenwich Village. In a premise incorporating both realistic and supernatural versions of a mixed marriage, their Italian father, Jerry, was a wizard, while their Mexican mother was a mortal. Once they completed their wizard training, the three siblings would have to compete to see which one of them would become the Family Wizard, while the other two would lose their wizard powers. As in previous shows about teens with magical powers, the Russo siblings tried to keep their wizard status secret, but as the series progressed, their secret gradually became known to a few of their friends. At the series' conclusion, Alex won the competition and became the Family Wizard.

Wizards of Waverly Place followed on the heels of *That's So Raven*, another Disney Channel live-action sitcom about a teen with magical powers, which featured an African American teen and her family. Premiering in 2003, *That's So Raven* starred actress Raven Symone, who had played the younger Huxtable daughter on *The Cosby Show*, as Raven Baxter, a teen with psychic powers that allowed her to see brief glimpses of the future. Raven was portrayed as a sassy girl with a big personality, whose psychic powers, ingenuity, and talent as a fashion designer would get her into and out of typical teen situations. She would often misinterpret her glimpses of the future, and her attempts at forestalling or changing what she thought was going to happen usually went awry. Raven had a number of catchphrases, including *"Oh Fudge!," "Oh snap!," "Ya nasty!," "How y'all doin'?,"* and *"Oh, no he/she didn't!"*

Before it ended its run in 2007, *That's So Raven* was the highest-rated series in the history of the Disney Channel. When it ended production, Disney replaced it with a spin-off, *Cory in the House*, featuring Raven's little brother Cory from *That's So Raven*. The premise for the new series was that, with Raven off to college and mom Tanya attending law school in London, dad Victor took a job as head chef at the White House under President Martinez. Father and son moved to Washington, D.C., where Cory had to deal with the President's bratty little daughter and various other annoying or ridiculous characters on the White House staff and at his new private prep school. Like *That's So Raven*, *Cory in the House* had a largely minority cast, including a Hispanic U.S. president.

Besides *That's So Raven* and *Cory in the House*, the Disney Channel aired several other shows in the 2000s that starred African American characters. *The Proud Family*, which debuted in 2001, was a cartoon about a middle-class African American family's day-to-day life. Stories revolved around teenage daughter Penny and her neighbors, friends, and classmates, as Penny dealt with typical teenage issues, like rivalry and bullying. The series also included references to African American history and culture.

In 2012, The Disney Channel and Disney Junior premiered *Doc McStuffins*, an educational cartoon about a six-year-old African American girl named Dottie, or "Doc," McStuffins, who wants to be a doctor like her mother and practices by "fixing" her stuffed animals and dolls. When Doc activates her magic stethoscope, her toys and dolls come to life and she can communicate with them. She helps sick toys "feel better" by giving them check-ups and diagnosing their illnesses with the help of "The Big Book of Boo-Boos" and "The Big Vet Book." In later seasons, a technology update had Doc consulting the books on a tablet. One of *Doc McStuffins'* educational goals was to allay children's fears about going to the doctor by demystifying the process. The series received critical and public acclaim for depicting Doc as an African American girl. The show was a ratings success and still runs on Disney Junior.

Nickelodeon had previously aired several shows starring African Americans, like *Gullah Gullah Island* and *Kenan and Kel*. In 2003, they added *Romeo!*, a tween-oriented live-action sitcom about an African American teenager, Romeo Miller, who was a rapper in a hip-hop group along with three of his siblings. The series followed Romeo's adventures as he tried to pursue a musical career, with guidance from his father, who was a famous record producer, as well as from Romeo's loving stepmother, an architect, and his eccentric nanny, a former circus performer.

On The WB, a new cartoon debuted in 2000 called *Static Shock*, a classic teen superhero show but one that starred an African American character. Based on a prior comic book, the series was about a black teenager, Virgil, who was accidentally exposed to a chemical mutagen in an event called "The Big Bang," which gave him the power to control and manipulate electromagnetism. Virgil used his powers to become a superhero named Static, and he fought against other teens called "Bang Babies" who had also gained special abilities in The Big Bang but used their powers for selfish or evil purposes. *Static Shock* was one of the first shows to star an African American superhero. It addressed a variety of real urban and teen issues, like gangs, gun violence, homelessness, racism, bullying, and drug abuse. Though the show included violent scenes, it depicted Virgil as always trying to reason with the villains first and using his powers only as a last resort.

With rare exceptions, like *The Mystery Files of Shelby Woo* on Nickelodeon in the late 1990s, there had been few children's shows starring Asian characters, other than those in Japanese anime or shows based on Asian celebrities, like *The Jackie Chan Adventures*, which began airing on the Cartoon Network in 2000. The Disney Channel took a step in correcting this meager record with the premiere of *American Dragon: Jake Long* in 2005. The animated series was about the adventures of a thirteen-year-old Chinese-American boy living in Manhattan, who could turn into a dragon. While secretly training to become the first American Dragon, Jake traveled around the city on a skateboard, befriending the unicorns, leprechauns, mermaids, and other magical creatures secretly living among the humans in the city. As the American Dragon, it would be Jake's responsibility to protect these magical creatures from harm. In the meantime, Jake also had to deal with the usual issues of being an adolescent, including his crush on a pretty blonde schoolmate who, unbeknownst to Jake, was actually a dragon slayer named Huntsgirl. Jake lived with his extended family: his China-born mother Susan, who came from a dragon family; his American dad, who was unaware that he had married into a family of dragons; seven-year-old sister Haley, who was another nascent dragon; Jake's maternal grandfather Lao Shi, who had recently immigrated from China to direct Jake's dragon training; and Grandpa's sidekick, a magical Shar-Pei named Fu Dog. Along with the magical plot elements, the show's storylines also dealt with Jake's Chinese heritage and the importance of family values.

Nickelodeon took another step in increasing diversity on children's television in 2000, with the debut of *Pelswick*, an animated series in which the lead character was a thirteen-year-old boy confined to a wheelchair. Pelswick Eggert was portrayed as a hip, independent, sarcastic teenager dealing with the usual challenges of growing up, in addition to the fact that he was "permanently seated," as he liked to describe himself. There was a magical element in the series, in that Pelswick had a laid-back, bearded, incompetent guardian angel named Mr. Jimmy, whom only Pelswick could see. Mr. Jimmy gave Pelswick cryptic advice that drove him crazy. Pelswick's girlfriend was African American, which added another element of diversity to the series.

Nickelodeon's other new shows in the 2000s continued the network's focus on representing children as savvy, spunky, independent, and peer-oriented, while adults were shown as disengaged, clueless, or irrelevant. One of Nick's most popular new shows in this tradition was *The Fairly OddParents*, an animated series that debuted in 2001. The show's premise was that the central character, ten-year-old Timmy, was neglected by his parents and tormented by his babysitter Vicky. One day, in the midst of his miserable life, Timmy was given two fairy godparents, Cosmo and Wanda, who would grant his every wish. But each wish that was fulfilled would lead to a series of unintended problems that Timmy would have to fix. Most of the adults in this series were portrayed as hapless, neglectful or evil. Timmy's parents were so disengaged that they were represented in the opening sequence by two cardboard cutouts sitting on the porch of Timmy's house.[38] Timmy's babysitter Vicky was the main antagonist in the show, and Timmy's teacher Mr. Crocker was also revealed to be a villain later in the series. *The Fairly OddParents* was Nickelodeon's most popular show until it was overtaken by *SpongeBob SquarePants*.

Jimmy Neutron: Boy Genius premiered on Nickelodeon in 2002. The first cartoon on Nickelodeon to be animated in full 3-D graphics, *Jimmy*

Neutron followed the adventures of Jimmy, his faithful robotic dog Goddard, and his friends and family, who lived in the town of Retroville. Jimmy was a typical fifth-grader who just happened to be a genius. He was constantly creating gadgets to improve his life or solve problems, but his inventions would often backfire, creating comical complications that Jimmy would have to sort out. Jimmy was depicted as smarter and more capable than the adults on the show, and every plot revolved around his superior intellect.

Several other new series that debuted on Nickelodeon after 2000 continued the network's focus on shows starring smart and spunky tween and teenage girls and helping adolescents navigate the transition from childhood to young adulthood. The idea of breaking out "tweens" as a distinct subgroup in between children and teenagers had become a popular marketing concept in the late 1990s, as the large cohort of Millennials began to reach this age. With more money to spend than children their age had ever had before, tweens became a sought-after target for advertisers and television networks.[39] In 2001, Nickelodeon created a new programming block addressed to tween viewers age nine to fourteen, called TEENick, which would air on Sundays from 6 to 8:30 p.m. One of the anchor shows in the new block was *As Told by Ginger*, an animated sitcom about the daily trials and tribulations of a dorky middle-schooler living with her divorced mother in the fictional suburban town of Sheltered Shrubs, Connecticut. The storylines generally revolved around Ginger's attempts to remain true to herself and to her old friends after she was befriended by the most popular girl in school and tried to become one of the "cool kids." The show addressed the usual preteen issues of social anxiety, jealousy, romance, and break-ups, but also dealt with more serious topics like depression, suicide, and death. The series was made to seem more realistic by having the characters age from season to season, so that Ginger entered high school by the time the series ended.

Nickelodeon followed up with live-action sitcoms *Unfabulous* in 2004 and *iCarly* in 2007, which also starred preteen girls and dealt with typical adolescent issues like friendships, dating, and break-ups. *Unfabulous* had a musical angle, since its starring character, Addie Singer, wrote and performed songs about her life in middle school. *iCarly* tapped into the growing role of the Internet in teenagers' lives and culture by depicting its central character, Carly Shay, as a teen whose life was turned upside down when her Internet show, "iCarly," suddenly became a web sensation. Carly and her friends were portrayed as almost completely independent, able to create and host their own web show and solve the various complications in their lives on their own as well. Carly lived with her 26-year-old brother and guardian, Spencer, while her father, a U.S. Air Force officer, was stationed on a distant submarine. There was no mother in Carly's life, an absence that the show did not address. Carly's father was seen only once, in the show's final episode, when he returned home to take Carly to Italy where he was being stationed next.

iCarly used the series' premise to make viewer interaction an integral element of the show. In a form of self-reflexive meta-reality, fans could actually go onto the iCarly.com site where the fictional Carly hosted her fictional webcast and send in comments, videos and suggestions, which were then incorporated into the show. This multi-level interactivity created an engaged and loyal fan base and helped to make *iCarly* one of Nickelodeon's most popular shows.

Nickelodeon had great success with its tween-oriented live-action sitcoms, and the Disney Channel followed suit in the new millennium, finding a winning formula with several coming-of-age sitcoms that significantly boosted the Disney Channel's ratings. In addition to *The Wizards of Waverly Place*, *That's So Raven*, and *Cory in the House*, discussed earlier, Disney's new crop of hit tween sitcoms included *Lizzie McGuire*, which debuted in 2001. The show followed the daily life and comical misadventures of a thirteen-year-old girl as she did her best to fit in and become popular at school while dealing with other normal preteen issues. Lizzie had an animated alter-ego who represented her true feelings and expressed them in monologues spoken directly to the viewer. Lizzie's best friend was Miranda Isabella Sanchez, giving the series a degree of cultural diversity.

Premiering on the Disney Channel in 2005, *The Suite Life of Zack and Cody* revolved around the adventures and misadventures of identical twin brothers Zack and Cody Martin, the tween sons of a divorced single mom who was a lounge singer at the fictional five-star Tipton Hotel in Boston, where the family got to live in an upstairs suite. Storylines often involved Zack and Cody getting into and out of trouble at the hotel, usually at the instigation of girl-obsessed Zack, the more rambunctious of the two. The boys regularly interacted with ditzy spoiled rich girl London Tipton, the daughter of the hotel's owner, and her unlikely best friend Maddie Fitzpatrick, the clerk at the hotel's candy counter. They also frequently ran afoul of the hotel's manager, Mr. Moseby, a rather affected character who favored pocket hankies and enjoyed the ballet. As on *iCarly*, London Tipton had her own web show, called "Yay Me! Starring London Tipton," which viewers could actually access online.

The Suite Life spawned a sequel series called *The Suite Life on Deck*, which debuted in 2008. In this spin-off, Zack, Cody, and London Tipton set sail on the *SS Tipton*, where they attended classes at Seven Seas High School while traveling to different countries around the world. Mr. Moseby, the hotel manager on *The Suite Life*, reappeared in the new series as the manager of the *SS Tipton*.

In 2006, Disney debuted a new tween sitcom called *Hannah Montana*, starring teen singer Miley Cyrus as Miley Stewart, who led a secret double life as an average schoolgirl by day but as famous recording artist Hannah Montana by night. The series followed Miley's day-to-day life with her brother, her friends, and her widowed dad, Robby, a successful country music singer played by Billy Ray Cyrus, who happened to be Miley Cyrus' real-life father. With Miley Cyrus' musical performances in her Hannah Montana role as a key feature of the show, the series quickly became a huge hit and multi-media licensing franchise, and it catapulted Miley Cyrus into teen idol stardom.

The Disney Channel also struck tween gold with another music-themed show that first aired in 2006, *High School Musical.* The show was the first installment in what became a highly successful trilogy of two made-for-TV movies and a theatrical film released over the next two years. This tween-targeted romantic comedy was described as a modern musical adaptation of Romeo and Juliet with a touch of West Side Story, in which two high school juniors from rival cliques, Troy Bolton, captain of the basketball team, and Gabriella Montez, a shy transfer student who is a math and science whiz, try out for the lead parts in their annual high school musical. Though other students try to thwart their ambitions, Troy and Gabriella succeed in landing the parts. Then scheduling conflicts for the busy teens threaten to interfere with their premiere performance, until the two use their computer skills to reschedule their conflicting school activities. The movie ended with Troy and Gabriella successfully performing in the school musical, to much acclaim. When it aired in 2006, *High School Musical* became the highest-rated original TV movie the Disney Channel had produced, and the movie's soundtrack was the best-selling album in the U.S. in 2006. That led to a television sequel, *High School Musical 2*, in 2007, and a feature film, *High School Musical 3: Senior Year,* released in theaters in 2008.

Girl Meets World, which debuted in 2014, continued Disney's string of coming-of-age sitcoms for tweens. The show was a sequel to ABC's popular 1990s primetime sitcom *Boy Meets World*. In this updated version, the two lead characters of the original series had grown up and married and were living in New York City with their tween-age daughter Riley, who was the central character in the new show. The series followed Riley's daily life as she traversed the normal challenges of adolescence, together with her best friend Maya. Critics praised the show for presenting a realistic look at "what it is like to be a young woman in America today—the struggle to define yourself, navigating the online world and its cyber bullies, and forging friendships to sustain you throughout those turbulent high school years."[40] Nevertheless, the show's ratings declined, and it ended its run in January 2017.

In addition to its new shows for tweens, the Disney Channel also continued to beef up its preschool lineup. Besides *Phineas and Ferb* and *Doc McStuffins*, there was *JoJo's Circus*, which premiered in 2003. This was a claymation-animated series about a six-year-old little girl clown named JoJo Tickle, who lived in Circus Town with her family and friends. JoJo and her pet lion Goliath attended the Little Big Top Circus School, where their teacher, Mrs. Kersplatski, instructed them in how to be circus performers. The show conveyed lessons about personal hygiene, responsibility, safety, and how to get along with others, but its main focus was on encouraging movement and exercise, at a time when childhood obesity was becoming a public concern. Using music, games, and humor, the show encouraged active participation by asking little viewers at home to walk, stretch, jump, clap, and dance along with the program.

In 2012, *Sofia the First* debuted on Disney Jr., as Disney's first television show to incorporate characters from Disney's series of princess movies. The animated musical series tells the story of Sofia, an eight-year-old village girl who suddenly becomes a princess when her mother marries the king. Storylines revolve around Sofia learning important life lessons as she adjusts to being a princess. With the help of a magical amulet the king gives her, Sofia can summon princesses from classic Disney movies, including Ariel, Belle, and Jasmine, to give her guidance in her transition to royalty. Sofia learns that having a title isn't what makes one worthy of being a princess but rather having qualities like honesty, loyalty, compassion, and grace.

The show's premiere was the highest-rated cable TV telecast among children 2–5 years old in TV history at the time, and its popularity proved very durable, perhaps not surprising given the series' connection to the Disney princess franchise. There was a brief controversy early in the show's run, when a producer referred to Sofia as Disney's first Latina princess. Disney management followed up by insisting that, while Sofia's mother came from a fictitious land with Latin influences, Sofia was a fairy-tale character not meant to represent any specific culture or ethnicity. While Disney's clarification may have been intended to broaden the show's appeal, it generated disappointed reactions from some Hispanic groups.[41]

Diversity was a popular topic on children's shows in the new millennium, but as Disney discovered with *Sofia the First*, it remained a sensitive issue. On PBS, a new series that began airing in 2004 also stirred up a controversy with its attempt to portray the diversity of life in America. The show, *Postcards from Buster*, was a spin-off from PBS' popular animated series *Arthur*, starring Arthur's best friend, eight-year-old rabbit Buster Baxter. Designed to build awareness and appreciation of America's diverse local cultures and to support English language learning, the series' premise was that Buster, whose parents were divorced, was traveling across America, Canada, Mexico, and Puerto Rico with his father, a pilot for a touring rock band. At each location they visited, Buster would meet children and families who lived there and learn about the local culture. To stay in touch with his friends back home, Buster would videotape each of his visits as "video postcards" that he would send back to his friends. While the rest of the show was animated, the video postcards were live-action sequences as seen from Buster's video camera.

The children and families shown in the series were meant to reflect the diversity of American life and culture, from a Mormon family in Utah to a Mestizo family in Texas. It was an episode in 2005 in which Buster visited Vermont to learn about the production of maple sugar that created a flap. In a complaint with overtones of the charge that televangelist Jerry Falwell had made about *Teletubbies* a decade earlier, the U.S. Secretary of Education, Margaret Spellings, objected to the fact that two of the families that Buster visited in that episode were headed by lesbian couples. Though no direct references were made to lesbians or homosexuals, a child in one of the families mentioned her "mom and stepmom," and at one point, Buster commented, "Boy, that's a lot of moms!" Claiming that parents would not want their children to be exposed to the "lifestyles" portrayed on that episode, Spellings demanded that PBS return all federal funding that had been used in its production.[42] PBS decided not to distribute the episode in question to their stations. However, WGBH, the public television station in Boston that produced the series, sent it out to the other PBS affiliates, and several did choose to air it.

The new millennium also saw the debut of a number of educational shows on PBS that dealt with math and science, topics that were generally not being addressed by children's shows on the commercial networks. Premiering in 2002, *Cyberchase* was an animated series intended to foster enthusiasm for math and inspire children to approach math with confidence. The cartoon's premise was that three ordinary children, Jackie, Matt, and Inez, were brought into the digital universe of Cyberspace to help protect it and its ruler, Motherboard, from the evil villain Hacker and his hench-bots, Hack and Delete. In each episode, the children would use their math and problem-solving skills to thwart Hacker's evil plans. Each episode would then be followed by a live-action segment called "*Cyberchase* for Real," which showed how the math concepts presented in the show could be applied to real-life experiences. To promote an interest in math among girls and minorities, two of the three lead characters on Cyberchase were girls, one African American and the other Hispanic.

Several other new science-oriented PBS shows were aimed at preschool viewers. *Curious George*, which debuted in 2006, is an animated show designed to inspire preschoolers to explore science, math, and engineering in the world around them. Based on the popular children's book series, the show revolves around the titular monkey, who loves to find new things to discover, touch, spill, and chew, teaching basic concepts in math, science, and engineering along the way. Each episode features two animated stories followed by short live-action segments in which real children investigate the ideas that George has introduced.

Sid the Science Kid was a 2008 computer-animated offering from the Jim Henson Company that used comedy and music to promote exploration, discovery, and science readiness. The characters on the show were computer-animated Muppets, including the central character Sid, a curious young Muppet boy and aspiring stand-up comedian. Sid would start each morning with a comedy monologue delivered to his stuffed animals, which focused on a single scientific question, like "Why do bananas get mushy?" With the help of his friends and family, Sid then spent the rest of the episode searching for the answer to his question, using basic scientific methods like observing, measuring, asking questions, and using words to communicate his findings.

The Cat in the Hat Knows a Lot about That!, which premiered in 2010, was an animated PBS series that drew on children's books and characters from Dr. Seuss to promote science literacy among preschoolers. With comedian Martin Short providing the title character's voice, each episode featured The Cat in the Hat as he led six-year-old neighbors Nick and Sally, the Fish, and Thing One and Thing Two on adventures around the world in his "Thinga-ma-jigger," a miraculous vehicle that could change size, sprout wings, pontoons, or booster rockets, or change in other magical ways needed to pursue their travels. As they explored places around the world, like the rain forest or the bottom of the ocean, they learned about the natural sciences.

The natural sciences were also the focus of another new show on PBS, *Wild Kratts*, which debuted in 2011. This cartoon series starred animated versions of real-life brothers Chris and Martin Kratt, hosts of prior live-action educational shows like *Kratts' Creatures* and *Zoboomafoo*, as they traveled to animal habitats around the world. The show's aim was to educate children about biology, zoology, and ecology. The real-life Kratt brothers would introduce each episode, then transform into their animated versions, who used their amazing Creature Power Suits to fly with peregrine falcons, swim alongside great white sharks, or dive to the bottom of the sea with a colossal squid, allowing viewers to observe these creatures up close in their natural habitats.

In 2015, PBS debuted an updated remake of popular animated British preschool series, *Bob the Builder*. Featuring the adventures of intrepid construction head Bob and his team of assistants and anthropomorphic construction machines, the show is aimed at introducing preschoolers to age-appropriate STEM (science, technology, engineering and math) concepts while fostering social-emotional growth. Bob and his team work on projects of all sizes, from fixing a leaky roof to installing an elevator in a skyscraper. Bob's team includes Wendy, his smart business partner and electronics specialist, and Leo, his enthusiastic young African American apprentice. Each episode includes a story about Bob and his team, sing-along music videos, and short live-action segments that teach lessons about problem solving, learning through trial and error, and the importance of friendship and teamwork.

The End of an Era

Throughout the 1990s, the commercial broadcast networks had struggled to find a children's programming strategy that would make it possible for them to successfully compete with the new child-focused cable channels. In the new millennium, not only did the competition from cable continue to grow, but additional viewing options from streaming services like Netflix, Hulu, Amazon Prime, and YouTube also seemed to be drawing away child viewers. By the start of 2017, all five broadcast television networks had thrown in the towel, outsourcing their Saturday morning airtime to syndication companies, who filled the hours with live-action lifestyle and documentary programming aimed at teens and families, which technically met the educational programming requirements defined by the Children's Television Act. The days when children across the country would gather around their TV sets on Saturday mornings to watch their favorite cartoons were over.

The broadcast networks are not the only children's television sources that have suffered audience losses as more video content has become available online. Cable television has also seen viewership for its children's programs erode. By 2015, Nielsen ratings for children's cable networks were down 30 percent from two years earlier.[43]

PBS has continued to provide educational programming for children, much of it now animated, devoting over eight hours per weekday and several hours each weekend to educational children's shows. But even *Sesame Street*, the foundational show of PBS' children's lineup, has had to adapt to the changing media environment. Competition from children's cable channels had been cutting into *Sesame Street*'s audience to the point that, by the show's 40th anniversary in 2009, *Sesame Street* had dropped from first place among children's shows to fifteenth, behind *SpongeBob* and *Dora the Explorer*. The show had also seen a decline in its licensing revenues, as DVR recording and Internet streaming replaced the purchase of DVD's, which had made up a major portion of the show's licensing income. After operating at a loss for several years, Sesame Workshop signed a five-season funding agreement with premium cable channel HBO in 2015, allowing HBO to air new episodes of *Sesame Street* nine months before they run on PBS.[44] Given *Sesame Street*'s beginnings as a service for educationally disadvantaged children, this seemed to some critics like a betrayal of the series' mission, but it gave the show a firmer financial footing from which to continue production in the years ahead.

Do these trends spell the end of children's television, at least as we know it, as more children continue to turn to digital media for entertainment? For now, children still spend more time watching television than using any other media, and digital media have actually extended the range of children's TV shows to even more viewers, who can now watch and interact with their favorite shows on other devices and screens whenever they want. Some think children's television is on the path to becoming another victim of the digital revolution, more road kill on the Information Highway, but the history of children's television suggests otherwise. Its resilience as an industry will more likely be invigorated by the new technologies, as shows become multi-platform brands and children are free to access their shows and find whatever content or interactive experience they wish with any devices and screens they have. The creators of children's television will always respond to the opportunity to tell stories and reach wider audiences in new ways, as they have since the medium was invented. Television is not just television anymore, but an integral and synergistic part of a vast digital environment, where it will continue to entertain and delight audiences as long as there are children to watch.

Epilogue

Like the superheroes on the old children's shows, children's television has "morphed" into new forms as it has adapted to changing technologies, changing regulations, changing media habits, changing social norms, and changing views about children and childhood. At its birth, children's television served as the electronic baby-sitter for the new postwar generation with shows like *Howdy Doody* and *The Lone Ranger*, which provided lessons in morals and values along with the puppets and shoot-'em-ups. Soon, *The Mickey Mouse Club* created a place just for children, where everyone could feel like they were a member of the club simply by putting on their Mickey Mouse ears and singing along. In the 1960s, Baby Boomers around the country took over the family TV set on Saturday mornings to watch their favorite cartoons, and adults joined in to watch *Rocky and Bullwinkle* provide comic relief from tense international saber-rattling. In the psychedelic 1970s, the youngest Boomers were introduced to the racially integrated *Sesame Street*, where they could learn their letters and numbers while being entertained by eye-grabbing graphics and cool pop culture parodies; meanwhile, shows like *Fat Albert and the Cosby Kids* used inner city issues as grist for comedy and prosocial learning. *The Smurfs* and "program-length commercials" took over children's television in the materialistic culture of the eighties. For boys, there was *He-Man* and *Transformers*; for girls, there was *My Little Pony* and *Care Bears*. In the prosperous but increasingly fractured society of the nineties, as Millennials rose and helicopter parents hovered, Nickelodeon declared "Kids Rule!," *Power Rangers* and *Pokémon* dominated the airwaves, and preschoolers fell in love with a big purple dinosaur named Barney. In the new millennium, when we seem to be on a roller-coaster ride of ever faster technological innovation and neck-snapping social change, children's television has served up postmodern shows for the postmodern child, with SpongeBob and Finn the Human making their innocent way through an increasingly surreal landscape where nothing is familiar or predictable, including childhood itself.

It may seem as if children's television in the 2000s bears little resemblance to the simpler and more innocent shows of the 1950s. If that is the case, it is because adults' conception of children and childhood has changed as well. We've gone from a time in the 1950s when parents in small towns and suburbs told their children to just "go outside and play," to an age when letting children roam their neighborhoods without parental supervision is seen as a form of parental neglect, if not child abuse. But the pendulum may be starting to swing back, as some parents are beginning to feel that a degree of risk is an acceptable price to pay for letting their children learn to navigate life on their own.[1]

The world has changed a great deal since the early days of television, and children's shows have kept pace, reflecting the evolution of society and inevitably contributing to it. What hasn't changed is the capacity of children's shows to offer a common ground and reference point for each generation of children, around which they can bond, build their shared vision of the world, and one day perhaps share fond memories.

Chapter Notes

Introduction

1. Steven Mintz, *Huck's Raft: A History of American Childhood* (Cambridge: Harvard University Press, 2004), 4.

2. David Buckingham, *After the Death of Childhood: Growing Up in the Age of Electronic Media* (Cambridge, UK: Polity Press, 2000), 6.

3. Stephen Kline, *Out of the Garden: Toys and Children's Culture in the Age of TV Marketing* (London: Verso, 1995), 46.

4. Mintz, *Huck's Raft*, 10, 76.

5. Kline, *Out of the Garden*, 64.

6. Kline, *Out of the Garden*, 74.

7. See, for example, Kline, *Out of the Garden*; Ellen Seiter, *Sold Separately: Parents & Children in Consumer Culture* (New Brunswick: Rutgers University Press, 1993); Gerald S. Lesser, *Children and Television: Lessons from Sesame Street* (New York: Vintage Books, 1975); Mark Collins and Margaret Mary Kimmel, eds., *Mister Rogers' Neighborhood: Children, Television, and Fred Rogers* (Pittsburgh: University of Pittsburgh Press, 1996).

8. Heather Hendershot, *Nickelodeon Nation: The History, Politics, and Economics of America's Only TV Channel for Kids* (New York: New York University Press, 2004).

9. Marion T. Bennet, *American Immigration Policies, A History* (Washington, D.C.: Public Affairs Press, 1963), 15; Michael R. Haines, "The Population of the United States, 1790–1920," in *The Cambridge Economic History of the United States, Vol. 2, The Long Nineteenth Century*, eds. Stanley L. Engerman and Robert E. Gallman (Cambridge: Cambridge University Press, 2000), 188, 194; Harold Evans, *The American Century* (New York: Alfred A. Knopf, 1998); Martha Olney, "The 1920s," in *Routledge Handbook of Major Events in Economic History*, eds. Randall E. Parker

and Robert Whaples (New York: Routledge, 2013).

10. Mintz, *Huck's Raft*, 255.

11. Mintz, *Huck's Raft*, 254–274.

12. Historian Marilyn Irvin Holt describes a polite but disputatious postwar encounter between 44 German educators and experts and American participants at a conference on this subject. See Marilyn Irvin Holt, *Cold War Kids: Politics and Childhood in Postwar America, 1945–1960* (Lawrence: University Press of Kansas, 2014), 148–149.

13. This description of children's and teens' lives during World War II is primarily based on Mintz, *Huck's Raft*, 254–274.

14. Robert Heide, *Home Front America: Popular Culture of the World War II Era* (San Francisco: Chronicle Books, 1995), 33–34.

15. Mintz, *Huck's Raft*, 265–268.

16. Lynn Spigel, *Make Room for TV: Television and the Family Ideal in Postwar America* (Chicago: University of Chicago Press, 1992), 33.

17. Mintz, *Huck's Raft*, 277.

18. David Halberstam, *The Fifties* (New York: Random House, 1994), 132.

19. Spigel, *Make Room for TV*, 32.

20. Tim Hollis, *Hi There, Boys and Girls! America's Local Children's TV Programs* (Jackson: University Press of Mississippi, 2001).

21. Spigel, *Make Room for TV*, 136–180.

Chapter One

1. Paul Charles Light, *Baby Boomers* (New York: Norton, 1988), 24; John Donovan, "Comic Books and the Cold War Red Menace on the Moon: Containment in Space as Depicted in Comics of the 1950s," in *Comic Books and the Cold War, 1946–1962: Essays on Graphic Treatment of Communism, the Code*

205

and Social Concerns, eds. Chris York and Rafiel York (Jefferson, NC: McFarland, 2012), 79–90.

2. Spigel, *Make Room for TV*, 36–72.

3. Gwendolyn Wright, *Building the Dream: A Social History of Housing in America* (New York: Pantheon Books, 1981), 255.

4. Benjamin Spock, M.D., and Michael B. Rothenberg, M.D., *Dr. Spock's Baby and Child Care*, Revised and Updated Edition (New York: Pocket Books, 1985).

5. Seiter, *Sold Separately*, 7–50.

6. Gary R. Edgerton, *The Columbia History of American Television* (New York: Columbia University Press, 2007), 127.

7. David Reisman, Nathan Glazer, and Reuel Denney, *The Lonely Crowd: A Study of the Changing American Character* (New Haven: Yale University Press, 1989).

8. Spigel, *Make Room for TV*, 128–129.

9. Mintz, *Huck's Raft*, 281.

10. Wright, *Building the Dream*, 246–248.

11. Wright, *Building the Dream*, 248.

12. Wright, *Building the Dream*, 257.

13. Mintz, *Huck's Raft*, 278.

14. Halberstam, *The Fifties*, 25–26.

15. Halberstam, *The Fifties*, 98–99.

16. "A Frightening Message for a Thanksgiving Issue," *Good Housekeeping*, November 1958, p. 61, in *A History of our Time: Readings on Postwar America*, 6th edition, eds. William H. Chafe, Harvard Sitkoff, and Beth Bailey (New York: Oxford University Press, 2003).

17. Stefan Kanfer, *A Journal of the Plague Years* (New York: Atheneum, 1973), 147–151; Wright, *Building the Dream*, 259.

18. Paul Buhle, *Hide in Plain Sight: The Hollywood Blacklistees in Film and Television, 1950-2002* (New York: Palgrave Macmillan, 2003), 4–6.

19. Gary H. Grossman, *Saturday Morning TV* (New York: Dell Publishing, 1981), 52.

20. Seiter, *Sold Separately*, 31–33.

21. Spigel, *Make Room for TV*, 45–47.

22. Spigel, *Make Room for TV*, 57

23. Spigel, *Make Room for TV*, 47.

24. Lynn Spigel, "Seducing the Innocent: Childhood and Television in Postwar America," in *The Children's Culture Reader*, ed. Henry Jenkins (New York: New York University Press, 1998), 110–135.

25. Tim Brooks and Earle Marsh, *The Complete Directory to Prime Time Network and Cable TV Shows 1946-Present*, Ninth Edition (New York: Ballantine Books, 2007), 1257–1258.

26. Harry Castleman and Walter J. Podrazik,

Watching TV: Six Decades of American Television (Syracuse University Press, 2003), 70.

27. Spigel, "Seducing the Innocent," 110–135.

28. Spigel, "Seducing the Innocent," 123–124.

29. Brooks and Marsh, *Complete Directory to Prime Time Network and Cable TV Shows*, 1243–1244.

30. Spigel, "Seducing the Innocent," 121.

31. Spigel, "Seducing the Innocent," 125.

32. Edgerton, *Columbia History of American Television*, 127.

33. Brooks and Marsh, *Complete Directory to Prime Time Network and Cable TV Shows*, 1062–1063.

34. Spigel, "Seducing the Innocent," 110–135.

35. Grossman, *Saturday Morning TV*, 119.

36. Spigel, "Seducing the Innocent," 110–135.

37. Brooks and Marsh, *Complete Directory to Prime Time Network and Cable TV Shows*, 725.

38. Grossman, *Saturday Morning TV*, 249.

39. Mintz, *Huck's Raft*, 298.

40. Grossman, *Saturday Morning TV*, 175–176.

41. George W. Woolery, *Children's Television: The First Thirty-Five Years, 1946-1981, Part II* (Metuchen, NJ: Scarecrow Press, 1983), 75.

42. Jenkins, *Children's Culture Reader*, 124.

43. Jenkins, *Children's Culture Reader*, 126.

44. Grossman, *Saturday Morning TV*, 228.

45. Grossman, *Saturday Morning TV*, 231.

46. Grossman, *Saturday Morning TV*, 225.

Chapter Two

1. Halberstam, *The Fifties*, 624–628.

2. Sidney Lens, *The Day before Doomsday: An Anatomy of the Nuclear Arms Race* (Garden City, NY: Doubleday, 1977), 128.

3. Melvin E. Matthews, *Duck and Cover: Civil Defense Images in Film and Television from the Cold War to 9/11* (Jefferson, NC: McFarland, 2011), 11–33.

4. Lens, *The Day before Doomsday*, 128–147.

5. Matthews, *Duck and Cover*, 34–127.

6. Lens, *The Day before Doomsday*, 128–130, 138–147.

7. Mintz, *Huck's Raft*, 287.

8. See, for example, Harrison E. Salisbury, *The Shook-Up Generation* (New York: Fawcett Publications, 1958).

9. Halberstam, *The Fifties*, 485–486
10. Mintz, *Huck's Raft*, 293–300.
11. Halberstam, *The Fifties*, 437.
12. Devery Anderson, "Widow of Emmett Till Killer Dies Quietly, Notoriously," *USA Today*, February 27, 2014, http://www.usatoday.com/story/news/nation/2014/02/27/emmett-till-juanita-milam/5873235/, https://perma.cc/26VC-6QX6. NB: Anderson is the author of the definitive history of the murder, *Emmett Till: The Murder that Shocked the World and Propelled the Civil Rights Movement* (Jackson: University Press of Mississippi, 2015). The January 24, 1956, *Look* article is reproduced at http://www.pbs.org/wgbh/amex/till/sfeature/sf_look_confession.html ("The Shocking Story of Approved Killing in Mississippi" by William Bradford Huie). Anderson has written that the *Look* article contains "gross inaccuracies." The woman involved recanted her story at the age of 72, as reported in Timothy Tyson, *The Blood of Emmett Till* (New York: Simon and Schuster, 2017).
13. Sheila Weller, "The Missing Woman: How Author Timothy Tyson Found the Woman at the Center of the Emmett Till Case," *Vanity Fair*, January 26, 2017, http://www.vanityfair.com/news/2017/01/how-author-timothy-tyson-found-the-woman-at-the-center-of-the-emmett-till-case, https://perma.cc/BGW8-3B72.
14. Halberstam, *The Fifties*, 539–563.
15. Mintz, *Huck's Raft*, 300, 302.
16. Mintz, *Huck's Raft*, 301.
17. Halberstam, *The Fifties*, 473–474.
18. Halberstam, *The Fifties*, 474.
19. Castleman and Podrazik, *Watching TV*, 119–120.
20. Seiter, *Sold Separately*, 32.
21. Edgerton, *Columbia History of American Television*, 197.
22. Edgerton, *Columbia History of American Television*, 198–201; Castleman and Podrazik, *Watching TV*, 122–124; Halberstam, *The Fifties*, 643–666.
23. Castleman and Podrazik, *Watching TV*, 118.
24. As discussed in Alex McNeil, *Total Television* (New York: Penguin Books, 1997), 546–547, the show was cancelled by ABC in fall 1959, but the series was revived in 1976 as *The New Mickey Mouse Club*, with a new cast that featured several African American Mouseketeers.
25. Grossman, *Saturday Morning TV*, 123.
26. Grossman, *Saturday Morning TV*, 123.
27. Grossman, *Saturday Morning TV*, 123.
28. McNeil, *Total Television*, 775.
29. Ross D. Petty, "Pedaling Schwinn Bicycles: Lessons from the Leading Post-World War II U.S. Bicycle Brand" (MA thesis, Babson College, 2007), 6.
30. Cy Schneider, *Children's Television: The Art, the Business, and How It Works* (Chicago: NTC Business Books, 1987), 12–37.
31. Schneider, *Children's Television*, 23.
32. Schneider, *Children's Television*, 24–37.
33. Castleman and Podrazik, *Watching TV*, 135.

Chapter Three

1. Mintz, *Huck's Raft*, 312.
2. David Farber, *The Age of Great Dreams: America in the 1960's* (New York: Hill and Wang, 1994), 190–211.
3. Terry Anderson, *The Movement and the Sixties* (New York: Oxford University Press, 1995), 176–177.
4. Anderson, *The Movement and the Sixties*, 325.
5. Farber, *Age of Great Dreams*, 221–224.
6. Betty Friedan, *The Feminine Mystique*, 50th Anniversary Edition (New York: W. W. Norton, 2013).
7. Farber, *Age of Great Dreams*, 239–261.
8. Paula S. Fass, *The End of American Childhood: A History of Parenting from Life on the Frontier to the Managed Child* (Princeton: Princeton University Press, 2016), 205.
9. Mintz, *Huck's Raft*, 313.
10. Mintz, *Huck's Raft*, 312–313.
11. James Davison, *Culture Wars: The Struggle to Define America* (New York: Basic Books, 1991).
12. Mintz, *Huck's Raft*, 313.
13. Mintz, *Huck's Raft*, 314–315.
14. J. Walker Smith and Ann Clurman, *Generation Ageless: How Baby Boomers Are Changing the Way We Live Today—and They're Just Getting Started* (New York: Collins, 2007), 4.
15. Castleman and Podrazik, *Watching TV*, 143–147.
16. Edgerton, *Columbia History of American Television*, 240–241.
17. Brooks and Marsh, *Complete Directory to Prime Time Network and Cable TV Shows*, 1370.
18. Jerry G. Bowles, *A Thousand Sundays: The Story of the Ed Sullivan Show* (New York: Putnam, 1980), 122, 187.

19. Gerald Nachman, *Right Here on Our Stage Tonight! Ed Sullivan's America* (Berkeley: University of California Press, 2009), 9–10.

20. Edgerton, *Columbia History of American Television*, 261–263.

21. Brooks and Marsh, *Complete Directory to Prime Time Network and Cable TV Shows*, 1262.

22. Castleman and Podrazik, *Watching TV*, 192–193; Edgerton, *Columbia History of American Television*, 266–267.

23. Timothy Burke and Kevin Burke, *Saturday Morning Fever: Growing up with Cartoon Culture* (New York: St. Martin's Griffin, 1999), 10.

24. Brooks and Marsh, *Complete Directory to Prime Time Network and Cable TV Shows*, 482.

25. Grossman, *Saturday Morning TV*, 374–377; Burke and Burke, *Saturday Morning Fever*, 144–145.

26. McNeil, *Total Television*, 73, 357, 382.

27. Burke and Burke, *Saturday Morning Fever*, 21–23.

28. Castleman and Podrazik, *Watching TV*, 142.

29. Newton N. Minow, "Television and the Public Interest," *Federal Communications Law Journal* 55, issue 3, article 4, 2003,http://www.repository.law.indiana.edu/cgi/viewcontent.cgi?article=1335&context=fclj, https://web.archive.org/web/20170321221352/http://www.repository.law.indiana.edu/cgi/viewcontent.cgi?article=1335&context=fclj.

30. Castleman and Podrazik, *Watching TV*, 197.

31. Mark Collins and Margaret Mary Kimmel, eds., *Mister Rogers' Neighborhood: Children, Television, and Fred Rogers* (Pittsburgh: University of Pittsburgh Press, 1996).

32. "Won't You Be my Neighbor?" http://www.cpb.org/aboutpb/mrrogers, https://web.archive.org/web/20170321221918/http://www.cpb.org/aboutpb/mrrogers.

33. http://www.cpb.org/aboutcpb/history-timeline.

34. Lesser, *Children and Television*, 35.

35. Heather Hendershot, "*Sesame Street*: Cognition and Communications Imperialism," in *Kids' Media Culture*, ed. Marsha Kinder (Durham: Duke University Press, 1999), 139–176.

36. Lesser, *Children and Television*.

37. Michael Davis, *Street Gang: The Complete History of Sesame Street* (New York: Penguin Books, 2008), 128.

38. Hendershot, "*Sesame Street*," 145.

39. Lesser, *Children and Television*, 196.

40. See Lesser, *Children and Television*.

41. Schneider, *Children's Television*, 23.

42. Jeffery Davis, *Children's Television 1947–1990* (Jefferson, NC: McFarland, 1995), 92.

43. Schneider, *Children's Television*, 56.

44. Andy Bennett, introduction to *Remembering Woodstock*, ed. Andy Bennett (Burlington, VT: Ashgate, 2004), xiv–xxi.

Chapter Four

1. Michael Grossberg, "Liberation and Caretaking: Fighting over Children's Rights in Postwar America," in *Reinventing Childhood: After World War II*, eds. Paula S. Fass and Michael Grossberg (Philadelphia: University of Pennsylvania Press, 2012), 19–37.

2. Fass, *End of American Childhood*, 211–212.

3. Bill Ong Hing, "Integrating New Americans," in *America's Americans: Population Issues in U.S. Society and Politics*, eds. Philip Davies and Iwan Morgan (London: Institute for the Study of the Americas, University of London, School of Advanced Study, 2007), 145–167.

4. Ruth Bader Ginsberg, "Some Thoughts on Autonomy and Equality in Relation to *Roe v. Wade*," in *The Abortion Controversy: 25 Years after Roe v. Wade: A Reader*, eds. Louis P. Pojman and Francis J. Beckwith (Belmont, CA: Wadsworth, 1998), 119–128.

5. Mintz, *Huck's Raft*, 332.

6. Richard M. Pious. *Civil Rights and Liberties in the 1970's* (New York: Random House, 1973).

7. Stephanie A. Slocum-Schaffer, *America in the Seventies* (Syracuse: Syracuse University Press, 2003), 176–177; Sarah Katherine Mergel, *Conservative Intellectuals and Richard Nixon* (New York: Palgrave Macmillan, 2010), 4.

8. Captain Timothy Guiden, "Defending America's Cambodian Incursion," *Arizona Journal of International and Comparative Law* 11 (January 10, 1994), 215; Charles N. Brower, "In Memoriam: William D. Rogers," *American Society of International Law, Proceedings of the Annual Meeting*, January 1, 2008, 509.

9. Thomas R. Hensley and Jerry M. Lewis, eds., *Kent State and May 4th: A Social Science Perspective* (Kent, OH: Kent State University Press, 2010), 58–59.

10. Frederick Stirton Weaver, *An Economic History of the United States: Conquest, Conflict, and Struggles for Equality* (Lanham, MD: Row-

man & Littlefield, 2016), 195–196, 208–209; Dean Baker, *The United States since 1980* (Cambridge: Cambridge University Press, 2007), 44–46.

11. Walter A. Rosenbaum, *Environmental Politics and Policy* (Washington, D.C.: CQ Press, 2002).

12. Castleman and Podrazik, *Watching TV*, 244–245.

13. Farber, *Age of Great Dreams*, 233.

14. Tom Wolfe, "The 'Me' Decade and the Third Great Awakening," *New York Times*, August 23, 1976, http://nymag.com/news/features/45938/, https://perma.cc/9B7A-JRZN.

15. Mintz, *Huck's Raft*, 334.

16. Mintz, *Huck's Raft*, 341.

17. Mintz, *Huck's Raft*, 358.

18. Paula S. Fass, "The Child-Centered Family? New Rules in Postwar America," in *Reinventing Childhood: After World War II*, 13.

19. Mintz, *Huck's Raft*, 343.

20. Mintz, *Huck's Raft*, 340–358.

21. Edgerton, *Columbia History of American Television*, 276.

22. Castleman and Podrazik, *Watching TV*, 217–219.

23. Castleman and Podrazik, *Watching TV*, 265–266.

24. Grossman, *Saturday Morning TV*, 355–357.

25. Grossman, *Saturday Morning TV*, 353.

26. Grossman, *Saturday Morning TV*, 358.

27. Burke and Burke, *Saturday Morning Fever*, 127.

28. See Richard A. Spears, *NTC's Dictionary of American Slang and Colloquial Expressions* (Lincolnwood, IL: NTC Publishing Group, 2000), 250. Not just slang for hat or cap, a lid was also 1970s slang for a small bag of marijuana.

29. David Martindale, *Pufnstuf & Other Stuff: The Weird and Wonderful World of Sid and Marty Krofft* (Los Angeles: St. Martin's Press, 1998).

30. Davis, *Children's Television*, 33.

31. McNeil, *Total Television*, 426.

32. McNeil, *Total Television*, 361, 424, 450.

33. McNeil, *Total Television*, 688.

34. At the time, Cosby was a beloved and highly-respected star whose involvement greatly enhanced the show's credibility and popularity.

35. Davis, *Children's Television*, 143–144.

36. Burke and Burke, *Saturday Morning Fever*, 39.

37. Grossman, *Saturday Morning TV*, 396.

38. Grossman, *Saturday Morning TV*, 274.

39. Grossman, *Saturday Morning TV*, 267.

40. McNeil, *Total Television*, 148, 885.

41. Seiter, *Sold Separately*, 99.

42. Burke and Burke, *Saturday Morning Fever*, 27–38.

43. Schneider, *Children's Television*, 176.

44. Burke and Burke, *Saturday Morning Fever*, 40.

45. Edgerton, *Columbia History of American Television*, 301.

Chapter Five

1. Garland A. Haas, *Jimmy Carter and the Politics of Frustration* (Jefferson, NC: McFarland, 1992), 83–84.

2. David R. Farber, *Taken Hostage: The Iran Hostage Crisis and America's First Encounter with Radical Islam* (Princeton: Princeton University Press, 2005), 12–13.

3. Steven R. Weisman, "Reagan Takes Oath as 40th President; Promises an 'Era of National Renewal'—Minutes Later, 52 U.S. Hostages in Iran Fly to Freedom After 444-Day Ordeal," *New York Times*, January 21, 1981, A1; Farber, *Taken Hostage*, 178.

4. Bruce J. Schulman. *The Seventies: The Great Shift in American Culture, Society, and Politics* (New York: Free Press, 2001), 218–219.

5. Michael McHugh, The *Second Gilded Age: The Great Reaction in the United States, 1973–2001* (Lanham, MD: University Press of America, 2006), 143.

6. Mark Setterfield, "Wages, Demand, and U.S. Macroeconomic Travails," in *After the Great Recession: The Struggle for Economic Recovery and Growth*, eds. Barry Z. Cynamon, Steven M. Fazzari, and Mark Setterfield (Cambridge: Cambridge University Press, 2013), 158, 162–164; Harold L. Wilensky, *American Political Economy in Global Perspective* (Cambridge: Cambridge University Press, 2012), 158–159.

7. Frederick Stirton Weaver, *An Economic History of the United States: Conquest, Conflict, and Struggles for Equality* (Lanham, MD: Rowman & Littlefield, 2016), 238.

8. Kevin Ferguson, *Eighties People: New Lives in the American Imagination* (New York: Palgrave Macmillan, 2016), 80–82.

9. David France, *How to Survive a Plague: The Inside Story of How Citizens and Science Tamed AIDS* (New York: Alfred A. Knopf, 2016), 6–21.

10. Craig Reinarman and Harry G. Levine, eds., *Crack in America: Demon Drugs and So-*

cial Justice (Berkeley: University of California Press, 1997), 2–5.

11. McHugh, *The Second Gilded Age*, 176–177; Harry G. Levine and Craig Reinarman, "Crack in the Rearview Mirror: Deconstructing Drug War Mythology," *Social Justice* 31, issue 1–2 (March 22, 2004), 182; Robert P. Weiss, "Privatizing the Leviathan State: A 'Reaganomic' Legacy," in *The 1980s: A Critical and Transitional Decade*, eds. Kimberly R. Moffitt and Duncan A. Campbell (Lanham, MD: Lexington Books, 2011), 89–108; Wilensky, *American Political Economy in Global Perspective*, 181–185.

12. In February 2017, a former convenience store clerk was convicted of Etan Patz's murder; a convicted serial killer admitted to Adam Walsh's murder on his deathbed in 2007, http://www.usatoday.com/story/news/2017/02/14/nyc-jury-reaches-verdict-etan-patz-murder-case/97894676, https://perma.cc/3TRP-5ZMS, http://time.com/4437205/adam-walsh-murder/, https://perma.cc/84X2-5ZVD.

13. Mintz, *Huck's Raft*, 337.

14. Mintz, *Huck's Raft*, 335–342.

15. N'Jai-An Patters, "A Culture in Panic: Day Care Abuse Scandals and the Vulnerability of Children," in *The 1980's: A Critical and Transitional Decade*, 295–297.

16. Castleman and Podrazik, *Watching TV*, 344.

17. *Frontline*, "The Way the Music Died," written, produced and directed by Michael Kirk, co-produced and reported by Jim Gilmore. http://www.pbs.org/wgbh/pages/frontline/shows/music/perfect/mtv.html, https://perma.cc/5HAV-GDF9.

18. Castleman and Podrazik, *Watching TV*, 315.

19. Blake J. Harris, *Console Wars: Sega, Nintendo, and the Battle that Defined a Generation* (New York: It Books, 2014), 11.

20. Paul Freiberger, *Fire in the Valley: The Making of the Personal Computer* (Berkeley: Osborne/McGraw-Hill, 1984), 144–145, 349.

21. John Markoff, "The Apple IIc Personal Computer," *Byte Magazine* 9, no. 5 (May 1984), 276–284, https://archive.org/details/byte-magazine-1984–05.

22. At the time, there was no hint of the sexual assault accusations that would later be lodged against Cosby.

23. Burke and Burke, *Saturday Morning Fever*, 161–163.

24. Horst Stipp, "The Role of Academic Advisors in Creating Children's Television

Programs: The NBC Experience," in *The Children's Television Community*, ed. J. Alison Bryant (New York: Routledge, Taylor & Francis Group, 2007), 122.

25. Donna Mitroff and Rebecca Herr Stephenson, "The Television Tug-of-War: A Brief History of Children's Television Programming in the United States," in *The Children's Television Community*, 18.

26. Terry Spencer, "Activist Protests War Toy Link: Fast Challenges Violence on TV," *Los Angeles Times*, January 4, 1988, http://articles.latimes.com/1988-01-04/local/me-22245_1_captain-power, https://perma.cc/8XZT-XNG3.

27. Robby London, "Producing Children's Television," in *The Children's Television Community*, 81.

28. McNeil, *Total Television*, 147.

29. Seiter, *Sold Separately*, 145–171.

30. Tom Englehardt, "Children's Television: The Strawberry Shortcake Strategy," in *Watching Television: A Pantheon Guide to Popular Culture*, ed. Todd Gitlin (New York: Pantheon, 1987), 97.

31. Seiter, *Sold Separately*, 145–171.

32. Seiter, *Sold Separately*, 161.

33. Ellen Seiter, "Children's Desires/Mothers' Dilemmas: The Social Contexts of Consumption," in *Children's Culture Reader*, 300.

34. http://www.nydailynews.com/entertainment/gossip/paul-reubens-pee-wee-playhouse-star-arrested-1991-article-1.2571832, https://web.archive.org/web/20170321135025/http://www.nydailynews.com/entertainment/gossip/paul-reubens-pee-wee-playhouse-star-arrested-1991-article-1.2571832.

35. James Sullivan, *Seven Dirty Words: The Life and Crimes of George Carlin* (Cambridge, MA: Da Capo Press, 2010), 206.

36. Sarah Banet-Weiser, *Kids Rule!: Nickelodeon and Consumer Citizenship* (Durham: Duke University Press, 2007), 89.

37. Seiter, *Sold Separately*, 115–144.

38. Kline, *Out of the Garden*, 236–276.

39. Seiter, *Sold Separately*, 135.

Chapter Six

1. Kurt Andersen, "The Best Decade Ever? The 1990s, Obviously," *New York Times Sunday Review*, Feb. 6, 2015. https://www.nytimes.com/2015/02/08/.../the-best-decade-ever-the-1990s-obviously.html.

2. Andersen, "The Best Decade Ever?"

3. Andersen, "The Best Decade Ever?"

4. https://www.w3.org/History/19921103-hypertext/hypertext/WWW/History.html ; https://perma.cc/MW5G-DDW9.

5. https://www.w3.org/People/Berners-Lee/FAQ.html#browser; https://www.w3.org/History/19921103-hypertext/hypertext/WWW/History.html; https://perma.cc/W5R8-MKXB.

6. http://arstechnica.com/articles/culture/total-share.ars/8 ; https://perma.cc/WY34-LJYS.

7. http://blog.cartesian.com/the-rise-of-mobile-phones-20-years-of-global-adoption, https://perma.cc/4KG9-6CKL.

8. Selma Taffe, "Trends in Fertility in the United States," *Vital and Health Statistics*, Series 21, Data from the National Vital Statistics System, No. 28, United States Department of Health, Education, and Welfare, DHEW Publication; No. (HRA) 78–1906, ISBN 0–8406–0108–5, accessed at http://files.eric.ed.gov/fulltext/ED162951.pdf (September 1977).

9. Gretchen Livingston, "In a Down Economy, Fewer Births," *Social and Demographic Trends*, Pew Research Center, October 12, 2011, http://www.pewsocialtrends.org/2011/10/12/in-a-down-economy-fewer-births/, https://perma.cc/4CAV-DSR6.

10. Richard Fry, "Millennials Overtake Baby Boomers as America's Largest Generation," Pew Research Center, April 25, 2016, http://www.pewresearch.org/fact-tank/2016/04/25/millennials-overtake-baby-boomers/, https://perma.cc/HL6X-5ZLG.

11. Mintz, *Huck's Raft*, 349.

12. Paula S. Fass, "The Child-Centered Family? New Rules in Postwar America," in *Reinventing Childhood after World War II*, 1–18; Steven Mintz, "The Changing Face of Children's Culture," in *Reinventing Childhood After World War II*, 38–50.

13. Foster W. Cline and Jim Fay, *Parenting with Love and Logic: Teaching Children Responsibility* (Colorado Springs: Pinon Press, 1990), 23–25. As quoted by Julie Lythcott-Haims in *How to Raise an Adult: Break Free of the Overparenting Trap and Prepare Your Kid for Success* (New York: St. Martin's Griffin, 2015), 4.

14. Fass, "The Child-Centered Family?" 1–18.

15. Steven Keslowitz, *The World According to the Simpsons: What Our Favorite TV Family Says about Life, Love, and the Pursuit of the Perfect Donut* (Naperville, IL: Sourcebooks, 2006).

16. "'The Simpsons' Becomes Longest Running Scripted TV Show," *TODAY* Show, NBC News, http://www.today.com/video/-the-simpsons-becomes-longest-running-scripted-tv-show-thanks-to-al-roker-802721347707, https://perma.cc/HA97-LJZQ.

17. Brooks and Marsh, *Complete Directory to Prime Time Network and Cable TV Shows 1946-Present*, 1276–1277.

18. Castleman and Podrazik, 377.

19. The Telecommunications Act of 1996 required the installation of "v-chip" technology in future television sets that would allow parents to block objectionable content from being received in their homes. Broadcasters and cable channels agreed to create a system of program content ratings to work with the v-chip technology, and this rating system was implemented in 1997. Shows were rated TVY, for children of all ages; TVY7, for children over the age of 7; TVG, for general audiences; TVPG, for shows where parental guidance was suggested; TV14, for children over 14; and TVM, for mature content not appropriate for children under 17. See Castleman and Podrazik, *Watching TV*, 382, 387.

20. Like HBO, premium cable channels usually do not carry advertising but charge subscribers an extra fee, in addition to the monthly fee for subscribing to "basic" cable service.

21. Banet-Weiser, *Kids Rule!*, 84.

22. Banet-Weiser, *Kids Rule!*, 50.

23. Banet-Weiser, *Kids Rule!*, 104–141.

24. Linda Simensky, "The Early Days of Nicktoons," in *Nickelodeon Nation*, ed. Heather Hendershot (New York: New York University Press, 2004), 87–107.

25. Terry Kalagian, "Programming Children's Television: The Cable Model," in *The Children's Television Community*, 148.

26. Mimi Swartz, "'You Dumb Babies!' How Raising the Rugrats Children Became as Difficult as the Real Thing," in *Nickelodeon Nation*, 108–119.

27. In 1996, Disney acquired the series, making some creative changes and retitling it *Brand Spanking New! Doug*.

28. See http://www.imdb.com/title/tt0101178/, https://web.archive.org/save/_embed/http://www.imdb.com/title/tt0101178/.

29. Lauren Duca, "How the Creator of 'Ren & Stimpy' Changed the Face of Cartoons (and then Got Fired)," *The Huffington Post*, December 1, 2014, www.huffingtonpost.com/2014/08/27/ren-and-stimpy_n_5647944.html, https://perma.cc/JP27-JFTZ.

30. Mark Langer, "*Ren & Stimpy*: Fan Culture and Corporate Strategy," in *Nickelodeon Nation*, 155–181.

31. Banet-Weiser, *Kids Rule!*, 158–160.

32. "Polliwog Helps Bring Gullah Culture to Life," *Sun Sentinel*, Features, July 7, 1996, http://articles.sun-sentinel.com/1996-07-07/entertainment/9606260243_1_natalie-daise-gullah-gullah-island-preschool-show, https://perma.cc/XV33-RFRP.

33. Daniel R. Anderson, "Watching Children Watch Television and the Creation of *Blue's Clues*," in *Nickelodeon Nation*, 241–268.

34. Mark I. West, ed., *The Japanification of Children's Popular Culture* (Lanham, MD: The Scarecrow Press, 2009).

35. Mark I. West, "Invasion of the Japanese Monsters: A Home-Front Report," in *The Japanification of Children's Popular Culture*, 17–24.

36. Cary Elza, "We All Live in a Pokémon World: Animated Utopia for Kids," in *The Japanification of Children's Popular Culture*, 55.

37. Caryn James, "TELEVISION REVIEW: Teletubbies Say Eh-Oh, and Others Say Uh-Oh," *New York Times*, April 6, 1998, http://www.nytimes.com/1998/04/06/arts/television-review-teletubbies-say-eh-oh-and-others-say-uh-oh.html, https://perma.cc/NH5N-9KA8.

38. Lawrie Mifflin, "Falwell Takes On The Teletubbies," *New York Times*, Business Day, Media Talk, February 15, 1999, http://www.nytimes.com/1999/02/15/business/media-talk-falwell-takes-on-the-teletubbies.html, https://perma.cc/W56Y-VQ2L.

39. Robert L. Mitchell, "Y2K: The good, the bad and the crazy," *ComputerWorld*, December 28, 2009, http://www.computerworld.com/article/2522197/it-management/y2k—the-good—the-bad-and-the-crazy.html, https://perma.cc/F7D3-R3VM.

Chapter Seven

1. Malise Ruthven, "How to Understand ISIS," *New York Review of Books*, June 23, 2016, http://www.nybooks.com/articles/2016/06/23/how-to-understand-isis/, https://perma.cc/75SL-VCAU.

2. Michael McHugh, *The Second Gilded Age: The Great Reaction in the United States, 1973–2001* (Lanham, MD: University Press of America, 2006), 157.

3. Wilensky, *American Political Economy in Global Perspective*, 136–137, 140–143; Weaver,

An Economic History of the United States, 218–220, 224–225; Barry Z. Cynamon, Steven M. Fazzari, and Mark Setterfield, "Understanding the Great Recession," in Barry Z. Cynamon, Steven M. Fazzari, and Mark Setterfield, eds., *After the Great Recession: The Struggle for Economic Recovery and Growth* (Cambridge: Cambridge University Press, 2013), 4–8; Alan Blinder, *After the Music Stopped: The Financial Crisis, the Response, and the Work Ahead* (New York: Penguin Press, 2013), 5.

4. Blinder, *After the Music Stopped*, 6; Wilensky, *American Political Economy in Global Perspective*, 158–185.

5. Clare Malone, "Barack Obama Won the White House, but Democrats Lost the Country. What Happened?" *FiveThirtyEight*, January 19, 2017, https://fivethirtyeight.com/features/barack-obama-won-the-white-house-but-democrats-lost-the-country/?ncid=newsltushpmgnews, https://perma.cc/S97C-4LGQ.

6. Raphael Israeli, *From Arab Spring to Islamic Winter* (New Brunswick: Transaction Publishers, 2013), 72–80.

7. http://www.pewinternet.org/2015/10/29/the-demographics-of-device-ownership/, https://perma.cc/AK7G-N2DX.

8. Nate Garrelts, introduction to *The Meaning and Culture of Grand Theft Auto: Critical Essays*, ed. Nate Garrelts (Jefferson, NC: McFarland, 2006), 3–5.

9. Timothy J. Welsch, "Everyday Play: Cruising for Leisure in San Andreas," in *The Meaning and Culture of Grand Theft Auto*, 132–135.

10. Alex Hern, "Will 2016 Be the Year Virtual Reality Gaming Takes Off?" *The Guardian*, U.S. Edition, December 28, 2015, https://www.theguardian.com/technology/2015/dec/28/virtual-reality-gaming-takes-off-2016, https://perma.cc/ZYV3-PJLQ.

11. Jessica Smith, "How the Early Days of VR Are Unfolding and the Challenges It Must Overcome to Reach Mass Adoption," *Business Insider*, The Virtual Reality Report, November 18, 2016, http://www.businessinsider.com/virtual-reality-report-2016-11, https://perma.cc/M66Y-GCNB.

12. "Digital Television," Federal Communications Commission, August 9, 2016, https://www.fcc.gov/general/digital-television, https://perma.cc/3VCS-3EKD.

13. Castleman and Podrazik, *Watching TV*, 442–443.

14. Ralph W. Larkin, *Comprehending*

Columbine (Philadelphia: Temple University Press, 2007), 8–14.

15. Mintz, *Huck's Raft*, 372–384.

16. See, for example, Neil Postman, *The Disappearance of Childhood* (New York: Vintage Books, 1994); David Buckingham, *After the Death of Childhood: Growing Up in the Age of Electronic Media* (Cambridge: Polity Press, 2000); Jyotsna Kapur, "Out of Control: Television and the Transformation of Childhood in Late Capitalism," in Marsha Kinder, ed., *Kids' Media Culture* (Durham: Duke University Press 1999), 122–138.

17. Postman, *The Disappearance of Childhood*, 80.

18. Buckingham, *After the Death of Childhood*, 96.

19. A.O. Scott, "The Death of Adulthood in American Culture," *The New York Times Magazine*, September 11, 2014, https://www.nytimes.com/2014/09/14/magazine/the-death-of-adulthood-in-american-culture.html.

20. Fass, *The End of American Childhood*, 215–267.

21. Amy Chua, *Battle Hymn of the Tiger Mother* (New York: Penguin, 2011).

22. Lenore Skenazy, *Free Range Kids: Giving Our Children the Freedom We Had Without Going Nuts with Worry* (San Francisco: Jossey Bass, 2009).

23. Jennifer Senior, *All Joy and No Fun: The Paradox of Modern Parenthood* (New York: HarperCollins, 2014).

24. Castleman and Podrazik, *Watching TV*, 419.

25. Heather Hendershot, "Nickelodeon's Nautical Nonsense," in *Nickelodeon Nation*, 182–208.

26. Tom Zeller, "How to Succeed without Attitude," *New York Times*, July 21, 2002, http://www.nytimes.com/2002/07/21/weekinreview/ideas-trends-cleaning-up-how-to-succeed-without-attitude.html, https://perma.cc/E9HJ-B3PH.

27. See Buckingham, *After the Death of Childhood*, 88–90; Tim Woods, *Beginning Postmodernism* (Manchester: Manchester University Press, 1999), 194–203.

28. Matt Blum, "Phineas and Ferb: Kid Inventors and a Secret Agent Platypus," *Wired*, July 9, 2008, https://www.wired.com/2008/07/phineas-and-fer/, https://perma.cc/V25E-HSHW.

29. Susan Stewart, "Bored Stepbrothers, Intrepid Platypus," *New York Times*, New York Edition, February 1, 2008, E27, http://www.nytimes.com/2008/02/01/arts/television/01phin.html?, https://perma.cc/ZS58-KQ66.

30. Brian Lowry, Phineas and Ferb Review, *Variety*, January 31, 2008, https://perma.cc/52Y6-AJBW?type=image.

31. "'Adventure Time' Creator Talks '80s," *USA Today*, November 1, 2012, https://perma.cc/8JBW-G3LA.

32. Neil Strauss, "'Adventure Time': The Trippiest Show on Television," *Rolling Stone*, October 2, 2014, http://www.rollingstone.com/tv/features/adventure-time-the-trippiest-show-on-television-20141002, https://perma.cc/XK72-5ZAQ.

33. Emily Nussbaum, "Castles in the Air," *New Yorker*, April 14, 2014. http://www.newyorker.com/magazine/2014/04/21/castles-in-the-air, https://perma.cc/464R-DE4Q.

34. Nussbaum, "Castles in the Air."

35. "Be Amazed by the Amazing World of Gumball," *Wired*, September 2, 2012, https://www.wired.com/2012/09/be-amazed-by-the-amazing-world-of-gumball/, https://perma.cc/V579-G2L3?type=image.

36. Mike Flaherty, "Meet the Cartoon Network's *Samurai Jack*," *Entertainment Weekly*, February 21, 2002, http://ew.com/article/2002/02/21/meet-cartoon-networks-samurai-jack/, https://perma.cc/D6XZ-ATZZ.

37. Brooks and Marsh, *Complete Directory to Prime Time Network and Cable TV Shows*, 189.

38. Banet-Weiser, *Kids Rule!*, 32.

39. Pat Wingert, "The Truth About Tweens," *Newsweek*, October 17, 1999, http://www.newsweek.com/truth-about-tweens-168306, https://perma.cc/4CE8-MELU.

40. Sabienna Bowman, "Girl Meets World Has Become a Landmark Show for a New Generation of Fans," *Bustle*, January 7, 2017, https://www.bustle.com/p/girl-meets-world-has-become-a-landmark-show-for-a-new-generation-of-fans-28517, https://perma.cc/P2U3-AGKM.

41. Cindy Rodriguez, "Backlash for Disney's First Latina Princess," *CNN*, October 22, 2012, http://www.cnn.com/2012/10/19/showbiz/disneys-first-latina-princess/, https://perma.cc/EB5T-2V52.

42. Lisa de Moraes, "PBS's 'Buster' Gets an Education," *Washington Post*, January 27, 2005, C1.

43. Brian Steinberg, "How Kids' TV Networks Are Fighting Off Their Frightening Decline," *Variety*, September 2, 2015, https://perma.cc/UL24-E6EQ?type=image.

44. Austin Siegemund-Broka, "B Is for Broke: Why 'Sesame Street' Is Moving to HBO," *Hollywood Reporter*, August 19, 2015, http://www.hollywoodreporter.com/news/b-is-broke-why-sesame-816105, https://perma.cc/62X5-M8DK.

Epilogue

1. Anna Noel Taylor, "Viacom Presents: Little Big Kids, Preschoolers Ready for Life," *Viacom Global Insights,* January 18, 2017, http://insights.viacom.com/post/viacom-presents-little-big-kids-preschoolers-ready-for-life/, https://perma.cc/SX4D-ER2B.

Bibliography

Adler, Richard P., ed. *All in the Family: A Critical Appraisal.* New York: Praeger, 1979.

Akass, Kim, and Janet McCabe, eds. *Reading Sex and the City.* London: I. B. Tauris, 2004.

Alley, Robert S. *Love Is all Around: The Making of the Mary Tyler Moore Show.* New York: Delta, 1989.

Andersen, Kurt. "The Best Decade Ever? The 1990s, Obviously." *New York Times Sunday Review,* February 6, 2015. https://www.nytimes.com/2015/02/08/.../the-best-decade-ever-the-1990s-obviously.html.

Anderson, Daniel R. "Watching Children Watch Television and the Creation of *Blue's Clues.*" In *Nickelodeon Nation,* edited by Heather Hendershot, 241–268. New York: New York University Press, 2004.

Anderson, Terry. *The Movement and the Sixties.* New York: Oxford University Press, 1995.

Andrews, Bart. *The "I Love Lucy" Book.* Garden City, NY: Doubleday, 1985.

Annenberg Public Policy Center's Annual Conference on Children and Television. Reports no. 6, 21, 25, 31, 39. Philadelphia: Annenberg Public Policy Center of the University of Pennsylvania, 1996–2000. http://www.annenbergpublicpolicycenter.org/Downloads/Media_and_Developing_Child/Conference_on_Child_Media/200006_Conference_on_Child_Media_report.pdf.

Arp, Robert, and Kevin S. Decker. *The Ultimate South Park and Philosophy: Respect My Philosophah!* Malden, MA: Wiley-Blackwell, 2013.

Baker, Dean. *The United States since 1980.* Cambridge: Cambridge University Press, 2007.

Banet-Weiser, Sarah. *Kids Rule! Nickelodeon and Consumer Citizenship.* Durham: Duke University Press, 2007.

Barcus, Francis Earle. *Children's Television: An Analysis of Programming and Advertising.* New York: Praeger, 1977.

Barcus, Francis Earle. *Romper Room: An Analysis.* Newtonville, MA: Action for Children's Television, 1971.

Barnouw, Erik. *Tube of Plenty: The Evolution of American Television,* Second Revised Edition. New York: Oxford University Press, 1990.

Bennett, Andy. Introduction to *Remembering Woodstock,* edited by Andy Bennett, xiv-xxi. Burlington, VT: Ashgate, 2004.

Bennet, Marion T. *American Immigration Policies: A History.* Washington, D.C.: Public Affairs Press, 1963.

Berger, Maurice. *Revolution of the Eye: Modern Art and the Birth of American Television.* Published in conjunction with exhibition organized by the Jewish Museum, New York, and the Center for Art, Design and Visual Culture, University of Maryland. New Haven: Yale University Press, 2014.

Bianculli, David. *Dangerously Funny: The Uncensored Story of The Smothers Brothers Comedy Hour.* New York: Simon & Schuster, 2009.

Blinder, Alan. *After the Music Stopped: The Financial Crisis, the Response, and the Work Ahead.* New York: Penguin Press, 2013.

Blum, Matt. "Phineas and Ferb: Kid Inventors and a Secret Agent Platypus." *Wired,* July 9, 2008. https://www.wired.com/2008/07/phineas-and-fer/. https://perma.cc/V25E-HSHW.

Bowles, Jerry G. *A Thousand Sundays: The Story of the Ed Sullivan Show.* New York: Putnam, 1980.

Bowman, Sabienna. "Girl Meets World Has Become a Landmark Show for a New Generation of Fans." *Bustle,* January 7, 2017.

https://www.bustle.com/p/girl-meets-world-has-become-a-landmark-show-for-a-new-generation-of-fans-28517. https://perma.cc/P2U3-AGKM.

Brooks, Tim, and Earle Marsh. *The Complete Directory to Prime Time Network and Cable TV Shows 1946-Present*, Ninth Edition. New York: Ballantine Books, 2007.

Brower, Charles N. "In Memoriam: William D. Rogers." *American Society of International Law, Proceedings of the Annual Meeting*, January 1, 2008, 509–510.

Brown, Ray, ed. *Children and Television*. Beverly Hills: Sage Publications, 1976.

Buckingham, David. *After the Death of Childhood: Growing Up in the Age of Electronic Media*. Cambridge: Polity Press, 2000.

Buhle, Paul. *Hide in Plain Sight: The Hollywood Blacklistees in Film and Television, 1950-2002*. New York: Palgrave Macmillan, 2003.

Burke, Timothy, and Kevin Burke. *Saturday Morning Fever: Growing Up with Cartoon Culture*. New York: St. Martin's Griffin, 1999.

Bryant, Alison J., ed. *The Children's Television Community*. New York: Routledge, 2007.

Calder, Jenni. *There Must be a Lone Ranger*. New York: Taplinger, 1974.

Campbell, Sean. *The Sitcoms of Norman Lear*. Jefferson, NC: McFarland, 2007.

Cantor, Muriel. *Prime-Time Television: Content and Control*. Beverly Hills: Sage Publications, 1980.

Castleman, Harry, and Walter J. Podrazik. *Watching TV: Six Decades of American Television*. Syracuse: Syracuse University Press, 2003.

William H. Chafe, Harvard Sitkoff, and Beth Bailey, eds. *A History of our Time: Readings on Postwar America*, 6th edition. New York: Oxford University Press, 2003.

Chan-Olmstead, Sylvia. "From Sesame Street to Wall Street: An Analysis of Market Competition in Commercial Children's Television." *Journal of Broadcasting & Electronic Media* 40, no. 1 (Winter 1996): 30–45.

Chua, Amy. *Battle Hymn of the Tiger Mother*. New York: Penguin, 2011.

Clark, Dick. *Dick Clark's American Bandstand*. New York: Collins, 1997.

Collins, Mark, and Margaret Mary Kimmel, eds. *Mister Rogers' Neighborhood: Children, Television, and Fred Rogers*. Pittsburgh: University of Pittsburgh Press, 1996.

Comstock, George, with Haejung Paik. *Television and the American Child*. San Diego: Academic Press, 1991.

Cook, Thomas. *"Sesame Street" Revisited*. New York: Russell Sage Foundation, 1975.

Coontz, Stephanie. *The Way We Never Were: American Families and the Nostalgia Trap*. New York: Basic Books, 2016.

Cotter, Bill. *The Wonderful World of Disney Television: A Complete History*. New York: Hyperion, 1997.

Cynamon, Barry Z., Steven M. Fazzari, and Mark Setterfield. "Understanding the Great Recession." In *After the Great Recession: The Struggle for Economic Recovery and Growth*, edited by Barry Z. Cynamon, Steven M. Fazzari, and Mark Setterfield, 3–30. Cambridge: Cambridge University Press, 2013.

Davies, Maire Messenger. *Children, Media and Culture*. Berkshire, UK: McGraw-Hill, 2010.

Davis, Jeffrey. *Children's Television 1947-1990: Over 200 Series, Game and Variety Shows, Cartoons, Educational Programs, and Specials*. Jefferson, NC: McFarland, 1995.

Davis, Michael. *Street Gang: The Complete History of Sesame Street*. New York: Penguin Books, 2008.

Davison, James. *Culture Wars: The Struggle to Define America*. New York: Basic Books, 1991.

Delaney, Tim. *Seinology: The Sociology of Seinfeld*. Amherst, NY: Prometheus Books, 2006.

Delmont, Matthew F. *Making Roots: A Nation Captivated*. Oakland: University of California Press, 2016.

Desjardins, Mary R. *Father Knows Best*. Detroit: Wayne State University Press, 2015.

Diffrient, David Scott. *M*A*S*H*. Detroit: Wayne State University Press, 2008.

Donovan, John. "Comic Books and the Cold War Red Menace on the Moon: Containment in Space as Depicted in Comics of the 1950s." In *Comic Books and the Cold War, 1946-1962: Essays on Graphic Treatment of Communism, the Code and Social Concerns*, edited by Chris York and Rafiel York, 79–90. Jefferson, NC: McFarland, 2012.

Duca, Lauren. "How the Creator of 'Ren & Stimpy' Changed the Face of Cartoons (and then Got Fired)." *The Huffington Post*. December 1, 2014. www.huffingtonpost.com/2014/08/27/ren-and-stimpy_n_5647944.html. https://perma.cc/JP27-JFTZ.

Edgerton, Gary R. *The Columbia History of American Television*. New York: Columbia University Press, 2007.

Edgerton, Gary Richard. *The Sopranos.* Detroit: Wayne State University Press, 2013.

Elliott, Philip. *The Making of a Television Series: A Case Study in the Sociology of Culture.* Beverly Hills: Sage Publications, 1972.

Englehardt, Tom. "Children's Television: The Strawberry Shortcake Strategy." In *Watching Television: A Pantheon Guide to Popular Culture,* edited by Todd Gitlin, 68–110. New York: Pantheon, 1987.

Erickson, Hal. *"From Beautiful Downtown Burbank": A Critical History of Rowan and Martin's Laugh-In, 1968–1973.* Jefferson, NC: McFarland, 2000.

Erickson, Hal. *Sid and Marty Krofft: A Critical Study of Saturday Morning Children's Television 1969–1993.* Jefferson, NC: McFarland, 1998.

Erikson, Erik H. *Childhood and Society.* New York: W.W. Norton, 1963.

Evans, Harold. *The American Century.* New York: Alfred A. Knopf, 1998.

Farber, David. *The Age of Great Dreams: America in the 1960's.* New York: Hill and Wang, 1994.

Farber, David R. *Taken Hostage: The Iran Hostage Crisis and America's First Encounter with Radical Islam.* Princeton: Princeton University Press, 2005.

Fass, Paula S. *The End of American Childhood: A History of Parenting from Life on the Frontier to the Managed Child.* Princeton: Princeton University Press, 2016.

Fass, Paula S., and Michael Grossberg, eds. *Reinventing Childhood: After World War II.* Philadelphia: University of Pennsylvania Press, 2012.

Faulk, Bruce, executive producer. *"Hiya, Kids!! A '50s Saturday Morning."* DVD compilation.

Federal Communications Commission. "Digital Television," August 9, 2016. https://www.fcc.gov/general/digital-television.

Feil, Ken. *Rowan and Martin's Laugh-in.* Detroit: Wayne State University Press, 2014.

Ferguson, Kevin. *Eighties People: New Lives in the American Imagination.* New York: Palgrave Macmillan, 2016.

Finn, Mark. "Political Interface: The Banning of *GTA3* in Australia." In *The Meaning and Culture of Grand Theft Auto: Critical Essays,* edited by Nate Garrelts, 35–48. Jefferson, NC: McFarland, 2006.

Fischer, Stuart. *Kids' TV: The First 25 Years.* New York: Facts on File Publications, 1983.

Flaherty, Mike. "'Meet the Cartoon Network's *Samurai Jack.*" *Entertainment Weekly,* February 21, 2002, http://ew.com/article/2002/02/21/meet-cartoon-networks-samurai-jack/. https://perma.cc/D6XZ-ATZZ.

France, David. *How to Survive a Plague: The Inside Story of How Citizens and Science Tamed AIDS.* New York: Alfred A. Knopf, 2016.

Freiberger, Paul. *Fire in the Valley: The Making of the Personal Computer.* Berkeley: Osborne/McGraw-Hill, 1984.

Friedan, Betty. *The Feminine Mystique,* 50th Anniversary Edition. New York: W. W. Norton, 2013.

Frontline. "The Way the Music Died." Written, produced and directed by Michael Kirk, co-produced and reported by Jim Gilmore. http://www.pbs.org/wgbh/pages/frontline/shows/music/perfect/mtv.html, https://perma.cc/5HAV-GDF9.

Fry, Richard. "Millennials Overtake Baby Boomers as America's Largest Generation." Pew Research Center, April 25, 2016. http://www.pewresearch.org/fact-tank/2016/04/25/millennials-overtake-baby-boomers/. https://perma.cc/HL6X-5ZLG.

Gans, Herbert J. *Popular Culture and High Culture: An Analysis and Evaluation of Taste.* New York: Basic Books, 1974.

Garrelts, Nate. Introduction to *The Meaning and Culture of Grand Theft Auto: Critical Essays,* edited by Nate Garrelts, 1–16. Jefferson, NC: McFarland, 2006.

Gillan, Jennifer. *Television Brandcasting: The Return of the Content-Promotion Hybrid.* New York: Routledge, 2015.

Gillard, Colleen. "Why the British Tell Better Children's Stories." *The Atlantic,* January 6, 2016. https://www.theatlantic.com/entertainment/archive/2016/01/why-the-british-tell-better-childrens-stories/422859/.

Gikow, Louise A., with Betsy Loredo, contributing ed. *Sesame Street, a Celebration: 40 Years of Life on the Street.* New York: Black Dog & Leventhal Publishers, 2009.

Ginsberg, Ruth Bader. "Some Thoughts on Autonomy and Equality in Relation to *Roe v. Wade.*" In *The Abortion Controversy: 25 Years after Roe v. Wade: A Reader,* edited by Louis P. Pojman and Francis J. Beckwith, 119–128. Belmont, CA: Wadsworth, 1998.

Gitlin, Todd, ed. *Watching Television.* New York: Pantheon Books, 1986.

Gray, Jonathan. *Watching with the Simpsons: Television, Parody, and Intertextuality.* New York: Routledge, 2006.

Grossman, Gary H. *Saturday Morning TV.* New York: Dell, 1981.

Guiden, Captain Timothy. "Defending America's Cambodian Incursion." *Arizona Journal of International and Comparative Law* 11 (January 10, 1994): 215–270.

Haas, Garland A. *Jimmy Carter and the Politics of Frustration.* Jefferson, NC: McFarland, 1992.

Haines, Michael R. "The Population of the United States, 1790–1920." In *The Cambridge Economic History of the United States, Vol. 2, The Long Nineteenth Century,* edited by Stanley L. Engerman and Robert E. Gallman, 143–206. Cambridge: Cambridge University Press, 2000.

Halberstam, David. *The Fifties.* New York: Random House, 1994.

Harris, Blake J. *Console Wars: Sega, Nintendo, and the Battle that Defined a Generation.* New York: It Books, 2014.

Hayes, Dade. *Anytime Playdate: Inside the Preschool Entertainment Boom, or, How Television Became my Baby's Best Friend.* New York: Free Press, 2008.

Heide, Robert. *Home Front America: Popular Culture of the World War II Era.* San Francisco: Chronicle Books, 1995.

Hendershot, Heather, ed. *Nickelodeon Nation: The History, Politics, and Economics of America's Only TV Channel for Kids.* New York: New York University Press, 2004.

Hendershot, Heather. *Saturday Morning Censors: Television Regulation before the V-Chip.* Durham: Duke University Press, 1998.

Henry, Matthew A. *The Simpsons, Satire, and American Culture.* New York: Palgrave Macmillan, 2012.

Hensley, Thomas R., and Jerry M. Lewis. "The May 4 Shootings at Kent State University: The Search for Historical Accuracy." In *Kent State and May 4th: A Social Science Perspective,* edited by Thomas R. Hensley and Jerry M. Lewis, 54–60. Kent, OH: Kent State University Press, 2010.

Hern, Alex. "Will 2016 Be the Year Virtual Reality Gaming Takes Off?" *The Guardian,* U.S. Edition, December 28, 2015. https://www.theguardian.com/technology/2015/dec/28/virtual-reality-gaming-takes-off-2016. https://perma.cc/ZYV3-PJLQ.

Higgin, Tanner. "Play-Fighting: Understanding Violence in *Grand Theft Auto III.*" In *The Meaning and Culture of Grand Theft Auto: Critical Essays,* edited by Nate Gar-

relts, 70–87. Jefferson, NC: McFarland, 2006.

Hing, Bill Ong. "Integrating New Americans." In *America's Americans: Population Issues in U.S. Society and Politics,* edited by Philip Davies and Iwan Morgan, 145–167. London: Institute for the Study of the Americas, University of London, School of Advanced Study, 2007.

Hollis, Tim. *Hi There, Boys and Girls! America's Local Children's TV Programs.* Jackson: University Press of Mississippi, 2001.

Holt, Marilyn Irvin. *Cold War Kids: Politics and Childhood in Postwar America, 1945–1960.* Lawrence: University Press of Kansas, 2014.

Holz, Josephine, and Amy B. Jordan. "Measuring the Child Audience: Issues and Implications for Educational Programming." Survey Series, Report No. 3. Philadelphia: Annenberg Public Policy Center, 1998.

Inglis, Ruth. *The Window in the Corner: A Half-century of Children's Television.* London: Peter Owen Publishers, 2003.

Israeli, Raphael. *From Arab Spring to Islamic Winter.* New Brunswick: Transaction Publishers, 2013.

Jackson, John A. *American Bandstand: Dick Clark and the Making of a Rock 'n' Roll Empire.* New York: Oxford University Press, 1997.

James, Caryn. "TELEVISION REVIEW: Teletubbies Say Eh-Oh, And Others Say Uh-Oh," *New York Times,* April 6, 1998. http://www.nytimes.com/1998/04/06/arts/television-review-teletubbies-say-eh-oh-and-others-say-uh-oh.html. https://perma.cc/NH5N-9KA8.

Jenkins, Henry, ed. *The Children's Culture Reader.* New York: New York University Press, 1998.

Johnson-Woods, Toni. *Blame Canada! South Park and Popular Culture.* New York: Continuum, 2007.

Jordan, Amy B. "Supplement: Children and Television: A Conference Summary." *The Annals of the American Academy of Political and Social Science* 550, issue 1 (January 3, 1997): 153.

Kalagian, Terry. "Programming Children's Television: The Cable Model." In *The Children's Television Community,* edited by J. Alison Bryant, 147–164. New York: Routledge, Taylor & Francis Group, 2007.

Kanfer, Stefan. *A Journal of the Plague Years.* New York: Atheneum, 1973.

Keslowitz, Steven. *The World according to the Simpsons: What Our Favorite TV Family Says about Life, Love and the Pursuit of the Perfect Donut.* Naperville, IL: Sourcebooks, 2006.

Kiger, Patrick J. "The 90s: The Last Great Decade?" *National Geographic.* http://channel.nationalgeographic.com/the-90s-the-last-great-decade/. https://perma.cc/75PT-SG7C.

Kinder, Marsha, ed. *Kids' Media Culture.* Durham: Duke University Press, 1999.

Kline, Stephen. *Out of the Garden: Toys and Children's Culture in the Age of TV Marketing.* London: Verso, 1993.

Landay, Lori. *I Love Lucy.* Detroit: Wayne State University Press, 2010.

Langer, Mark. "*Ren & Stimpy*: Fan Culture and Corporate Strategy." In *Nickelodeon Nation*, edited by Heather Hendershot, 155–181. New York: New York University Press, 2004.

Larkin, Ralph W. *Comprehending Columbine.* Philadelphia: Temple University Press, 2007.

Lavery, David, ed. *Reading the Sopranos: Hit TV from HBO.* New York: Palgrave Macmillan, 2006.

Lavery, David, with Sara Lewis Dunne. *Seinfeld, Master of Its Domain: Revisiting Television's Greatest Sitcom.* New York: Continuum, 2006.

Lear, Norman. *Even This I Get to Experience.* New York: Penguin, 2014.

Lens, Sidney. *The Day before Doomsday: An Anatomy of the Nuclear Arms Race.* Garden City, NY: Doubleday, 1977.

Lesser, Gerald S. *Children and Television: Lessons from Sesame Street.* New York: Vintage Books, 1975.

Light, Paul Charles. *Baby Boomers.* New York: Norton, 1988.

Livingston, Gretchen. "In a Down Economy, Fewer Births." *Social and Demographic Trends*, Pew Research Center, October 12, 2011. http://www.pewsocialtrends.org/2011/10/12/in-a-down-economy-fewer-births/. https://perma.cc/4CAV-DSR6.

London, Robby. "Producing Children's Television." In *The Children's Television Community*, edited by J. Alison Bryant, 77–94. New York: Routledge, Taylor & Francis Group, 2007.

Lowry, Brian. "Phineas and Ferb Review." *Variety*, January 31, 2008. https://perma.cc/52Y6-AJBW?type=image.

Lythcott-Haims, Julie. *How to Raise an Adult: Break Free of the Overparenting Trap and Prepare Your Kid for Success.* New York: St. Martin's Griffin, 2015.

Malone, Clare. "Barack Obama Won the White House, but Democrats Lost the Country. What Happened?" *FiveThirtyEight*, January 19, 2017. https://fivethirtyeight.com/features/barack-obama-won-the-white-house-but-democrats-lost-the-country/?ncid=newsltushpmgnews. https://perma.cc/S97C-4LGQ.

Markoff, John. "The Apple IIc Personal Computer." *Byte Magazine* 9, no. 5 (May 1984): 276–284. https://archive.org/details/byte-magazine-1984-05.

Martindale, David. *Pufnstuf & Other Stuff: The Weird and Wonderful World of Sid and Marty Krofft.* Los Angeles: St. Martin's Press, 1998.

Matthews, Melvin. *Duck and Cover: Civil Defense Images in Film and Television from the Cold War to 9/11.* Jefferson, NC: McFarland, 2011.

McGrath, Tom. *MTV: The Making of a Revolution.* Philadelphia: Running Press, 1996.

McHugh, Michael. *The Second Gilded Age: The Great Reaction in the United States, 1973–2001.* Lanham, MD: University Press of America, 2006.

Mcneil, Alex. *Total Television: The Comprehensive Guide to Programming from 1948 to the Present.* New York: Penguin Books, 1997.

Mergel, Sarah Katherine. *Conservative Intellectuals and Richard Nixon.* New York: Palgrave Macmillan, 2010.

Michaud, Nicholas, ed. *Adventure Time and Philosophy: The Handbook for Heroes.* Chicago: Open Court, 2015.

Mifflin, Lawrie. "Falwell Takes on the Teletubbies," *New York Times*, Business Day, Media Talk, February 15, 1999. http://www.nytimes.com/1999/02/15/business/media-talk-falwell-takes-on-the-teletubbies.html, https://perma.cc/W56Y-VQ2L.

Minow, Newton N. "Television and the Public Interest." *Federal Communications Law Journal* 55, issue 3, Article 4 (2003). http://www.repository.law.indiana.edu/cgi/viewcontent.cgi?article=1335&context=fclj. https://web.archive.org/web/20170321221352/http://www.repository.law.indiana.edu/cgi/viewcontent.cgi?article=1335&context=fclj.

Mintz, Steven. *Huck's Raft: A History of Amer-*

ican Childhood. Cambridge: Harvard University Press, 2004.

Mitchell, Robert L. "Y2K: The Good, the Bad and the Crazy." *ComputerWorld*, December 28, 2009. http://www.computerworld.com/article/2522197/it-management/y2k—the-good—the-bad-and-the-crazy.html. https://perma.cc/F7D3-R3VM.

Mitroff, Donna, and Rebecca Herr Stephenson. "The Television Tug-of-War: A Brief History of Children's Television Programming in the United States." In *The Children's Television Community*, edited by J. Alison Bryant, 3–34. New York: Routledge, Taylor & Francis Group, 2007.

Moraes, Lisa de. "PBS's 'Buster' Gets an Education." *Washington Post*, January 27, 2005, C1.

Morreale, Joanne. *The Dick Van Dyke Show*. Detroit: Wayne State University Press, 2015.

Morrow, Robert W. *Sesame Street and the Reform of Children's Television*. Baltimore: Johns Hopkins University Press, 2006.

Nachman, Gerald. *Right Here on Our Stage Tonight! Ed Sullivan's America*. Berkeley: University of California Press, 2009.

Nussbaum, Emily. "Castles in the Air." *New Yorker*, April 14, 2014. http://www.newyorker.com/magazine/2014/04/21/castles-in-the-air. https://perma.cc/464R-DE4Q.

Okuda, Ted, and Jack Mulqueen. *The Golden Age of Chicago Children's Television*. Chicago: Lake Claremont Press, 2004.

Olney, Martha. "The 1920s." In *Routledge Handbook of Major Events in Economic History*, edited by Randall E. Parker and Robert Whaples, 105–118. New York: Routledge, 2013.

Ortved, John. *The Simpsons: An Uncensored, Unauthorized History*. New York: Faber and Faber, 2010.

Palmer, Edward. *Television and America's Children: A Crisis of Neglect*. New York: Oxford University Press, 1988.

Palmer, Edward L. *Children in the Cradle of Television*. Lexington, MA: Lexington Books, 1987.

Patters, N'Jai-An. "A Culture in Panic: Day Care Abuse Scandals and the Vulnerability of Children." In *The 1980's: A Critical and Transitional Decade*, edited by Kimberly R. Moffitt and Duncan A. Campbell, 295–312. Lanham, MD: Lexington Books, 2011.

Pious, Richard M. *Civil Rights and Liberties in the 1970's*. New York: Random House, 1973.

Postman, Neil. *The Disappearance of Childhood*. New York: Vintage Books, 1994.

Reinarman, Craig, and Harry G. Levine. "Crack in the Rearview Mirror: Deconstructing Drug War Mythology." *Social Justice* 31, no. 1/2 (2004): 182–99. http://www.jstor.org/stable/29768248.

Reisman, David, Nathan Glazer, and Reuel Denney. *The Lonely Crowd: A Study of the Changing American Character*. New Haven: Yale University Press, 1989.

Reiss, David S. *M*A*S*H: The Exclusive Inside Story of TV's Most Popular Show*. Indianapolis: Bobbs-Merrill, 1980.

Ricci, Franco. *The Sopranos: Born Under a Bad Sign*. Toronto: University of Toronto Press, 2014.

Rodriguez, Cindy. "Backlash for Disney's First Latina Princess." *CNN*, October 22, 2012. http://www.cnn.com/2012/10/19/showbiz/disneys-first-latina-princess/. https://perma.cc/EB5T-2V52.

Rosenbaum, Walter A. *Environmental Politics and Policy*. Washington, D.C.: CQ Press, 2002.

Ruthven, Malise. "How to Understand ISIS." *New York Review of Books*, June 23, 2016. http://www.nybooks.com/articles/2016/06/23/how-to-understand-isis/. https://perma.cc/75SL-VCAU.

Salisbury, Harrison E. *The Shook-Up Generation*. New York: Fawcett Publications, 1958.

Santo, Avi. *Selling the Silver Bullet: The Lone Ranger and Transmedia Brand Licensing*. Austin: University of Texas Press, 2015

Schneider, Cy. *Children's Television: The Art, the Business, and How It Works*. Chicago: NTC Business Books, 1987.

Schodt, Frederik L. *Dreamland Japan: Writings on Modern Manga*. Berkeley: Stone Bridge Press, 1996.

Schulman, Bruce J. *The Seventies: The Great Shift in American Culture, Society, and Politics*. New York: Free Press, 2001.

Scott, A.O. "The Death of Adulthood in American Culture." *New York Times Magazine*, September 11, 2014. https://www.nytimes.com/2014/09/14/magazine/the-death-of-adulthood-in-american-culture.html.

Scott, Keith. *The Moose That Roared: The Story of Jay Ward, Bill Scott, a Flying Squirrel, and a Talking Moose*. New York: St. Martin's Press, 2000.

Seiter, Ellen. *Sold Separately: Parents & Children in Consumer Culture*. New Brunswick: Rutgers University Press, 1993.

Seiter, Ellen. "Children's Desires/Mothers' Dilemmas: The Social Contexts of Consumption." In *The Children's Culture Reader*, edited by Henry Jenkins, 297–317. New York: New York University Press, 1998.

Setterfield, Mark "Wages, Demand, and U.S. Macroeconomic Travails." In *After the Great Recession: The Struggle for Economic Recovery and Growth*, edited by Barry Z. Cynamon, Steven M. Fazzari, and Mark Setterfield, 158–185. Cambridge: Cambridge University Press, 2013.

Shore, Michael. *The History of American Bandstand: It's Got a Great Beat and You Can Dance to It.* New York: Ballantine Books, 1985.

Siegemund-Broka, Austin. "B Is for Broke: Why 'Sesame Street' Is Moving to HBO." *Hollywood Reporter*, August 19, 2015. http://www.hollywoodreporter.com/news/b-is-broke-why-sesame-816105. https://perma.cc/62X5-M8DK.

Simensky, Linda. "The Early Days of Nicktoons." In *Nickelodeon Nation*, edited by Heather Hendershot, 87–107. New York: New York University Press, 2004.

Skenazy, Lenore. *Free Range Kids: Giving Our Children the Freedom We Had without Going Nuts with Worry.* San Francisco: Jossey Bass, 2009.

Slocum-Schaffer, Stephanie A. *America in the Seventies.* Syracuse: Syracuse University Press, 2003.

Smith, Jessica. "How the Early Days of VR are Unfolding and the Challenges It Must Overcome to Reach Mass Adoption." *Business Insider*, The Virtual Reality Report, November 18, 2016. http://www.business insider.com/virtual-reality-report-2016-11. https://perma.cc/M66Y-GCNB.

Smith, J. Walker, and Ann Clurman. *Generation Ageless: How Baby Boomers are Changing the Way We Live Today—and They're Just Getting Started.* New York: Collins, 2007.

Spencer, Terry. "Activist Protests War Toy Link: Fast Challenges Violence on TV." *Los Angeles Times*, January 4, 1988. http://articles.latimes.com/1988-01-04/local/me-22245_1_captain-power.

Spigel, Lynn. *Make Room for TV: Television and the Family Ideal in Postwar America.* Chicago: University of Chicago Press, 1992.

Spock, Benjamin, M.D., and Michael B. Rothenberg, M.D. *Dr. Spock's Baby and Child Care*, Revised and Updated Edition. New York: Pocket Books, 1985.

Stabile, Carol A., and Mark Harrison, eds. *Prime Time Animation: Television Animation and American Culture.* New York: Routledge, 2003.

Steinberg, Brian. "How Kids' TV Networks Are Fighting Off Their Frightening Decline." *Variety*, September 2, 2015. https://perma.cc/UL24-E6EQ?type=image.

Sterling, Christopher H., and John M. Kittross. *Stay Tuned: A Concise History of American Broadcasting.* Belmont, CA: Wadsworth Publishing Company, 1978.

Stewart, Susan. "Bored Stepbrothers, Intrepid Platypus." *New York Times*, New York Edition, February 1, 2008, E27. http://www.nytimes.com/2008/02/01/arts/television/01phin.html?, https://perma.cc/ZS58-KQ66.

Stipp, Horst. "The Role of Academic Advisors in Creating Children's Television Programs: The NBC Experience." In *The Children's Television Community*, edited by J. Alison Bryant, 111–128. New York: Routledge, Taylor & Francis Group, 2007.

Strauss, Neil. "'Adventure Time': The Trippiest Show on Television." *Rolling Stone*, October 2, 2014. http://www.rollingstone.com/tv/features/adventure-time-the-trippiest-show-on-television-20141002. https://perma.cc/XK72-5ZAQ.

Swartz, Mimi. "'You Dumb Babies!' How Raising the Rugrats Children Became as Difficult as the Real Thing." In *Nickelodeon Nation*, edited by Heather Hendershot, 108–119. New York: New York University Press, 2004.

Sullivan, James. *Seven Dirty Words: The Life and Crimes of George Carlin.* Cambridge, MA: Da Capo Press, 2010.

Taffe, Selma. "Trends in Fertility in the United States." *Vital and Health Statistics* 21. Data from the National Vital Statistics System, No. 28, United States Department of Health, Education, and Welfare. DHEW Publication No. (HRA) 78–1906, ISBN 0–8406–0108–5. http://files.eric.ed.gov/fulltext/ED162951.pdf.

Taylor, Anna Noel. "Viacom Presents: Little Big Kids, Preschoolers Ready for Life." *Viacom Global Insights*, January 18, 2017. http://insights.viacom.com/post/viacom-presents-little-big-kids-preschoolers-ready-for-life/. https://perma.cc/SX4D-ER2B.

Telotte, J. P. *Disney TV.* Detroit: Wayne State University Press, 2004.

Tobin, Joseph, ed. *Pikachu's Global Adventure: The Rise and Fall of Pokémon.* Durham: Duke University Press, 2004.

Tschiggerl, Martin, and Thomas Walach. *The Simpsons Did It! Postmodernity in Yellow.* Vienna: Ferstl & Perz Verlag, 2015

Tuchman, Gaye, ed. *The TV Establishment: Programming for Power and Profit.* Englewood Cliffs, NJ: Prentice-Hall, 1974.

Turner, Chris. *Planet Simpson.* London: Ebury, 2004.

Walker, Cynthia W. *Work/text: Investigating The Man From U.N.C.L.E.* New York: Hampton Press: 2013

Weaver, Frederick Stirton. *An Economic History of the United States: Conquest, Conflict, and Struggles for Equality.* Lanham, MD: Rowman & Littlefield, 2016.

Weinstock, Jeffrey Andrew, ed. *Taking South Park Seriously.* Albany: State University of New York Press, 2008.

Weisman, Steven R. "Reagan Takes Oath as 40th President; Promises an 'Era of National Renewal'—Minutes Later, 52 U.S. Hostages in Iran Fly to Freedom After 444-Day Ordeal." *New York Times,* January 21, 1981.

Weiss, Robert P. "Privatizing the Leviathan State: A 'Reaganomic' Legacy." In *The 1980s: A Critical and Transitional Decade,* edited by Kimberly R. Moffitt and Duncan A. Campbell, 89–108. Lanham, MD: Lexington Books, 2011.

Weller, Sheila. "The Missing Woman: How Author Timothy Tyson Found the Woman at the Center of the Emmett Till Case." *Vanity Fair,* January 26, 2017. http://www.vanityfair.com/news/2017/01/how-author-timothy-tyson-found-the-woman-at-the-center-of-the-emmett-till-case.

Welsch, Timothy J. "Everyday Play: Cruising for Leisure in San Andreas." In *The Meaning and Culture of Grand Theft Auto,* edited by Nate Garrelts, 127–142. Jefferson, NC: McFarland, 2006.

West, Mark I., ed. *The Japanification of Children's Popular Culture: From Godzilla to Miyazaki.* Lanham, MD: The Scarecrow Press, 2009.

Wilensky, Harold L. *American Political Economy in Global Perspective.* Cambridge: Cambridge University Press, 2012.

Wingert, Pat. "The Truth About Tweens." *Newsweek,* October 17, 1999. http://www.newsweek.com/truth-about-tweens-168306. https://perma.cc/4CE8-MELU.

Wolfe, Tom. "The 'Me' Decade and the Third Great Awakening." *New York,* August 23, 1976. http://nymag.com/news/features/45938/. https://perma.cc/9B7A-JRZN.

Woolery, George W. *Children's Television: The First Thirty-Five Years, 1946–1981, Parts I and II.* Metuchen, NJ: Scarecrow Press, 1983.

Wright, Gwendolyn. *Building the Dream: A Social History of Housing in America.* New York: Pantheon Books, 1981.

Zeller, Tom. "How to Succeed without Attitude." *New York Times,* July 21, 2002. http://www.nytimes.com/2002/07/21/weekinreview/ideas-trends-cleaning-up-how-to-succeed-without-attitude.html. https://perma.cc/E9HJ-B3PH.

Index